The Anteater And The Jaguar

The Anteater And The Jaguar

Is This Our Destiny? A Story From the Oasis of Peace

Rayek R. Rizek

© 2017 Rayek R. Rizek
All rights reserved.

ISBN-13: 9781545184189
ISBN-10: 1545184186
Library of Congress Control Number: 2017907010
CreateSpace Independent Publishing Platform
North Charleston, South Carolina

This book is dedicated to my life partner, Dyana Shalloufi Rizek, who has never stopped believing in me and encouraging me and who has brought me to the Oasis of Peace.

Contents

Acknowledgments · ix
Foreword · xiii
Preface · xvii

Part I: The Oasis of Peace · 1
One	Between a Doctorate and a Café · · · · · · · · · · · · · · ·	3
Two	Born Without a Charter · · · · · · · · · · · · · · ·	13
Three	Father Bruno Hussar, 1911–1996 · · · · · · · · · · · · · · ·	18
Four	All About This Bit of Land · · · · · · · · · · · · · · ·	24
Five	The Primary School: Eleven Kids, Two Teachers, And An Idea · · · · · · · · · · · · · · ·	27
Six	The School for Peace · · · · · · · · · · · · · · ·	31
Seven	My First Years in the Oasis of Peace · · · · · · · · · · · · · · ·	39
Eight	Financial Support and its Ramifications · · · · · · · · · · · · · · ·	43
Nine	An Accidental Radical · · · · · · · · · · · · · · ·	47
Ten	Embracing the Evolution of our Expectations · · · · · ·	56
Eleven	To Leave or to Stay · · · · · · · · · · · · · · ·	60
Twelve	Yesterday and Today · · · · · · · · · · · · · · ·	66

Part II: Within the Middle East · 77
Thirteen	My Public-Relations Work · · · · · · · · · · · · · · ·	79
Fourteen	About Geography · · · · · · · · · · · · · · ·	89
Fifteen	About Religion · · · · · · · · · · · · · · ·	101
Sixteen	About People · · · · · · · · · · · · · · ·	114

Part III: Life Experiences **121**

Seventeen	My Parents	123
Eighteen	In Jerusalem and the West Bank	130
Nineteen	Between Nazareth and the Americas	140
Twenty	More Stories About Nazareth	150
Twenty-One	Aliens on our Own Planet	158
Twenty-Two	The Gaza Experience	164
Twenty-Three	My First Visit to a Refugee Camp	169
Twenty-Four	The First Intifada Begins	173
Twenty-Five	The Death of Abu Ahmad	178

Part IV: Reaching an End to Conflicts **199**

Twenty-Six	Our Responsibility	201
Twenty-Seven	I am Responsible	208
Twenty-Eight	US and Them	221
Twenty-Nine	As a Palestinian	230
Thirty	To Divide Or Not To Divide	238
Thirty-One	The Choice is Ours	253
Thity-Two	Our Destiny	263

Acknowledgments

Thanks to Howard Shippin; Daniella Kitain; Deb Reich; Debra and Ted First; David Matz; Ann Solange Noble; Bob Fenton; Gorge Khleifi; Zuhair Sabbagh; David Yoshpi; Ariela Bairey Ben Ishay; Basma Kewar Rizik; Marc Gopin; my wife, Dyana; and my two sons, Hilal and Taj, for reviewing the draft of this book at different stages and for giving me valuable notes and ideas that have helped bring it to fruition. I want to thank my maternal aunt Yosra (ninety-three years old at this writing) for providing me with much important information about the family. I want to thank Daniel Warner for encouraging me to send my book to Brian Mooney, the president of Border Stone Press, and to thank Brian for his support and generosity, which were critical in bringing the book to its present level. Naturally, I owe a debt of gratitude to my parents, because they loved me and did not mind my moving to live here in the Oasis of Peace. I thank my two older brothers, Basheer and Bassam, who, in different ways, motivated my curiosity. Thanks also to my brother Basheer for supporting me during my seven-year stay in the United States. I am indebted to my father's friend the late journalist Ibrahim Shbat, whose intervention was critical for getting my visa to the United States back in 1975. I am also indebted to my cousin and friend, Sohail Abu-Nowara. Sohail, a writer, an artist, and a philosopher, advised me whenever I complained about some people in my community not to waste my energy trying to fix or challenge them but to make my point by building and living in my own oasis of peace. I remember with thankfulness, too, my late friend and roommate in Austin, Texas, Makram Qobty. When I was still in my early twenties, Makram taught me to think outside the box.

I owe a debt of gratitude as well to those friends who cared for me and supported me when I was in great need. I refer here to Sayed Khattari and Raji Badwan, my brother Basheer's friends in the United States; my high school classmate Muneer Qobty; my cousins Najeeb Rizik and Ramzi Abu Nowara; my friends Sobhi Damouni, Dahoud Hayek, and Bishara Matar; CEO of sonara newspaper, Vida Mashour; my younger brother, Shibly; my sister, Afaf; my community neighbors, Voltaire Shamshoom, Abdelrahman Abu Ajami, Eli bin-Ari, Kamel Tibi, and Daoud Boulos; my nearby neighbors Zakaria Sonbaty from Beit Sera and Mohammad Al-Obra from Rahat; Omar and Isoldi Abu-Elhaija from Germany; and Bishara and Zuhair Sabbagh. I would also like to thank my cousin Azmi Zeibak and his wife, Ghada Shalloufi, who connected between me and Dyana, and my classmates from my peace-studies course at Bradford University, including Veronica Green from Iowa, USA; Chinatsu Baba from Japan; my Jordanian fellow student at Coventry University, Ibrahim Abu-alsokar; and Ingrid Jradat from Beit Lahem. Others to whom I owe thanks are Richard Goodwin, Joan Golder, Judy and Don Dubin, Barbara Meislin, Elaine Rubenstein, and Debra and Ted First, who have been longtime supporters of my community and who helped me financially so I could pursue my doctoral studies.

For helping me learn to write, I owe thanks to my teachers at the peace-studies department at Bradford University, especially Davina Miller, Tom Woodhouse, and Oliver Ramsbotham. My thanks must go to Uri Davis as well, who showed me the way to Bradford. Special thanks are also due to Marwan and Lou Darweish from Birmingham and to my friend and PhD supervisor at Coventry University, Andrew Rigby, who insisted I write a book about my community.

Thanks to Hagit Ra'anan, who gave me a book that has changed my understanding of myself and helped me to fathom the meaning of life. In addition, I would be remiss if I did not thank the literally *hundreds* of volunteers who have come over the past forty years from all over the world to lend a helping hand in building the Oasis of Peace. Many people have worked sincerely and diligently to promote knowledge of our community in their various countries through our community's Friends Associations. These associations have helped locate and secure needed financial and moral support for our programs and maintenance, and for this support, we are all extremely grateful. My sincere appreciation goes to all those generous people and organizations who have donated their money toward our cause, for they—like we—believe Jews and Palestinians have no other choice but to share their life in this land as equals.

I would like to thank all the members of the Oasis of Peace, but I am particularly grateful to those early pioneers who believed enough in the future of our community to persist in their common dream and make that dream a reality, despite many hardships.

Nor shall I forget to thank everyone who has hurt me, because the hurt has also been a cause for my awakening and has made me the human I am today.

Finally, I would like to extend special thanks and deep gratitude to Professor Randall Bush and to Deb Reich for editing and refining my book, help that was much needed and critical, as English is not my mother tongue.

Thank you all.

Foreword

Storytelling has emerged in recent centuries as perhaps the most powerful way to connect strangers and to bring unprecedented levels of compassion and empathy to human social life and political transformation. In fact, some experts on violence and peace have argued—I think quite convincingly—that extraordinary storytelling, as at the hands of Émile Zola, Marcel Proust, Victor Hugo, John Steinbeck, and great film directors such as Richard Attenborough and Steven Spielberg, transformed human rights from an abstract philosophical and political construction into something that sparked the imagination and commitment of literally billions of people. Those affected demanded and achieved political and legal evolution in dozens of societies in a way that has completely changed human history and saved millions of lives. Some have noted that you can't hate people after you have heard their stories, and the act itself of telling a story has become part of what affirms our humanity. As Masha Hamilton of the Afghan Women's Writing Project has said, "To tell one's story is a human right."

As an activist and a writer my whole life, I have been listening to and telling the stories of peacemakers—their sorrows and triumphs. For thirty-two years in the Middle East I have done this, because so many of us have seen the power of story to transform even the most hard-hearted, to build healing and incremental change where none was thought possible.

Rayek R. Rizek

The story you are about to read by Rayek Rizek about his life journey in his native Palestine and Israel will enthrall you. It will enthrall you because it is hard for me, after thirty-two years of challenging work, to recall a human being like Rayek Rizek when it comes to introspection and the telling of the story of his society's conflict from such a deeply honest perspective. I have never seen such self-examination and reflection based on the life experience of his many identities: as a son; as a Palestinian; as an Israeli; as a community leader of one of the boldest experiments in coexistence ever undertaken; as an on-site historian; as a vulnerable and courageously penitent man; and as a devoted husband to his ever-patient and ever-wise life partner, Dyana, to whom this book is dedicated.

This is an ethical/spiritual journey with so much to teach the world, to teach Palestinians and Israeli Jews, to teach Middle Eastern citizens. Confessional honesty and self-reflection are almost unheard of in massive and violent conflict settings. The sheer expanse of injury that human beings experience when they have fought, suffered, and died in large numbers makes it often unlikely that the most important ingredient of healing conflicts, self-examination, can take place. And yet here we have a model of just that. Sometimes we can evolve as human beings by just one model of how to be different, how to be more enlightened, even in the most difficult situations, and that is why this story is seminal.

This book is about much more than the Oasis of Peace experiment, in which Rayek and Dyana have played a key role. It is about conflict itself, peace building as such, and the critical role of an individual's inner journey to its outward results, in terms of effective engagement with masses of people. As Rayek has understood, true peace building begins only in the inner life, and from there to community, and from community to the world.

I will teach this book in my graduate program, certainly in terms of Middle Eastern conflict analysis, and the power of story and personal history to complexify and illuminate poorly understood, oversimplified conflicts. But I will teach this book also in my course on cutting-edge approaches to healing and transforming global conflicts, a process that must begin with our inner selves, with the war inside of us and with the

The Anteater And The Jaguar

peace inside of us. The inner suffering that Rayek speaks of so often is actually a symbol of and a gateway toward analyzing and transforming the suffering that we all feel in places of tragic conflict, including conflict in our own families. As such, Rayek's inner and outer journey has crucial lessons to teach all of us, as to how to live, as to how to build peace even when surrounded by destructive conflict.

Thirty-three years ago, as a young, sheltered Orthodox American Jew, I met Rayek for the first time. In under twenty-four hours, we walked along the hills and surveyed the valleys below suffused with history and sorrow; I slept in his simple, poor house at the Oasis of Peace; and he simply changed the entire course of my life. His passionate love of every herb of the land, his model of sensitivity, his introspective style, his quiet determination and courage, simply transformed me. I believe he reminded me much of an unforgettable picture of my courageous, angry, determined grandfather in Boston circa 1945, doggedly determined to rebuild a Jewish world buried in ashes, despite the outrage of a Holocaust. And there we were in 1984, Jew and Palestinian, locked in separation, but bonded completely at the same time, overlooking the ancient land of Israel and ancient land of Palestine. Quiet, stubborn determination would become my way of life.

Here in this story you will find a true model of building peace, from the depths of inner honesty to the unstoppable determination to make an Oasis of Peace between human beings. It is a long journey that foreshadows the journey that all citizens of the earth must someday travel, and that is why it is vital reading.

Rabbi Dr. Marc Gopin,
James H. Laue Chair,
Director of the Center for World Religions, Diplomacy, and Conflict Resolution,
The School for Conflict Analysis and Resolution,
George Mason University
Arlington, Virginia

Preface

For many years now, I have wanted to write a book about my community. In many ways, it is a one-of-a-kind place—where Jews and Palestinians (Christians and Muslims) live together intentionally. It deserves a book.

Early on, however, I realized I could not hope to write such a book without providing the reader with some context. The community where I live came into being, developed, and exists to this day against the backdrop of the bitter, ongoing conflict between Jews and Palestinians, who dwell together in this land. Our community indeed conceives of itself as embodying the seed of a more hopeful alternative reality for us all.

The founding purpose of our community, its educational activities, its structure, and even its location make sense only against the backdrop of the conflict around us. Visitors in search of context, after listening to a basic description of who we are and what we are doing here, always question us further about our place on the map of the conflict, our attitudes to the conflict, and so on. I have fielded such questions from hundreds of visiting groups over the years. To find out what I've learned in those encounters, read on.

The members of our community share a common calling. We strive to be agents of peace in a deeply troubled land. Understanding the deeper context, which I hope to provide here, will equip you to better appreciate the many challenges we have faced in our village—starting

Rayek R. Rizek

with the choice to come and live in a community like ours in the first place.

Meanwhile, having begun to write, I discovered that I could hardly write about the conflict without writing about myself, too. While I understand myself as first and foremost a *human being*, I am also a member of various groups, with which I identify to varying degrees—by religion, ethnicity, nationality. Unavoidably, my life story, my experiences and affinities, have influenced my thinking about the issues that concern us here, including the Israeli-Palestinian conflict and the possibilities for constructively addressing and, perhaps, ultimately resolving it. I will share all of this as candidly as I can.

Our conflict has some deep roots that are entangled with the variety of religions and faiths that exist in the region known as the Middle East. Clearly, then, my own religious background as an Arab Orthodox Christian must be relevant to my perceptions of the conflict affecting us all, and I will present my thoughts along those lines, too. My perspective, moreover, may be unusually helpful, because it stands in a middle place between the other two great monotheistic religions in our region: Judaism and Islam. I feel myself to be closely connected to both of these other religions, in ways I will discuss.

As you read, you may find that I tend to have an unusual perspective, one that may allow me to be more objective than most Jewish or Palestinian commentators are able to be. Most write exclusively from the standpoint of their separate side, whereas my sense of standing between Judaism and Islam prompts me to look beyond my own group to consider how opponents see things. This informs my intentional efforts to reach beyond my own awareness, as formed by my own life experiences, and enhances my ability to expand my own outlook to incorporate the different identities of others with whom I have been in conversation in this Palestinian-Jewish community where I have lived more than half my life so far.

As the book proceeds, I will describe challenges I have faced. I will share emotionally painful associations. I will tell of my search for a life free of suffering—a search begun more than ten years ago.

The Anteater And The Jaguar

Throughout the book I shall raise critical issues and ask probing questions. Some of what I present may not agree with what every reader thinks are established facts. I could not separate my perspective on the facts from the facts as I see them, even if I tried, and the attempt would not be helpful. Still, and especially for thoughtful people interested in the question of peace in the Middle East, my narrative is, I trust, worth consideration.

Living and working in this unusual community has made it possible for me to converse with thousands of people—not only Jews and Palestinians from our area or elsewhere but a broad cross section of people coming from all across the globe. It amounts to conducting my own field research with a large and diverse population, the like of which is available to very few. The time has come, after thirty-two years of this, to share what I've learned.

I hope you can bring a spirit of fairness and openness to your reading here. My aim is to bring you a different, less one-sided, and perhaps more objective version of the Palestinian-Israeli conflict than is commonly offered. I make an effort not to think of myself as *right* and others with whom I disagree as *wrong*. Nor do I wish to portray myself as a victim and others as aggressors, although some parts of the text could perhaps be interpreted that way; my goal is rather to enable you to feel my own humanity and the collective humanity of Palestinian Arabs—who have been a target of distortion ever since they appeared on the political and historical scene. I hope to persuade you that our humanity is equal to everyone else's and that the Palestinian people deserve to be recognized as equally human and equally a people. Here, I am reminded of the slogan on a banner I saw a few years ago, displayed by a young German amateur rock group performing at a festival in Italy: "Nobody Is Illegal."

That we, as residents of this planet, still divide ourselves into "legal" and "illegal" is sad—almost as though the people fortunate enough to be labeled "legal" were born on this planet and all the "illegals" were aliens from outer space. This theme is a central one here. Once we accept the idea that we are all *legal citizens* of this planet, we realize that we can

Rayek R. Rizek

no longer tolerate the oppression, killing, exploitation, exclusion, and humiliation of our fellow human beings. No longer can we accept or justify excuses for such activities, however compelling the excuses may seem to be.

If you, my reader, detect here some degree of frustration, I hope you can parse it. It's about the fact that, for most of my people, the tragedy continues, showing little hope of coming to an end anytime soon. I remain frustrated by, and disappointed in, the numerous influential leaders, politicians, and intellectuals who know much more about the real reasons for the present impasse between Jews and Palestinians than they let on, yet do little or nothing to generate movement toward a solution. I hope you will bear with me, in the chapters that follow, when I express some of that frustration and disappointment, alongside my hopes and dreams. I have been searching all my life for peace. I seek a life without suffering not only for myself but for everyone else as well. I hope this book will inspire many of you to join me in my quest.

Part I: The Oasis of Peace

One

Between a Doctorate and a Café

You should write a book!

People have made this remark to me many times during the nearly thirty years I've spent living in our Palestinian-Jewish shared community. In English we are called the *Oasis of Peace*, which in Hebrew is *Neve Shalom* and in Arabic *Wahat Al-salam* (pronounced *Wahat Assalam*).

My wife, Dyana, and I decided to come live at the Oasis of Peace in 1984, and we have remained ever since. In the interim, I have given many talks about our life and experiences here to diverse audiences. Of the hundreds, even thousands, of people who have heard these talks, a great many have encouraged me to write them down.

Over the years, I've made several fitful starts at writing, but I always got stuck after a few pages when I realized the dimensions of the commitment and hard work required. I kept putting it off. I lacked confidence in my ability to carry out the task properly. Could I deal adequately with the complexity of the Israeli-Palestinian conflict? I didn't know. I made up my mind to forge ahead regardless.

So today, at the age of fifty-six, after spending twenty-eight years living in the Oasis of Peace, I feel ready and more determined than ever to meet the challenge of writing a book. I have done enough thinking and talking about it. I have some relevant academic qualifications, too, having spent one year (2000–2001) at Bradford University in the United Kingdom for a master's degree in peace studies and later a part of 2002–2003 doing research at Coventry University, also in the United Kingdom, toward a doctorate in their department of reconciliation and forgiveness. I did a lot of reading on intentional communities and alternative communities during my time there. The course of study was a logical one for me, because my intention was that my doctoral thesis would examine life in our Palestinian-Jewish community. My readings at Coventry immersed me in exploring the complexities of life in different types of communities and, in hindsight, became excellent preparation for writing this book.

The book project got another boost in the summer of 2007, when Dyana and I rented a place at the entrance to our community and turned it into a combination gift shop and café. We didn't intend to turn our place of business into a kind of public relations department for the Oasis of Peace community, but that's what happened. People both local and from around the world visit our community every day. Groups small and large who are planning a visit generally call our community's office of communications and development (not us) to make the appropriate arrangements. Many of these folks, whether part of a previously arranged visit or not, end up in our café anyway. They venture in, they sit down, they order something to eat and drink, they ask questions, and we talk. And for the many visitors who arrive unannounced, we are often the primary, even the only, point of contact in the community. Our shop, a welcoming spot of green facing the main parking lot, is the first place they see on arrival.

Even though our PR function sort of naturally evolved out of our gift shop and café functions, I am still taken aback sometimes when total strangers walk in and immediately strike up a conversation that is typically longer rather than shorter. I suppose, though, that I should not think of this as unusual, because our place *is* different. It is, after all, a *gateway* to a strange and unique community.

The Anteater And The Jaguar

Here is a picture of how such an encounter typically begins: Some visitors come into our gift shop/café. Before we know it, they begin asking probing questions: *Tell us about yourself. Tell us about your community. Do you live here? Where did you come from? How long have you lived here? How old is the place? How did it get started? What is it like to live here? Do the Jews and the Palestinians get along here?* The questions just keep on coming.

Many times our café guests invite us to join them at their table so we can continue our talks. I answer their questions as honestly and forthrightly as I can. This is something I do almost every day, and frankly, I mostly do not mind doing it. I end up feeling pretty good after I tell them the truth about our relations as Jews and as Palestinians here in the community. Many are surprised to learn that our conflicts, and our agreements and disagreements, are not necessarily between Jews and Palestinians but between people who either share or do not share similar values and attitudes. Our visitors realize then that we are people like everybody else.

Until about ten years ago, I was not yet ready to do this intensive sort of PR work, especially with the Israeli Jews who comprise the majority of our customers, because I was still burdened with a great deal of unresolved emotional pain. Today I understand that I first had to go through a number of serious changes in my attitudes toward life. Changing my own attitudes was necessary if I was ever to overcome the pain and emotional baggage I'd been carrying around for so long. Had I not succeeded in working through my own issues, then even *starting* my business, much less *succeeding* in it, would have been unimaginable and probably impossible. Now, though, as I look back on our venture in hindsight, I am gratified by the astonishing success Dyana and I have enjoyed. We now have many regular customers, not only because we serve good food and provide a calm, relaxing atmosphere for our patrons but also because we harbor convictions and attitudes that give them hope.

And we have benefited in other ways as well. I have learned a lot during these last years from talking and listening to people. Since our place of business is not always busy, I have also had time to read many books that have given me valuable knowledge about how to live my life with less emotional pain. I have shared and discussed these insights with my wife, with my two sons, with numerous friends—in fact, I've discussed them with anybody who wants to listen.

Throughout my personal struggles, I have learned that nothing happens to us as a matter of sheer coincidence. There is always a purpose to what we go through, even if that purpose at first seems unclear. I find many examples as I look back over my life's journey. For instance, at one point a number of years ago, I decided to leave the United States and return to my hometown of Nazareth. (Note that *Nazareth* in Arabic is *Al-Nasira* [pronounced *An-Nasira*], and *Nazarene* is *Al-Nasiri* [*An-Nasiri*]. *Yasoua Al-Nasiri* [*Yasoua An-Nasiri*] is *Jesus the Nazarene*.)

I left the United States and returned home to Nazareth, having been away for about seven years. Many people thought I had gone mad and all but said so: *How could you leave America and come back to live in this country?* A few months after I returned, though, the purpose became clear. Through my family, I met Dyana, the woman who was to become my wife. Had I not returned, I never would have met the love of my life. What a tragedy that would have been! It was Dyana, too, who introduced me to the Oasis of Peace, the community where we would spend our whole married life.

This is not to say that my life in the Oasis of Peace community has always been easy. Despite the many good outcomes, I have had my share of emotional pain, conflicts, and challenges. But looking back at my time here as a whole, I do not regret having chosen to live here. Indeed, I have come to think that if my awakening resulted from all I've been through—including the fact that I was born a member of a minority and a Palestinian—then it is a good thing I had to go through it all. How many times have the bad things that happened to us actually turned out to be those very things that caused some greater good to come to fruition years later?

During my six months as a graduate student at Coventry, I often spent time with a Jordanian friend and fellow student, Ibrahim. We would go

The Anteater And The Jaguar

almost every day to a café just across the street from the university campus. In addition to my appreciation for what we ate and drank at that café, I also very much enjoyed the music I heard there. Although conscious of the fact that the point of my being in England was to achieve a PhD, hopefully for an academic career, I nevertheless felt somewhat envious of the young woman who owned the café. *Wouldn't it be great—* I would say to myself—*if I could have work like hers, with my own café, so I could be independent and host people with good food, a good atmosphere, and good music?*

As my first six months there drew to a close, I was unable to find the money to continue my studies; I was forced to quit and did so with great regret. Back home at the Oasis of Peace and needing to earn a living, I spent a few months doing temporary translation work until my Palestinian friend Zakaria, who has always been a friend in my times of need, suggested I open a garden nursery and loaned me some money to get started. About a year later, Dyana and I turned the nursery into a gift shop, selling handcrafts and other things produced locally and abroad. Within three years, we added a small café. We did this not only because the gift shop was not proving itself sustainable financially but also in response to comments often made by customers at the gift shop, who expressed disappointment at not finding some sort of café in our beautiful community, where folks could sit down to rest for a while and enjoy some food and drinks.

And so in the summer of 2007, after much deliberation, our café was born. An appropriate space became available when the community kindergarten moved to a new building next to the community primary school on the other side of the village. We decided to take the plunge and rent the former kindergarten, which we then gradually renovated for our purposes: a compact kitchen and gift shop inside and most of the seating outside, surrounded by lots of greenery.

Some months passed in our new café before it dawned on me that I had actually fulfilled the wish I'd hesitated to voice, even to myself, back at the café in Coventry. And as time goes by, I've come to realize that

Rayek R. Rizek

in running this café with Dyana, I am actually doing the most enjoyable and fulfilling work I have ever done in my whole life, because it provides most of what I look for in my work.

In the Gallery Café Ahlan, as we finally named it, I am independent. Rather than having to commute every day to the city, as most of my neighbors do, I have a five-minute walk to work through a scenic village in serene pastoral surroundings. I am not subject to an unvarying routine of daily work hours, because we close our doors around sunset each evening, an ever-changing time frame. In our country, we have four lovely seasons of winter, spring, summer, and fall, with sunset coming at about four in the afternoon in winter and about eight in the evening in summer. I host people from all over the world, and I share my favorite music with my guests. I share my ideas and thoughts about the Israeli-Palestinian conflict and about life in general. In between stocking the café and sharing the food prep, cooking, serving, and cleanup with Dyana and part-time help in our busy seasons, I have time to read, to write, to create some artwork, and to host and socialize with my friends. And most importantly, I spend a lot of time with Dyana. My feelings are exactly in line with what the great Chinese sage Confucius advised: *choose a job you love, and you will never work a day in your life.*

Another source of satisfaction from our café has to do with my previous life in Nazareth, where I grew up having Sundays off. Nazareth schools and businesses are closed on Sundays all over town, even though it is a mixed town of Christians and Muslims. Those Sundays in Nazareth live on in my memory as some of the most beautiful days of my childhood, not only because I didn't have to go to school; Sunday was always a day for visiting and socializing within the circle of my large, loving family. The day began when, dressed neatly in our best clothes, we set out for the morning service in the Arab Orthodox community's church, only a five-minute walk from our house. Lots of our relatives would be there, along with my classmates and other kids from the neighborhood. We would play marbles and *ghommayda* (hide-and-seek) near the church, which was next to our primary school. As a youngster, I enjoyed listening

The Anteater And The Jaguar

to the prayers chanted by the priests and the choir, which sang beautiful Byzantine melodies in both Arabic and Greek. There were frequent holy days, when we could walk along with the community's scouts as they paraded in their neat uniforms to the music of marching drummers and horn players.

Around noon there was a family lunch, always a delicious meal that included everyone's highlight of the week: my mother's cooking. Later in the afternoon, we would go to one of four cinemas in town to enjoy the indescribable pleasure, some years before the advent of television, of seeing a Western or a James Bond film on the magical big screen. In the evening, it was time to visit Sitti Meladi, my maternal grandmother. Sitti (Arabic for *granny*) was the only grandparent I knew, as all the others had passed away before I was born. Those early Sunday evening visits to Sitti Meladi in her 130-year-old house live on in my mind as the most beautiful family gatherings of my childhood and adolescence. We were always joined there by my aunts Mariam and Yosra and my uncles Elias and Fadell, with their families—more than thirty people altogether.

I remember Sitti Meladi, who lived to the age of eighty-six, sitting in her bed and reading the Bible in Greek, which she learned in a private girls' school that she attended in Nazareth. Later she worked as a teacher in the same school until she was married to her cousin, my grandfather Jeryis, who was a carpenter, around 1908.

We must digress long enough for me to tell you something about their house. Its structure was common in the old city of Nazareth, as well as more widely in Palestine and the region. This kind of building style is called, in Arabic, *aaqed* (meaning "vault"). The traditional method calls for building the shape of a dome by laying rows of stones around a central mound of earth in smaller and smaller circles or squares as the construction ascends. When the dome is locked in place at the apex by the final stone, the *qafell* (lock), the mound of earth is removed from the inside, and the walls are plastered inside and out.

A family house could include several such spaces connected with and open to one another. Often the aaqeds form a square around an open courtyard, a *hoshe* that would commonly include a well or a cistern for rainwater and sometimes a small pond with a fountain. Typical landscaping in the hoshe included jasmine, at least one lemon tree, and grapevines. A grape arbor provided shade for part of the hoshe, and the grapes themselves are a valued food, of course; the fresh vine leaves are traditionally boiled and rolled into oblong wraps stuffed with rice and ground lamb or beef. The lemon tree is a necessity for lemon juice, a major ingredient in most dishes from Palestinian and nearby Arab kitchens. And the jasmine is for the scent. A small paradise.

What is unique about this type of construction, with its one-meter-thick walls, is that the building's internal temperature remains nearly constant through all four seasons of the year. Most of Nazareth's old city, still inhabited and active today, was built using this traditional construction, which dates back thousands of years. The method is rarely employed these days—at least not in our region—apparently due both to a lack of expertise and to the introduction of modern architecture.

But to return to my family's Sunday gatherings at Sitti Meladi's house, one pair was missing at those gatherings. My aunt Zbaydi had left Palestine with her husband, George, in the mid-1940s, when Uncle George, a journalist and editor, was offered a position at the United Nations headquarters in New York. Since they were out of Palestine during the 1948 war, they—like many other Palestinians—were denied their right to return to their home, their birthplace, under Israeli law. They lived for some years in New York until Uncle George was transferred to the UN headquarters in Geneva and finally to Baghdad. On his retirement, they went to live in Amman, Jordan. I visited Aunt Zbaydi there in 1998, some years after Uncle George had passed away. She told me that she once asked him where he thought they would go when he retired, and he replied, "Amman." When she asked him why, he said, "Because it is closest to Palestine."

When I myself left Nazareth right after finishing high school, I continued to enjoy Sundays as a day of rest during the next seven years, which I spent in the United States. Later, when Dyana and I came to live in Neve Shalom, that would change. We had to adapt to a new life in which Saturday is the day off, as in the majority Jewish culture in Israel, and Sunday is a working day. And so it was—until we opened the café.

The café changed a lot for us, including our day of rest. Given that most of our customers are Jews who live in nearby cities, towns, and villages, we found that Saturdays are usually the busiest time of the week at the café. So Sunday became our day off again, for the first time in more than twenty years of working in various branches of the community. This issue of when people have their day off may seem insignificant, but remember that our community is all about mutual compromise and balance, and everyone is encouraged to live out their cultural identity as broadly as circumstances permit. In pursuit of that very necessary and humane ideal, we strive to ensure that no one in the community will feel he or she has given up more than anyone else to make it possible. For Dyana and me, as Christians, having Sundays off serves very well—especially when we decide to visit our families in Nazareth, who are always available on Sundays, or to host them in our house in Wahat Assalam.

There is one more thing about the café. Our place of work has not only been dedicated to sharing positive feelings with other human beings; it also has become a shelter for many feral cats in our community. Over the past nine years, probably over two hundred cats have lived for some period of time at our café (though not all of them at once). Regrettably, since they are wild, most of them do not live long. But on any given day, at least fifteen of them may be seen lounging in or near the café courtyard. It all began when we adopted one female cat that was hanging around. In addition to the kittens she, and later her descendants, bore, other feral cats began appearing, drawn by the presence of food. When the cat population ballooned, we started feeling a bit uncomfortable. We had neither expected nor planned to take on such a job. But over time we have learned to accept it and to devote time and money to it as needed, not only for their food but also for medical treatment. One cat, called Kotkot, ran up a $3,000 bill with the veterinarian for treatment against some virus. When we brought Kotkot back more than three weeks later, the vet sent us home with ten different kinds of pills and eye drops to give him over the next two weeks. We decided to adopt him and take him home to our house so the treatment would be easier. Later we adopted two more cats, Noosho and Tuti, and all three became fairly good friends with our dog, a Pinscher named Kalboushi.

The transformation of our café courtyard into a center for feral cats may seem strange to some people, but it grew naturally out of our belief that peace can be real only if we live life with compassion and that life is not just about taking chances but is also about fate. I believe Dyana and I were meant to meet each other, to come to this community, and to end up in this corner of the world at this time of our lives. We were meant not only to work for money and receive all kinds of visitors who are curious about the story of our community but also to take care of the feral cats in the village. These experiences have complemented the sense of serenity I have increasingly achieved in my personal life over the last few years here at the Oasis of Peace. Serenity of mind has enabled me to write this book, and I hope it will help in our shared challenge to bring world peace.

Two

Born Without a Charter

Living in an intentional community like ours means that each of us has chosen to share our life, in its many dimensions, with others. Committing to do this does not guarantee that we shall live in a ready-made utopia. Sustainable living in a community always involves hard work, and in our community in particular, it requires unstinting effort.

Living here is not quite like living anywhere else in the world. In most other places, we would be freer to build physical and emotional barriers to set some limits on our contact with others; that is much harder to do here. Choosing to live in a small rural community like ours means we have agreed to live our lives most of the time within a very small space and to interact most of the time with a relatively small group of fellow residents. We see the same people every day passing by on the street, picking up mail, and attending meetings—and for those of us who work here in the community and don't commute to a job outside, we see one another quite a lot during the workday, too. To a great degree, the limited physical dimensions of our village and the logistics of living in close proximity to one another define our social as well as physical boundaries, and only with great difficulty can someone disconnect socially from someone else here for any length of time. This remains true even if someone says or does something that hurts our feelings. Sustaining civility under these circumstances is clearly not simple.

We have learned that community life requires a lot of proactive involvement on the part of each member of the group. Each person must work at maintaining a positive attitude toward others. Taking the path of least resistance is not an option. Attitudes of disrespect and the kinds of behaviors that push other people's buttons cannot be tolerated for long, because these affect everyone. Conflicts must be addressed and resolved as they arise. There are times when we may need to turn over a new leaf every day and readjust our attitudes—again. We cannot afford here to carry around unresolved feelings of frustration, anger, resentment, or hatred toward others. Closely connected to one another as we are by the restrictions of the physical space, unresolved negative energy is too powerful and our social fabric too delicate to ignore it. Even if we could manage to disconnect ourselves from others *physically*, we would never be able to do this *emotionally*. Instead, we would only end up at a hopeless impasse in our efforts to promote the idea of community, to build our community up, and to foster its ongoing development.

A whole spectrum of conflict-related issues familiar to most people take on heightened importance in a case like ours. Although there were some general foundational aspirations to begin with (about which I'll write more later), our community at its inception was not based on any specific ideology, in contrast to many other intentional communities. Ours started with people who represented at least two different and contradictory overarching narratives. These narratives were deeply rooted in a very complex political conflict. Against all odds, these people chose intentionally to live together for the purpose of building a new reality where compassion, tolerance, and peace would replace hatred, intolerance, and conflict.

I learned a great deal from my readings at the University of Coventry, affording me a considerable acquaintance with some of the literature about community life in general. To begin with, I was surprised and even shocked—given the unique parameters of our project at Wahat

The Anteater And The Jaguar

Assalam—at some of the similarities between the communities I studied and our own. The various kinds of social and ideological conflicts we struggle with are not new; they have been occurring in communities throughout history, as I discovered in my readings about groups from the 1500s onward. As I continued reading, I began to realize that the choice I'd made to live in the Oasis of Peace also meant I would have to learn how to process a very complex social and psychological environment. This step had brought me into a landscape that was totally new for me, but that wasn't the case for all my fellow residents, especially not for those Jewish members who came from living in some other intentional community, such as a kibbutz. And yet, among all the communities I read about, I did not find a single one with a story like ours. Our community seems to be alone in having been founded as the result of a political conflict. All the others I learned about were typically founded for religious, economic, or social reasons. (Religion does, of course, come into play at Neve Shalom, but apart from an early interfaith orientation that did not last, religion per se was never the driving force behind our purpose.)

Most of the other communities I studied were homogeneous, inhabited by people belonging to the same nationality or the same religion—but Wahat Assalam is unique in that respect. It is the only intentional community whose members come from two or more discrete national groups in conflict and belong to three different monotheistic religions and where the intention is to nurture and reinforce (not set aside) these respective identities while honoring all the others. (Perhaps I should mention here that we have always had a few members who are neither Jewish nor Palestinian; our intentional orientation is just that—a set of intentions—and is not intended to exclude anyone.)

All the other intentional communities I studied were founded to foster a specific way of life and advance a specific set of beliefs; most were also founded or organized by a person who was thought of as a leader or guru. The leader retained an important role as a kind of referee for the community, someone who could sort out problems as they arose and to whose judgment people deferred. The founder of Neve Shalom, Father

Rayek R. Rizek

Bruno Hussar (I will tell more of his story shortly), in contrast, did not request or require members of our community to follow a specific way of life or to embrace a specific set of beliefs, and though he was the community's founder, he never assumed the role of the community's leader. For him it was enough to start by accepting others as equals. From that point forward, matters would be decided based on this belief in equality.

I should digress long enough to note here that residentially mixed neighborhoods of Jews, Muslim Palestinians, and Christian Palestinians are to be found in cities such as Jaffa, Haifa, Ramleh, Lod, Acre, and Upper Nazareth. The difference between them and us, however, is that we choose intentionally to live together for the purpose of figuring out a different way of relating to one another, seeking a dynamic very unlike the uneasy tensions prevailing most of the time in those places. Most of the people living in mixed neighborhoods elsewhere in Israel did not seek out a mixed neighborhood on purpose—they found themselves there for historical reasons. Around the time of the 1948 war, for example, in many cities and towns, a lot of houses left empty by their Palestinian Arab residents were eventually turned over to Jewish families after the houses were declared the property of the state of Israel.

Nazareth was a special case with a different set of circumstances. The mixed neighborhoods of Upper Nazareth (*Natzrat Illit* in Hebrew) developed gradually in recent decades, when housing became impossible to find in the increasingly overcrowded precincts of the original Arab Nazareth down the mountain. Young couples and families, desperate for a place to live close to home, saw no option but to look for apartments in Upper Nazareth, which had been founded originally in 1957 as a new Jewish town overlooking the Arab town below. Immigrant Jews flocked to the new town built on land partly confiscated from Arab owners who had lived in Arab Nazareth and nearby Arab villages. Today, Arabs in Upper Nazareth constitute more than 17 percent of its forty thousand residents. This Arab population is currently represented by three members out of seventeen on the municipal council, and one of the Arab members was appointed deputy mayor recently. That appointment, which brought new benefits for the Arab minority community of the town, including an agreement to build the first Arab school in Upper Nazareth, came about as a result of a new coalition within the municipal council. This new coalition was formed with the Arab members in support of one of the Jewish members of the municipal council for the position of mayor, after the forced resignation of the previous mayor due to charges of corruption on his watch.

Wahat Assalam thus remains the only community inhabited *by choice* by Palestinian Arabs and Jews in the whole of Israel/Palestine. Members of our community are among the very few in the general population who are wholly open to discussing every issue that has to do with the Israeli-Palestinian conflict, past, present, and future. Tensions exist in our oasis, but they go with the territory, so to speak. They bring teachable moments. They are, for us, fodder for enlightenment.

You might think a reasonable beginning for our community would have been for the future residents to first create some kind of charter. Since, as Jews and Palestinians, they represented two groups of people from opposing sides of a deep-rooted conflict, they could have sought initially to address the very important questions and critical issues bound to confront them in this new project of living their lives together—before they went ahead. But no such founding charter was created.

To live together is fine (they might have reasoned), but how should we share the management and governance of our community as equals in a wider environment rife with inequality? How should we educate our children? How should we represent ourselves to the world outside? Who are we exactly? How do we relate to the main conflict? Where do we stand on the political map? What do we agree about, and what do we not agree about?

None of these questions was addressed in any organized fashion ahead of time. I imagine that, had the beginning really been like that, our community would not have found any practical starting point and would never have been established at all.

So what exactly did happen here? And how did it start?

Three

FATHER BRUNO HUSSAR, 1911–1996

Father Bruno Hussar, founder of the Oasis of Peace, was born in Egypt to a secular Jewish-French-Hungarian family early in the twentieth century.

The more one learns about his life, the less one is inclined to wonder why Father Bruno came to found the Oasis of Peace on a hilltop in the Holy Land and the more one is inclined to ask how, given his biography, he could have ended up doing anything else.

The future Nobel Peace Prize nominee (1988) was born in 1911 to a Hungarian father and a French mother who were living at the time in Cairo, where Bruno grew up. (In the Oasis of Peace, he is referred to universally as Father Bruno, or just Bruno, and I shall do likewise here.) After finishing high school, Bruno traveled to France to continue his studies in civil engineering. During his first years there, through the influence of a group of friends and his own spiritual searching, he became a Christian. Later, in his late thirties, he joined the Dominican order of the Roman Catholic Church and became a priest.

Bruno's conversion to Christianity, far from disconnecting him from Judaism, actually helped him to reconnect to it. This was further aided by his reading of the Bible and his becoming familiar with Jewish

The Anteater And The Jaguar

experiences of the Holocaust. He learned to feel fully at home, apparently, with both these identities. If you visit his grave at the small cemetery at the Oasis of Peace, you will find that the cross and the Star of David are both engraved on his headstone. To get a sense of the man in his own words, I recommend *Oasis of Dreams* by Grace Feuerverger, which includes a long interview with Father Bruno.

Father Bruno came to Israel for the first time in 1953, and some years later, he opened a center for Jewish-Christian reconciliation in Jerusalem called the House of Isaiah. The issue of reconciliation, to which he dedicated his entire life, drove him to look for places where it was most urgently needed—and reconciliation, he concluded, was urgently needed between Jews and Palestinians. Both, he insisted, were the children of Abraham.

Toward the end of the 1960s, Father Hussar conceived the idea of forming a community that would be called *Neve Shalom*—Hebrew for the "Abode of Peace"—where followers of the three monotheistic religions could live, work, and bring up their children together in what he called a "permanent encounter." The reestablishment of relations between East and West Jerusalem, cut off from each other by the war of 1948 and then brought back into contact again by the war of 1967, influenced this specific idea. The opening of the borders that had, for a time, divided Palestine into three parts (Israel, the West Bank, and the Gaza Strip) contributed, as well, to Hussar's belief that the two peoples should share this land equally.

After a long search, at some point in the early 1970s, Father Bruno approached the Trappist Monastery of Latroun, which had been established in Palestine in 1890. The monastery is located midway between Jerusalem and Jaffa-Tel Aviv. Bruno requested from the Trappists a piece of land where he could start his community. The monks welcomed the idea and decided to support the project, leasing Bruno one hundred acres of nearby land for a period of one hundred years, in exchange for a symbolic payment by Bruno of one hundred Israeli pounds.

In 1999 the Neve Shalom community signed a new agreement with the Latroun Monastery. The community relinquished fifty of the leased acres to the monastery, and in return, the monastery made a permanent gift to the community of the other fifty acres. This was undoubtedly the most important—and the most generous—donation the community ever received.

By early 2016, about sixty families were living on those fifty acres, and another ninety lots had been set aside for future residential use. I imagine that, at some point in the near future, Wahat Assalam will have grown from a tiny community to a small but sustainable village with 150 resident families. In percentage terms, the distribution between Jews and Palestinians (the latter both Christians and Muslims) will be about fifty-fifty. Moreover, considering the number of people who have been approaching our community over the years with an interest in joining it, I would imagine that if we had enough land, we could easily grow into a town of several hundred more families.

I knew Father Bruno Hussar personally for twelve years, but I have learned to appreciate him even more since his death. I have learned to appreciate him especially when I consider, in light of my readings about other communities, how remarkable his contributions really were and how different Father Bruno himself was from so many other community founders. His humility and selflessness set him apart. Bruno, when I knew him, was already in his seventies, whereas most of the other members of Neve Shalom in those early days were in their late twenties or early thirties. Despite his seniority in age and breadth of experience, however, and despite (or perhaps because of) his considerable wisdom, he did not assign himself the role of leader. In community meetings, he was not a talker, as most others were. Sometimes he would share his opinion about a subject under discussion, but he would always do so very quietly and without the expectation that others would necessarily accept it.

One unforgettable discussion between Father Bruno and me occurred around the beginning of the First Intifada. He expressed a political view that greatly angered me, and I told him so and left. To my surprise, some minutes later, Bruno appeared at my house to tell me he had not intended to hurt my feelings. If he had done so, he told me, it was unintentional, and he wanted me to know he was sorry he had upset me. I was shocked, because in my own culture, it was most uncommon that a man my father's age would apologize to me, a much younger man. Bruno's apology left me bewildered and somewhat embarrassed; yet, at the same time, I gained a great respect for this unusual person who did not mind apologizing to a man so many years his junior.

Accounts of the community's earliest years are not entirely uniform, but according to the various chronologies available, Father Bruno evidently came to live atop what was then the barren hill of Neve Shalom sometime in 1972. He purchased an old bus and converted it into his first house. A short time later, a French woman by the name of Ann LeMeignen joined him. Ann, who was to become one of Father Bruno's lifelong supporters, still lives in the community. Her friendship with Bruno had a significant influence on his project of forming the community and persevering in its successful development.

Many people, I am told, were drawn to join Father Bruno during the community's early years, but few stayed for very long. An exception was one couple, Ilan and Tamar, and their young daughter, Hila. They joined Father Bruno in 1977. Now Ilan and Tamar are grandparents. They are still living in our community and are known as our first family.

I have met some of the people who spent brief periods of time with Father Bruno during the community's early years, and I have heard about others whose contributions aided in its founding. Clearly there was a good deal of help and support given to Father Bruno by the comrades of those first few years. Yet the impression persists that the community's evolution from an idea into a reality is attributable above all to the depth of Bruno's own conviction and the strength of his will to persevere. Few others seem to have the same degree of determination, persistence, and patience in standing behind the dream until it eventually became a reality. Father Bruno spent about six years living on that hill before there was anything like a stable community there with him.

Father Bruno had a remarkable capacity to accept people whose personal beliefs differed from his, welcoming them as members of the

Rayek R. Rizek

community he had founded. Thanks to Bruno's liberal convictions, our community ended up being much more representative of the diverse social and political reality of the entire country than any of the other intentional communities I came to know through my reading. In that way, Wahat Assalam is quite unlike most of these communities, which feature a uniform credo and a homogeneous outlook. Some visitors criticized Father Bruno for accepting into the community people who did not practice prayer, and his response was incisive: he believed these people were doing the work of God simply by being willing to live in such a community.

When Father Bruno passed away in 1996, he left behind a community of more than thirty families and a number of thriving institutions, including the School for Peace (an award-winning training and encounter institution); the Oasis of Peace Primary School, which includes a kindergarten and nursery; a cheery guesthouse used to host visitors and to accommodate a variety of programs offering educational and spiritual activities; the Corner of Silence (*Doumia* in Hebrew and *Sakinah* in Arabic); a plan for a Pluralistic Spiritual Center; and numerous other facilities. By the time of Bruno's death, the community had also become internationally known. Thousands of visitors, both domestic and international, traveled every year from across the country and around the world to visit it. Among these were diplomats, artists, spiritual leaders, students, and ordinary people from all walks of life and of all ages. The stream of visitors continues to the present. Some are celebrities, such as Hillary Clinton, who came in late 1998, when she was first lady of the United States; actor and activist Jane Fonda; actor Richard Gere; Ian Anderson of the British rock group Jethro Tull; and Roger Waters of Pink Floyd, who came and performed in our community in June 2006 for an audience of more than seventy thousand people. Professor Stephen Hawking visited our community in December 2006 for a physics seminar and presented a lecture about black holes.

Father Bruno Hussar fulfilled his dream against all odds; enormous hardships, challenges, and doubts could not deflect him. The creation of the Oasis of Peace in the face of such seemingly insurmountable odds shows us what an individual can achieve if she or he has enough faith, conviction, and determination. I see Father Bruno and his work as living proof that the realities we create outside ourselves are manifestations of our internal realities.

When Dyana and I joined the community on May 1, 1984, there were, besides Bruno, Ann, and us, six married couples (four Jewish, one Arab, and one mixed couple of a Swedish Christian married to an Israeli Jew) and another eight single people, some Arab and some Jewish, plus twelve children and a few resident volunteers.

During the summer of 1984, another three families joined our community. Two of these were Arab (one Muslim and one Christian), and the third was another mixed couple, a Jewish Israeli married to a British Christian. These couples brought with them an additional six children, so that by the end of the summer of 1984, the community had increased by an additional eight adults and six children, making the number of Jews and Arabs almost equal for the first time. Two of the Arab families and their children left two years later, but their time with us had helped the momentum for expansion to continue.

My guess is that 1984 must have been a special year for Father Bruno, as he witnessed for the first time, after almost twelve years, the real beginnings of a community of thirty adults and eighteen children. Together, these residents were representative of the Jewish, the Arab-Palestinian Christian, and the Arab-Palestinian Muslim population of the whole land of Israel/Palestine, in addition to few European Christians.

Four

ALL ABOUT THIS BIT OF LAND

According to copies of official documents I obtained, the land where our community is built was registered under the ownership of the Monastery of Latroun in 1935. One document notes that the monastery paid the amount of seventeen Palestinian pounds as surveying fees. The papers also revealed that this land fell into the category of *Miri mauqufa waqf Khalil Al Rahman*—that is, state-owned land endowed as an Islamic charity under the name of Abraham, whom the Quran refers to also as the *friend of Allah* or as *Khalil Alrahman* ("Friend of [God who is] Merciful"). *Khalil* means *friend*, and *Alrahman* means *the merciful.* Alrahman is one of the ninety-nine names of God mentioned in the Quran.

"Al Khalil" also happens to be the Arabic name for the city of Hebron. Indeed, the Quran is full of Arabic names for figures familiar to readers of the Bible: *Musa* for Moses, *Isa* for Jesus, *Yahya* for John, *Yunis* for Jonah, *Ibrahim* for Abraham, *Daud* for David, *Sulayman* for Solomon, *Is-haq* for Isaac, *Ismail* for Ishmael, *Yakub* for Jacob, and *Yusuf* for Joseph.

The precise location of our community is rather interesting. By the end of the 1948 war, under the cease-fire agreements that came into effect in 1949, a strip of land in the area was marked off as a buffer zone at the boundary between Jordan (the West Bank) and Israel. The

The Anteater And The Jaguar

land offered to Father Bruno was located within this strip, which from 1949 to 1967 was designated as no-man's-land. One kilometer wide and ten kilometers long, this land was also a demilitarized zone. However, at the conclusion of the 1948 war, the monastery's main building had ended up inside the boundary of the West Bank, while the lands that the monastery owned were divided among the West Bank, Israel, and the demilitarized zone. (The location of this land can be viewed on Google Earth.) Following the 1967 war, the monastery regained its ownership of the land within the demilitarized zone, and in 1970, they leased part of it to Father Bruno so he could start his community.

Some years ago, Palestinian scholar Walid Khalidi published a book entitled *All That Remains*. (Khalidi, a prolific writer, is also the author of *Before Their Diaspora*, a fascinating photographic history of the Palestinians from 1876 to 1948.) In *All That Remains*, Khalidi documents the history of the Palestinian villages that were occupied, depopulated, and destroyed in 1948 by the Jewish forces. He also cites the names of new Israeli settlements that were built either in the same locations or nearby. Khalidi's book, however, errs in reporting that the colony of Neve Shalom (our community) was built on the lands of the [Palestinian] village of Latroun. I contacted all the concerned parties involved in publishing Khalidi's book and gave them documents so they could correct the mistake; unfortunately, they did not do this. It is true that a small village of Latroun existed near the monastery, but the land on which our community was built was not part of that village's lands.

All that information became available to me only in 1998, after I obtained copies of the official documents from the monastery's adviser. When I came to live in the village in 1984, I knew no details of the history of the land in that precise place. Even so, I learned the particulars only because I was serving as secretary general (equivalent to mayor) of the community when we conducted negotiations for a new agreement with the monastery. Father Bruno Hussar and Father Elie Corbisier, then head of the Latroun Monastery, signed the first long-term lease agreement on 6 November 1970. Then, in the late 1990s, an updated agreement,

Rayek R. Rizek

dividing the original hundred-acre parcel between our community and the monastery, was drafted following negotiations between the parties; our community was represented by Ilan Frish, Ahmad Hijazi[1], and me (in my role as secretary general of the village). The two signatories to the new agreement were to be Father Paul Sauma, a Lebanese who had become the head of the monastery, and me. I was asked if, as a symbolic gensture, I would agree to have a Jewish member cosign the agreement with me. I said yes and asked Ilan to do it. We signed the agreement with Father Paul on 31 December 1999.

---

1 When I had just begun writing this book, in August 2012, we were shocked and saddened to hear that Ahmad Hijazi and his young son Adam were killed in an automobile accident while on a holiday in Zanzibar. They were our neighbors and our friends. Ahmad was 45 at the time; Adam was 9.

Five

The Primary School: Eleven Kids, Two Teachers, And An Idea

Unusual schools in this world tend to begin with love and an idea. The Oasis of Peace Primary School certainly began that way.

In September 1984, our primary school opened its doors for the children of the community. The first bilingual and binational school in the entire country, it started with eleven girls and boys at first-, second-, and third-grade level. Seven younger children were already being cared for in our community preschool, which had begun operating a few years earlier.

When the primary school opened, Ety Edlund (Jewish) and the late Abdelsalam Najjar (Arab) taught these eleven children around one table. While the efforts of many people were important in moving the idea of the school from wishful thinking to reality, Ety and Abdelsalam should be acknowledged as the founders of the primary school. Moreover, their classroom launched an experiment that would become an important component of our approach to education, whether for children or adults: every classroom would have one Jewish and one Arab teacher, and both Arabic and Hebrew would be spoken there.

The school grew to encompass the first through the sixth grade, but to achieve that growth and put the school on a sustainable footing, we

Rayek R. Rizek

had to open our doors wider. In the early 1990s, we started accepting students, both Jewish and Arab, from surrounding villages and towns.

The number of children enrolled in the primary school increased gradually and now exceeds two hundred. Children from outside the community became a majority of the student body a long time ago. They brought needed expansion numerically but also new challenges: most of them, for example, unlike most of our own children, were not bilingual in Arabic and Hebrew; some had had literally no prior experience with or exposure to children from the other national group. I will discuss this in greater depth later on. For now, suffice it to say that, while the various educational and training institutions of our community have done important work for several decades in bringing the two sides of the conflict closer to each other, the primary school remains the jewel in the crown of the community's educational and peace-building work.

Since the school's founding, thousands of children from Wahat Assalam and surrounding Jewish and Arab communities have passed through it. These children, including my own sons, Hilal and Taj, spent their formative years in this school, and I think they are lucky to have had this experience. Everyone knows that what we experience and learn during our childhood years influences the direction of our entire life. These early influences are written on our children's minds like "an inscription on stone," as one Arab proverb goes. Unfortunately, since almost all children in this land attend nationally separate schools, we can expect that they will continue to relate to one another as strangers and enemies. Stereotypes will be reinforced, too, as long as the conflict remains unresolved. Meanwhile, a school like ours breaks stereotypes and helps raise children into tolerant, broad-minded, humane adults. This forming of character results from personal and direct exposure to others whose backgrounds are different, as well as to their languages, their religions, and their cultures. Considering the successes of our school in promoting these virtues in its graduates, it is not hard to imagine that peaceful and respectful coexistence in this land is truly possible. While accompanying outside visitors on tours of our school, I often think about what

The Anteater And The Jaguar

could happen if all the children in our country could have opportunities similar to the ones our school provides. Conflicts, no doubt, could be resolved more easily. (Aiming to address this, two educators who were influenced by our school, Lee Gordon and Amin Khalaf, founded an NGO known today as Hand in Hand, through which they have opened four bilingual schools in different parts of the country since 1998.)

Throughout the school year at the Oasis of Peace Primary School (and doubtless at the Hand in Hand schools, too), activities are offered that bring together not just the children but their parents, too, including ones that celebrate the start of each school year in the fall, commemorate an array of different religious and national holidays, and mark the end of the school year in the spring. The end-of-school activities usually draw a few hundred people—students, siblings, parents, and friends. Everyone gathers to celebrate and to watch the children dance, recite, and sing together in Hebrew and in Arabic.

When attending such occasions, I almost always feel I am inside a magical world. When I look around me and see such harmonious occasions for Jewish and Palestinian families to gather for a common cause, my heart fills up with intense feelings of joy and hope. I cannot help but get emotional during such events. It is easy to imagine as they are taking place that it is not complicated, as some tend to believe, for Jews and Palestinians to enjoy their time together and to demonstrate mutual respect toward one another. Nothing could better describe such a gathering than to say it is beautiful!

However, even if mixed schools such as ours are not always possible, we still must consider a new approach to the educational system—an approach that says, "Yes, we are members of different nations, different communities, and different religions, but we are still equal as human beings." How can we expect any constructive change if we insist on teaching our children stories and giving them experiences that breed division and discord? Even as we keep talking about peace and hoping for it, can we not see how we ourselves stand in the way of peace? Must we persist in passing on our unresolvable arguments, irreconcilable differences, and entrenched stereotypes from generation to generation? What profit has there been, or will there ever be, if we persist in doing these things?

Even in our unique school, most teachers and parents believe that commemorating and celebrating historical occasions and events is important, even though some of these occasions and events can consciously or unconsciously increase separation and help sustain the conflict. Who really needs these celebrations? The children…or the adults? Perhaps our courageous decision to teach and to bring up our children in such an unusual school environment is just the beginning; perhaps we ourselves need to learn *how* to help them let go of certain convictions that foster resentment, division, and discord.

It is fine to recall past events in our separate histories, but *how* we remember them makes all the difference in the world. Do the histories we commemorate foster separation, or do they help us share aims and common human values, in the way our school tries to emphasize? Do we teach our kids that our narrative is the only right story that explains the causes of the conflict, or do we teach them that there are (at least) two narratives that are equally valid in spite of their contradictions? Do we ask them to take responsibility for the past, even though they were not part of it, or do we ask them to take responsibility for the present moment, which is the only time we can build a different future? Do we have to continue relating to *our* fatalities as martyrs while considering *theirs* as terrorists, or could we commemorate all the dead as victims? I hope that someday all countries will adopt a day to remember all the victims of all the wars that have ever taken place on this planet and that they will do so in the spirit of Kahlil Gibran, who wrote, "Was the love of Judas' mother of her son less than the love of Mary for Jesus?" (*Sand and Foam*, 1926).

Six

The School for Peace

The School for Peace (SFP) was the first institution serving the general public to operate inside our community. It began because of Father Bruno's wish to invite Jews and Palestinian for encounters and workshops. In his own words, Father Bruno explains that he intended for the village to be "the setting for a school for peace." In his memoir, *When the Cloud was Lifted*, which was translated by A. Megroz and published in Dublin by Veritas Press in 1989, he continued:

> For years there have been academies in the various countries where the art of war has been taught. Inspired by the prophetic words: "Nation shall not lift up sword against nation, neither shall they learn war anymore," we want to found a school for peace; for peace, too, is an art. It does not appear spontaneously; it has to be learned. People would come here from all over the country to meet those from whom they were estranged, wanting to break down the barriers of fear, mistrust, ignorance, misunderstanding, preconceived ideas—all things that separate us—and to build bridges of trust, respect, mutual understanding, and, if possible, friendship. This aim would be achieved with the help of

Rayek R. Rizek

courses, seminars, group psychology techniques, shared physical work, and recreational evenings.

Through the School for Peace, tens of thousands of Palestinians and Jews have had the chance to meet face-to-face, most of them for the first time in their lives. Indeed, our community's School for Peace has pioneered the work of facilitating encounters between Jews and Palestinians, beginning in 1980. Although the efforts of many people were crucial along the way, the main credit for establishing the SFP belongs to Nava Sonnenschein and the late Abdelsalam Najjar. Today there are many organizations doing similar work, but the experience that participants undergo is somewhat different at our School for Peace, partly due to the fact that ours is the only institution of its kind operating from within the supportive embrace of a mixed Palestinian-Jewish intentional community.

Until the early 1990s, most participants in the SFP workshops were Jewish-Israeli and Palestinian-Israeli high school students. After the Oslo agreement in 1993, however, further encounters were initiated between Jewish-Israeli students and Palestinian students from the West Bank. The school added binational encounters between groups of women, as well as programs to conduct encounters between groups of professionals, including teachers, lawyers, physicians, professors, journalists, and others, and to prepare them to serve as agents of egalitarian social change in their family networks, communities, and professional circles.

Throughout the School for Peace's years of operation, many individuals and a number of foundations have funded its work. Coming mainly from Europe and the United States, these funders have helped to cover the expense of hosting anywhere from thirty to seventy or more participants in our community's guesthouse for each of the two-day, three-day, or longer workshops offered.

Our community built the forty-room guesthouse during the early 1990s with the support of the Association of German Friends of our community (with much credit to its chairman for many years, Herman

Sieben). Its purpose from the beginning was to host participants in the encounters facilitated by the School for Peace. Today the guesthouse also welcomes foreign and local tourists and is quite busy throughout the year. Before the guesthouse opened, we used to host the School for Peace encounter program participants in a somewhat more basic, forty-bed youth hostel built in the late 1970s thanks to a generous donation by Lotte Shifler, a German friend of the community.

Over time, the School for Peace developed its own pioneering model for facilitating encounters between groups in conflict, after experimenting for some years with workshop models imported from social psychology and other disciplines abroad, notably from the United States. Some trial and error was necessary, because no projects quite like ours were available to learn from when the SFP was being established, and there was scant literature on the subject to guide us. The work became increasingly rigorous, and the model continued to evolve as young staff members from the early days earned master's degrees and doctorates and plowed their new knowledge back into their work. By that time, the SFP was giving courses in partnership with leading universities and undergraduate colleges in Israel, and its model was earning recognition and awards overseas.

The story of how the SFP operating model evolved is an interesting one. When it was getting started in the late 1970s and early 1980s, the general consensus among groups doing similar work was that merely bringing people together was good enough: the encounter, in and of itself, would yield a peace dividend. Then the SFP was awarded a grant by the Ford Foundation for the years 1985–1989, and it began carefully documenting every aspect of its work and publishing its first professional research.

To begin with, the research showed that the encounter was taking place within an asymmetrical context, in which the Jewish and Palestinian participants were unequally empowered in several crucial ways. For example, the Jewish-Israeli participants came to the encounter having a much more solid collective identity than did their Israeli-Palestinian counterparts. This was typical, because most Israeli Jews had learned a narrative covering a history that spanned thousands of years. They had learned through that narrative, as well, what had happened to their people in the past, and they had also gained skill in advancing arguments and justifications that could fend off accusations raised against them, specifically accusations relating to their conflict with Palestinian Arabs.

The Israeli-Palestinian students, on the other hand, were disadvantaged, because they had been subjected to the curriculum imposed by the Israeli ministry of education. They had not learned much about their own narrative as a result but were instead taught a version of the Israeli narrative—which, perhaps unsurprisingly, tended to put all the blame on the Palestinian people for whatever had gone wrong between them and the Jews during their common conflict.

As the Israeli establishment continued to solidify the collective identity and commitment of Israeli Jews, it was projecting a questionable kind of fragmented identity onto Israeli Palestinians. Rather than being seen as a collective, Israeli Palestinians were characterized as a disparate collection of people separated into Muslim, Christian, Druze (an eleventh-century offshoot of Ismaili Shia Islam), and Bedouin subgroups. This collection of people was not viewed as a larger cohesive *national* minority that could be said to have had a real *national* identity. This version of Palestinian identity, as promoted by the Jewish establishment, focused on which group's political and historical rights should be favored and which should not—although, in fact, the various Palestinian-Arab communities within Israel shared a much higher degree of cultural cohesion than the newer Israeli-Jewish communities shared among themselves. Palestinian communities of different faiths and traditions had been sharing their lives as neighbors for hundreds of years, while the Jewish communities in Israel, most of whom arrived as immigrants after 1948 from a diverse list of countries, had been meeting and learning about one another for a relatively short period of time.

The ongoing research led the SFP to adopt an alternative model of encounter. One component of the new model was that, early in the encounter process, the Jewish and Palestinian participants would undergo uni-national workshops to equip them better for a more balanced and productive binational encounter. Disparities between the two groups could be highlighted and explored. As stereotypical ways of thinking were abandoned, the complexity of the conflict could be addressed more effectively. Other components, such as the assurance that participants could speak their mother tongue, with translation provided, buttressed this process of achieving an experience that, while never fully symmetrical given the reality outside, was still a lot more balanced than it had been. Even today, the School for Peace stands out for its insistence that, if the goal is an egalitarian encounter on an equal footing, then speaking Arabic must be as legitimate as speaking Hebrew in any Jewish-Palestinian workshop or event.

The SFP trajectory was not always a smooth one, however. In 1989, an ideological rift, complicated by financial issues and personal frictions, led to dissension among the staff, and a majority of the staff resigned. Subsequently, the remaining staff, along with newcomers, abandoned much of the unique approach to encounter developed at the SFP up to that point. For some time, the SFP proceeded to run workshops in a manner harking back to earlier methods, in contradiction to the conclusions of its own research. Eventually, however, the alternative methodologies were reintroduced, and the SFP continued to elaborate and develop its model. The SFP courses taught in academic settings today reflect the hard-won conclusions of all that research into the conduct of a more egalitarian type of encounter.

Ironically enough (considering the institution's name), the 1989 crisis at the School for Peace led to the first major breakdown between members of the community. When most of the staff resigned, I found myself siding with those who had left. Although my own wife was then coadministering the School for Peace and was among those who resigned, my reasons for taking sides were not purely personal; I simply could not accept the approach advocated by the other faction as a useful means of ever resolving the Palestinian-Israeli conflict. How could we go on with the workshops using the method that had preceded the research? How could we, as a community, go on claiming we were different in our approach to conflict resolution if we insisted on behaving just like those practitioners whose methods we had been criticizing?

So I found myself resigning, too. I resigned from participation in the community while continuing to live in it. Thus began the most difficult period of my life as a resident of the Oasis of Peace, and it continued for seven years. During that time, Dyana and I, along with several other members, boycotted the community from within. We abstained from attending community meetings, and we no longer socialized with members whom we believed had caused the breakdown.

But just as one crisis caused me to resign from the community, another caused me to return—and not only did I return, but I also ended up becoming mayor of the community. This time it was about the death of Tom, a young man from our community who was killed doing his army service. I will discuss this episode in more detail at a later point.

For the School for Peace, however, despite its name, the crisis of 1989 was neither the first nor the last ideological/financial/personal crisis to occur. The institution has witnessed many such conflicts over the years. Some of these have occurred among the staff members themselves. Others have involved conflict between the staff and other community members. Most have been ideological in nature, resulting mainly from differing views of the causes of the Israeli-Palestinian conflict and how the conflict should be approached. Indeed, a turnover of staff has taken place every few years at the SFP. Still, I believe most of those who have served there were searching honestly for a better understanding of the complex reality existing in our country. They merely had different ideas about how to assess that complex reality and how to go about addressing it and offering solutions to it.

The reality for Palestinians—as well as for Israelis—has been and remains both complicated and painful. Issues of identity, in particular, can be painful. Palestinians of the West Bank and the Gaza Strip, for example, have a more solid collective identity than do their Palestinian counterparts living in Israel, because the former have lived through similar collective experiences under Israeli occupation. Israeli Palestinians have been subject to Israeli *civil law* since 1966 and are classified as Israeli citizens; Palestinians residing in the West Bank and the Gaza Strip have been subject to Israeli *military law* since 1967.

No attempt to explain or justify military rule over a civilian population can persuade me that a military occupation allows for real freedom or normal human rights for the people living under its laws. Military rule cannot avoid violating the individual and collective human rights of its subjects. Military rule cannot tolerate any political activity directed against it; if such activity does take place, then those participating in it are considered terrorists in need of being punished, imprisoned, or executed. Again, the identity formed by those living under military rule is not determined only by what they choose: It is also determined by the occupying power that usually ends up exacerbating whatever problem it is trying to resolve. The occupier appears to be trying to extinguish a fire by pouring gasoline on it.

So, despite all the reasons we may cite for unbalanced kinds of encounters between people, I am not sure today if those with a solid national identity are destined to be the winners and those with a less solid national identity are doomed to be the losers. I am not sure today if the Palestinians need to become more like their Israeli-Jewish counterparts by fostering a more solid national identity or whether Israeli Jews should become, like us Palestinians, less solid in their national identity. Can conflicts like ours in this land be resolved by means of a confrontation between equally solid national identities? Or do the national identities make up a big part of the problem? What can I do with a solid national identity anyway, except separate myself from others and create and sustain conflicts with them? What benefit would I get from strengthening my national identity except to increase my pain and anger? What gain would I get except to keep feeding my vanity and illusion? Aren't national identities, whether they are solid or fluid, often based on anecdotal stories or highly selective and subjective narratives, after all? Do national identities need to be dismantled so we can become again what we were before turning into members of an invented community? What would happen if we were all to waive our national identities and develop a common human identity instead? Indeed, what courses of action would be best for reaching a humane solution to the Palestinian-Israeli conflict? These are questions I have been dealing with lately through my search for peace between our two peoples. I am not sure how these questions should be answered, but I believe they are questions we must seriously consider.

I believe my rights to live as an equal and to prosper in this land should not depend on whether I am a member of this or that nationality. I believe, rather, that my rights should be valued simply because I am a human being who just happens to have been born in this land. My relationship to this or that community or nation should not negate any of my fundamental human rights.

Seven

My First Years in the Oasis of Peace

I knew nothing of the existence of Neve Shalom until 1982. I learned of it through Dyana while we were courting; we were married in summer 1983. Dyana had had her first contact with the community in 1979, while she was studying the arts at the University of Haifa. Being politically active within the university, she was attracted to the ideals that Wahat Assalam stood for, even though the community was still in an embryonic stage at that time. She visited the place a few times, and later she took a course in how to facilitate youth encounters at the community's School for Peace.

After Dyana and I met in 1982, we went to visit the community together. I still remember that first visit and the people I met there, who already knew her. The place at that time included a few wooden huts, which had been salvaged from other locations and rebuilt on this hilltop across from the Latroun Monastery. There were no paved roads, and services such as electricity and water were available for only a few hours a day. There were a few trees and plenty of wild grass, but also flies, snakes, and scorpions.

Despite these inhospitable conditions, I was attracted to the place, because it reminded me of my childhood summers at Mount Tabor, which is near my hometown. Called *Jabal Al-Tur* in Arabic and *Har Tavor* in Hebrew, this mountain is thought by local Arab Christians and many others around the world to be the site at which the Transfiguration of Jesus occurred. This is the traditional view, though Mount Hermon is another candidate. Tabor is also mentioned in the Old Testament as a mountain that overlooks the Jezreel Valley (*Marj ibin Amer* in Arabic and *Emek Yezre'el* in Hebrew), where many wars were fought through thousands of years. The historic panorama seen from Mount Tabor has a certain kinship, for me, with the Ayalon Valley, as seen from the hilltop where my community is located.

During the 1950s and 1960s, my parents took us to Mount Tabor to spend the whole month of August for our summer vacations. My father would rent a small pickup truck, which we would load with mattresses, clothes, and other basic goods. On Tabor's summit are two churches, built a few hundred meters apart. One is Roman Catholic, and the other is Greek Orthodox. Both had facilities to host pilgrims. Near the Orthodox Church, there is a complex with a two-story house and another thirteen separate rooms; altogether, this complex could host about fifteen families. For many years, the same families, most of them related to one another, spent their summers there.

The rooms themselves had no electricity and no running water. Kerosene lamps provided light, and a well in front of the church supplied water that had to be drawn daily. During the day, mothers would take care of family needs and spend time socializing over coffee while baking bread and cooking. The men did the shopping at the nearby Arab village of Dabboriah, or at Nazareth, and spent the majority of their time playing backgammon or cards. Some men brought rifles and hunted partridges and wild doves during the early morning hours. Others devoted themselves to picking figs and cactus fruit to be eaten for breakfast along with watermelon and *labaneh*, the traditional sour white Arab cheese made from strained yogurt that is generally eaten with pita bread and olive oil. In the evenings, the families usually enjoyed their dinners together, sitting outside in front of the rooms. They drank lots of *Arak*—a

The Anteater And The Jaguar

traditional Levantine alcoholic beverage distilled from grapes and seasoned with anise—as they sang and danced most of the night away, rarely retiring before well past midnight. We children spent our days playing and wandering in the woods on the mountain with our slingshots. In the early evening hours, we flew kites, and we also enjoyed a daily walk with the rest of the families toward the Catholic Church and back, a pleasant stroll of an hour or so. Many times these walks would include a welcome rest, sitting by the path, surrounded by nature's greenery, with some *tabbouleh* for a snack, followed by singing and dancing just for the fun of it. I can still remember the taste of that tabbouleh—it's a famous, traditional vegetarian dish popular in Palestine, Syria, and Lebanon: finely chopped parsley, mint, and onion mixed with bulgur wheat (*burghul* in Arabic); seasoned with olive oil, lemon juice, and salt; and garnished with finely chopped tomatoes and cucumber. It is best eaten rolled in grape leaves or lettuce. Those vacations remain vivid memories and seem like the most precious and most enjoyable days of my childhood.

As soon as I visited Neve Shalom with Dyana that first time and was reminded so strongly of the flavor of those summers at Mount Tabor, I knew I was destined to live there. Even my parents remarked when they visited me for the first time that Wahat Assalam was a lot like Mount Tabor.

I was also drawn to the community because of its philosophy. Dyana told me the people living in Neve Shalom were searching together for a different kind of life between Jews and Palestinians, a harmonious life unlike any that could be found in the rest of the country. Their engagement in this common quest meant that joining this community would add additional value to my life, beyond the ordinary existence I had lived in Nazareth and in Texas during the seventies.

The option of living in the community presented itself at a point when I had already been feeling unsure about staying in Nazareth. Nazareth had changed greatly during the seven years I was away, as a result of its need to expand vertically. It was much more crowded and noisy. Vertical expansion was inevitable, because the Israeli state had confiscated most of the surrounding lands after 1948. This situation is also the case for most other Arab communities in the state of Israel.

About two years later, in May 1984, Dyana and I formally joined the community. We had been married for only ten months. Dyana had already been invited to join the School for Peace as a facilitator. She was very interested in this position, so we applied to become members of the community, were screened, and were accepted by the Absorption Committee. Soon we moved into our new residence.

Dyana was clear about what she would be doing. As to what my role in the community was to be, however, I had no clue. Still, there was much good work to be done there, so I volunteered for a few months. I soon got my first official job as a kindergarten teacher with Dorit Shippin when I was accepted as a replacement for Aisha Najjar, who took a one-year leave to continue her studies. (Aisha was, in fact, cofounder of the original nursery in the community, which came into being when a caregiving framework was needed for the first few babies, and the community realized that sending the children elsewhere, to separate Jewish and Arab preschools, was just not an option.)

The following year, I spent a few months teaching in the primary school with Ety Edlund, standing in for Abdelsalam Najjar after he became ill. Later I moved to the School for Peace, where I worked as the office manager. After that, I moved on to the guesthouse, where I worked as a receptionist and as manager of the dining room.

Apart from those positions, I served about five years, during two different periods, as the elected secretary general of the community. I also spent about a year and a half as a night guard in the village. All through the years, I was also involved in outreach activities, both as a member of the community's public-relations committee and as a guide conducting tours of the village and its institutions and giving talks to visiting groups.

Eight

Financial Support and its Ramifications

Wahat Assalam is unusual, because it is one of very few privately initiated and supported communities in the whole country. (Most other communities are built by the state of Israel.) Father Bruno's main idea was to build a community where Jews and Palestinians (Christian and Muslim) would live, work, rear their children together, and work to create encounters between the people of this land. When Father Bruno applied for permission to establish a community, his application was rejected, so he settled for an educational project. This project later became the School for Peace.

Only about two decades later, in 1989, did the state of Israel recognize Neve Shalom as a legitimate community. This enabled it to receive those basic services the state provides to every such community. In addition, the state granted the community permission to build homes and other buildings legally for the first time.

Through the years, both before and after the community's recognition by the state of Israel, all the funding for its infrastructure and communal projects was provided by donations from private individuals and organizations, alongside what the residents themselves contributed. Most of these donors are located in North America, Europe, and Japan.

Rayek R. Rizek

The donations helped the community to develop infrastructure by making possible the building of public facilities such as the primary school, the School for Peace, the guesthouse, the swimming pool, the pluralistic spiritual center, and various other buildings and halls. Without any help from the state, the community even managed twice to pave the road that connects the village to a state road. (More recently, the state finally repaved and widened the access road, in addition to building a sports hall funded by the Israeli national lottery.)

The community's public-relations department (eventually renamed the department of communications and development) garnered most of the external funding. The principal credit for establishing the PR department goes to Pinhas Welsley Ahron and his wife, Coral Ahron, who were British Jews. They joined the community in the early eighties, when he was eighty years old, and she was in her midsixties. Over the years, the community established Associations of Friends in ten different countries. Most members of the Friends Associations have visited the community at some point. Enthused by the idea of peaceful coexistence and equality between Jews and Palestinians, they organized themselves and worked in a volunteer capacity to secure financial and moral support for us from sources in their home countries. All these people have persevered in their efforts, often over many years, and have visited the community from time to time, developing friendships with members of our community across the years and the generations. Their work and efforts have helped make the community a normal place to live, with the basic amenities every community aspires to; they have aided materially in the establishment of our educational institutions and have provided the stimulus that has helped these institutions to flourish.

In many ways, our supporters have shared our goals. They believed our community was based on a humane idea that deserved their support. Still, many and perhaps most of them did not fully realize the complexity of the challenges they were choosing to become involved in. Sometimes, disillusioned, one or more of them withdrew their membership from a given Friends Association. Still, by and large, they persevered in their support, regardless of conflicts and arguments that waxed and waned in the community and regardless of what they eventually learned about the complexity of the political situation and the challenges we faced in bringing the communal idea to bear upon our particular context.

Despite their good intentions, some supporters were not always up to the expectations we Palestinians had of them. Some supporters seemed unable to accept our narrative as we presented it as being fully legitimate. To a certain extent, their inability to accept our narrative reflected attitudes that could even be found inside our own community. So not only were we ourselves sometimes confused and in conflict about what the political identity of our community actually was, but our supporters living abroad were, too.

One hot issue revolved around terminology. Until at least the late 1980s, outsiders rarely used the term *Palestinian* to refer to Palestinian citizens of Israel, who were usually called by others "Israeli Arabs"—an artificial identity they did not choose. Some of our supporters overseas complained about "Israeli Arabs" who kept defining themselves as Palestinians, noting that this was hindering fundraising efforts abroad.

As this issue became prominent, Palestinians of our community were unwilling to compromise on our narrative and our affiliations just for the sake of money. Some people inside the community and elsewhere preferred to compromise on the Palestinian narrative so as not to damage the flow of funding.

The Palestinian members of our community faced another problem from abroad, as well. Most money raised for the support of the community and its educational institutions came from the Western world, where most media outlets and influential public figures were pro-Israel and usually also anti-Palestinian. And yet, a number of people, including Jews, did not automatically conclude that being pro-Israeli had to mean being anti-Palestinian. These people saw the injustice that had befallen the Palestinians, and they wanted to do something about it. Like us, these people rejected violence as a means of dealing with conflict. Instead, they preferred peaceful approaches and solutions. Like us, they also realized that two native peoples inhabited this land and that each had equally legitimate claims that needed to be taken seriously. They further recognized that the inhabitants of this land would eventually have to accept one another and live together as equals, not as masters and slaves.

To some external observers, our efforts to bring about communal harmony seemed futile for a number of reasons: First, any Palestinians and Jews who tried to nourish such a community faced an unbelievable challenge in addressing the historical obstacles that one of the world's most divided regions had put in their way. Second, none of us who were trying to make this communal ideal work had the practical experience we actually needed to make it work. In particular, no one had any prior experience of *choosing* to live in a mixed community like ours. Third, none of us came to the community project with adequate knowledge of the dynamics of conflict management or conflict resolution. We were just normal people like everybody else. We were, of course, willing to face whatever challenges would come our way; we were just unable to know in advance what the difficulties would be. And fourth, we had no specific ideology to provide a foundation for our community, a circumstance which set us apart from all the other intentional communities I know about.

One way to view this confusion and conflict was to see it as proof that our idea of community, which we were struggling to actualize in a practical way, was doomed to fail. Some people undoubtedly viewed the situation that way. Others may have viewed all the confusion and uncertainty as a predictable outcome of our attempts to encourage encounters between two groups so deeply alienated from each other. Perhaps we were trying to do the impossible. Certainly it may have seemed so.

Nine

AN ACCIDENTAL RADICAL

At some point during my first months in the community in the mid-1980s, I was asked to give a talk to a small group of British visitors. I presented myself as a Palestinian, unwittingly giving rise to my first political conflict inside the community. The group's guide called the head of the village's public-relations committee to complain, because she felt I should have defined myself as an Israeli Arab and not as a Palestinian.

I do not want to enumerate the series of episodes that gradually, cumulatively resulted in my being portrayed as a radical. The main factor in my earning this image was that I insisted on defining myself as a Palestinian, but I was also viewed as provocative because I referred to the Palestine Liberation Organization (PLO) as a legitimate organization at a time when Israel and many other countries still considered it a terrorist organization. In the 1980s, mentioning the word *Palestinian* evoked harsh accusations. Some people started claiming that I was trying to legitimize something everyone knew was illegitimate, while, at the same time, daring to delegitimize Israel.

As an ideologically vibrant mixed group in its earliest stages of evolution, our political, cultural, and social challenges were many. By the summer of 1985, we had embarked on a series of whole-day meetings to try to address what was happening. An external adviser charged with helping us clarify and understand our differences facilitated these meetings, which continued for about two years under three different advisers. As a result, we ended up understanding and knowing one another better than before, though we did not reach agreement on everything. We did, however, gain a greater realization of how complex our choice to live together really was.

The fact that we were Palestinians or Jews did not have much impact on our arguments and disagreements about administrative issues—but it did encumber our efforts to build a common political identity. The task was hard, because none of us seemed willing or able to accept the other side's narrative and commitments. It became clear that the challenges posed by the whole idea of living together were not only internal and personal; they were also immensely broad, because virtually every aspect of the Israeli-Palestinian conflict exacerbated the difficulties at every turn. Our struggle began attracting attention from beyond the confines of our own community.

I am not sure how fully any of us realized that this challenge from the outside was looming, but on it came, a powerful wave. Without intending it, we suddenly became the center of attention. The main cause seemed to be simply that the idea behind our community was so unusual. The public spotlight turned our way as local and international media suddenly started scrutinizing us. Everybody wanted to know what was happening here: Who were these Jews and Palestinians who had chosen to live together? Had they figured out something no one else had? What did they agree and disagree about? How committed were they to their respective national causes? Were they serious people or just naïve and silly fools?

No one among us was prepared for this challenge; no one had the tools, the knowledge, or the qualifications to deal with all the questions being thrust at us. Indeed, the major question suddenly was: *What do we do?* Should we abandon the whole idea of the community, break up into our separate groups, and go back to where we came from? Or should we boldly face this challenge, despite not having answers to all the questions that we ourselves and numerous outsiders were raising?

"How can we live with Jews who define themselves as Zionists and engage in army service?" the Palestinians would ask. "How can we live with Israeli Arabs who define themselves as Palestinians and identify with or recognize the PLO?" the Jews would want to know. Usually, Jews or Palestinians who have not visited us tend to express a negative opinion even about their own people who live in our community. Jews, in general, are sure the Jews who live in Wahat Assalam are not serious or realistic Jews but are the type who give up their identity so Palestinians will accept them. Likewise, Palestinians think the Palestinians who live here are unrealistic and unfaithful to their people's cause.

If I mention our community to Palestinians I meet on the outside, I then have to expend an enormous effort to convince them that I am still committed to the Palestinian narrative and to our rights in Palestine, even though I happen to be living with Jews. Sometimes I just don't have the energy and patience to explain or justify my choice to live in Neve Shalom; sometimes I simply tell people I am from Nazareth when they ask where I come from. The good news, however, is that most people who are skeptical initially, whether Palestinians or Jews or others, tend to change their opinion and become more positive after they learn more about our community or visit it. They realize after talking with us that people here are realistic and serious. They recognize that we are trying hard to face our common challenges together instead of avoiding them. They also see that this group of people has succeeded in building a fine project and that it has known progress and enjoyed success on many levels, despite differences and disagreements.

We have also encountered people who seem pained to learn that, all in all, we are doing all right together in our community. Perhaps the tableau of our well-being does not resonate with their fixed opinions and their negative stereotypes about how impossible it is for Jews and Palestinians to get along. I regret to say that such reactions are also common among local Jewish and Arab journalists, most of whom tend to

Rayek R. Rizek

write about our community only when there are problems. It is almost as though they want to say, "We *told* you Jews and Palestinians could not live together." Their editors top their articles with sensational headlines: "The Failure of Wahat Assalam/Neve Shalom" or "Coexistence Is Not Working." They make mountains out of molehills, fixing on trivial issues that could cause problems in any community anywhere and blowing them out of proportion. Certainly we have our share of serious issues, both political and social, to deal with, but these have not even come close to causing the total breakdown or failure of our central idea. More often than not, when unexpected challenges from the reality "out there" come along, we are the first people among the Jews and Palestinians inhabiting this land to deal with them.

At the beginning of my time living at Wahat Assalam/Neve Shalom, I thought things were going to be easy. I felt that all I had to do was to convince the other side they were wrong and I was right. Later, I discovered that, as much as I believed in my story, they had the same conviction about theirs.

Somehow, we have managed to live with our differences and disagreements. Most of us have realized that we will need a much longer time to reach agreements on things than we originally anticipated. Meanwhile, accepting the right of each member of our community to present his or her point of view without censorship or intimidation has been enough. After all, each one has had the difficult task of reconciling the various contradictions that can arise between his or her beliefs and choice to live in a mixed community such as ours. Each one also has had to prove that his or her beliefs and values are real and realistic, rather than mainly theoretical, as is the case with most Jews and Palestinians outside of our community.

At some point, it becomes clear to each of us that if we decide to stay in the community, then we all must choose to live together with our different stories as inclusively and expansively as possible. This is something we will do someday anyway when we have to share this land equally. After all, if we all came here with good intentions and a higher level of awareness of the humanity of the other, then why should we give up just at the beginning of our journey? We would be foolish to do so, especially when we are here, now, living out in practice the most utopian solution to the conflict available. Who says that someone must give up his or her own story for another's or that there is no way to share our life together? Is ours not the same kind of challenge that opponents face in any conflict?

Many years have passed for a lot of us in our community, but we still have not reached a consensus about many issues, not even about what shape the exact solution to the Israeli-Palestinian conflict might take. Should the land be divided, or should it be kept whole? Opinions vary not only between Palestinians and Jews but also between Palestinians and Palestinians and between Jews and Jews. Some think the solution should be an Undivided Land solution. Others think it should be a Divided Land one. And some believe that the fact of living together is by itself a political and humane statement that does not need any more elaboration.

I personally do not see anything wrong with such disagreements. After all, we joined this community in order to find the way forward together in spite of the conflict. We had no preconditions, except for agreeing to accept one other's equal rights in this land. We are basically a group of Palestinians and Jews who have chosen to live the peace now, since we refuse to tolerate any further excuses for why it is not possible. We are a group of people who have taken personal responsibility for our fate and the fate of our children. By the way, I consider these children to be the luckiest in the land, since they play and argue with one another not as Palestinians and Jews but as normal children.

What we have learned also is that our knowledge about the history of the conflict is not final and never will be. We used to argue as if what we knew was the whole truth. But groundbreaking books are still being published with fresh information that was previously kept in classified archives and has been released only recently. There is still more information to be revealed, of course, especially pertaining to the period of 1948 and before.

With regard to conflicts in general, though, people tend to be divided into two main groups—those who are willing to compromise and those who are not. This is true whether the conflict is personal or collective. With time I have learned that in order to resolve any particular conflict peacefully, there must be a willingness to compromise, and I learned that it is much easier to achieve a good compromise if we consider compromise a process that is about accepting for others what we accept for ourselves—rather than about giving up or giving in to one another.

I have also learned that if the intention of a dialogue is to exchange information about those unknown sides of different personal narratives, about what we were told by parents and grandparents, and about what we read in books, then our dialogues have a good chance of being profitable and productive. However, if the intention of our dialogues is to turn them into arguments, to try to convince others that we have more rights than they do, or to persuade them that our story is right and theirs is wrong, then the dialogue is sure to be useless, even destructive. Arguments that refuse to acknowledge the other side only sharpen the lines of separation and sustain conflict. Nobody likes to be challenged or proven wrong in his or her opinions. Many are not even willing to admit that they are wrong over the most trivial of issues. Many instead are all too willing to fight, to kill, and to die to prove themselves right.

Finally, there is the question of language. This is another very significant personal challenge I have had to face while living at Neve Shalom. In Israel it is possible to live without knowing Arabic, but not knowing Hebrew would make life here very difficult. Most Israeli-Palestinian Arabs speak Hebrew at different levels of proficiency, while most Israeli Jews cannot speak Arabic at all. Arabs are expected to study Hebrew throughout their school years, but Arabic has been introduced only recently as a curriculum in some Jewish schools. In spite of this, to meet an Israeli Jew who can speak fluent Arabic is very rare. Regrettably, too, among the descendants of those Jews whose native language *was* Arabic—known in Hebrew as Mizrahi (Eastern) Jews, who comprise about half the Jewish population of Israel—too few are able to speak the Arabic spoken by their parents.

In my case, unlike most Arabs living in the community when I joined it, I had a problem with Hebrew. I could read and write Hebrew but not

The Anteater And The Jaguar

speak it. I had studied Hebrew during the years I spent in Nazareth's elementary and secondary schools. The study of the Hebrew language included grammar, literature, and the Bible, but it did not include conversation. Thus I ended up, like many other students in my situation, finishing high school with fairly good command of written Hebrew but with a limited ability to converse. What little competence I had in spoken Hebrew, I lost during my seven-year stay in the United States. For some years after I joined Wahat Assalam, my inability to converse in Hebrew severely limited my participation in the various community forums. Though I attended all the meetings, I was unable to present my point of view or even just to follow the discussions and arguments. My only chance at meaningful participation was in the public-relations committee, where we all spoke English.

I carried on for a time, somehow accepting this reality. I accepted it, I suppose, because I had already internalized the psychological "minority complex." Like so many other Israeli-Palestinian Arabs, I believed it was normal for *us* to speak Hebrew, but if the Jews could not speak Arabic, then that was fine. I awoke to this unconscious reality, though, after hearing a Jewish member of the community comment, "Rayek does not have much to say." In fact, my not saying much was not because I had nothing to say but because I was not fluent in Hebrew. At some point, I expressed my anger about the comment.

Still, there was little I could do to improve my situation. The meetings had to take place, and there was much of importance to be discussed. The other members could not afford to wait until I could understand them and respond. Eventually I found a different solution that addressed my dilemma and also changed the way others viewed me. I decided, every once in a while, to write letters. Through them, I talked about myself, about my political convictions, and about many issues concerning our life as a community and its administration. The process was very demanding, because I had to write every letter in Arabic, Hebrew, and English to ensure that every member could read it. Even after I became fluent in Hebrew, I continued writing letters in all three languages to reflect my respect for my fellow residents and my understanding of the meaning of equality.

I remember that my letters sometimes made some members of the community uneasy, because what I said in them included my political opinions. I spelled out my expectations and demanded that others respect and recognize my Palestinian identity when the nature of Jewish Zionist identity was not at issue in the argument. Even though most of the Jews who had been living in the community were politically at the center or left-leaning, some nonetheless behaved in a patronizing way toward us Palestinian Arabs. I thought maybe they acted this way because they had comprised the majority of the community's founding group or because most of the Palestinian Arabs had been late joiners. Or maybe they still believed they were right and we were wrong, as they had been taught. Whatever the reason, it seemed as though we were being expected to join a *Jewish* community and to accept norms and principles that had already been established according to their (collective, primarily Jewish) understanding.

To give an example, by the time I joined the community, it had already produced a leaflet that told its basic story. But at one particular public-relations committee meeting, I objected to the main definition of Neve Shalom as a community inhabited by *Israeli Arabs* and Jews, to the omission of the Arabic name of our community, and to the avoidance of the term *Palestinian*. After I raised this issue several times, Coral, a fellow member of the committee, said, "Rayek, you just keep complaining while expecting us to do something about it. Why don't you suggest something practical?"

This was a very important comment that would subsequently prove to be a great help to me in my life at Wahat Assalam/Neve Shalom. Thanks to Coral, I realized that criticism is not enough. We have to offer alternative solutions. Prompted by her comment, I spent a few days drafting my own suggested version of a new leaflet with my wife's help and, on the English, with some assistance from a young American Jewish woman by the name of Lauren, who was volunteering in our community at the

The Anteater And The Jaguar

time. After producing my alternative with their help, I presented my suggestion to the committee, but it was immediately clear that the members were not going to be willing to adopt it. Why not? Because I mentioned that those living in Wahat Assalam/Neve Shalom were Jews and *Palestinians having Israeli citizenship.* In hindsight, I think that for most of the members it was not a problem to use the word *Palestinian*, but at the same time they were worried about giving people outside the community the impression that we were a radical group. This would have been a problem at the time, because we were still struggling for official state recognition of ourselves as a village. These concerns notwithstanding, however, I made some copies of what came to be known as "Rayck's Leaflet." I translated it into German with the help of a German-speaking member of our community, Evi Guggenheim, who hails originally from Switzerland. "Rayek's Leaflet" was later translated into additional languages. Some years passed, during which two different brochures were used. Finally, another community member, Smadar Kramer, introduced a new leaflet that merged the two versions and included the changes I had suggested.

The issue of language is still raised every once in a while, especially when Jews and Palestinians begin to compete about who has sacrificed the most by joining Neve Shalom. Sometimes, various Palestinian members insist on speaking Arabic in the meetings just to let the Jewish members know that, by not becoming functionally fluent in Arabic, they may not be doing enough to uphold the principle of equality.

The language issue bothered me greatly during my first years in the community, until I began to understand and accept that the process we are engaged in is a long-term one. In that context, perhaps it was enough if we could guarantee that the second generation would be bilingual, even if we ourselves were unable to achieve that goal. The fact is that we have made slow but steady progress, because the majority of the second generation living in Wahat Assalam *is* bilingual.

Language is not only a tool for communication; it also gives us access through a wider door that can meaningfully connect us with others.

Ten

EMBRACING THE EVOLUTION

OF OUR EXPECTATIONS

Though we are defined both outside and inside our community as a binational project, the idea of our being a binational collective has never worked out well here. Some members, myself included, and many outsiders have thought it imperative for us to view ourselves as binational. Yet even when we tried to think of ourselves in this way, we did not succeed in creating two separate national groups. Even after the Jewish members were able to accept the idea that the Arabs they were living with were not only Israeli Arabs but also *Palestinians*, the binational label did not really apply. I will explain to you as well as I can half a dozen or so of the reasons for our inability to deal with most of our conflicts as two separate national groups.

First and foremost, we have been living and managing our life in the community under a constitution that treats everyone as equal with no discrimination. This differs from the reality existing within the state of Israel. Though Israeli democracy is advanced with regard to many issues, it nonetheless has, because of its identification with Judaism, been unable to offer its non-Jewish citizens the level of equality enjoyed by citizens of most Western democracies—and Israel does consider itself to be this kind of democracy.

Another reason our identity as a community is not based on binationalism is that our life here transcends politics. We have, by and large, transcended politics, because guided by our common pursuit of peaceful coexistence, we have lived together and busied ourselves with building up our community and its institutions. Our encounters with one another have taken place twenty-four hours a day for many years; over these years, we have formed friendships and built a shared neighborhood. We have cared for one another in illness and through other family crises. Sharing our experiences on many occasions, both happy and sad, we have also laughed together and cried together. During the Gulf War of January 1991, for instance, most members of our community, both Jews and Palestinians, took refuge together in the community bomb shelter, because there was talk at the time that Iraq might use unconventional weapons against Israel. Dyana and I felt secure enough to stay in our newly built brick house, and we gladly hosted our Jewish neighbors, Eli and Naomi, and their three daughters, who took refuge with us because they did not feel secure enough staying in their old wooden house. Eli and Naomi wanted to reduce the risk in case unconventional weapons *were* deployed. (They were not.)

Indeed, over time, the social interaction among us has created subgroups that are mixed in the sense that they cut across the boundaries of nationality and religion. Sometimes, over a period of years, we have made close connections with coworkers in one department or another of the community. At other times, we have made connections with other parents whose children were our children's friends. Mutual interests, family life, and shared work have often bound us together more meaningfully than our identity as Jews or Palestinians has done.

As time has progressed, our associations with one another as people have subjectively influenced us to see one another first, and mainly, as people. At the same time, we have become less objectively judgmental by not stressing the differences between our particular national and religious identities. This means we might vote for somebody to occupy a particular position based on the closeness of our friendship with that person or on our belief that one particular person would be better for a specific job than another, rather than looking to a candidate's national or religious identification.

Moreover, our agreements and disagreements, along the spectrum of opinion that exists concerning many issues and decision, have almost always cut across all our national and religious distinctions. More often than not, divisions, when they do occur, are between or within mixed groups. This seems to be the case whether our discussions pertain to administrative, economic, social, cultural, educational, or even political issues.

Another probable reason that Neve Shalom has transcended a strictly binational identity is that it has been a dynamic community for many years. This dynamism is generated naturally as new members have continued to join us throughout the years of our existence as a community. New arrivals come from a variety of different backgrounds, bringing fresh infusions of diversity. As a result, the nature of our agreements and disagreements has not remained static and fixed; there is always an evolving dialogue. This was true of the community even when Dyana and I joined. Though there were only twenty-two adults at that time, the community was diverse and fluid in its perspectives. Even when we first joined, our community was not what most people tended to think we were—or even what most of us thought we should aspire to be at the time. We Jews and Palestinians are not like two football teams facing off against each other all the time. Indeed, as soon as we started taking part in different meetings about community issues, disagreements and agreements between individual participants in the discussion were almost never defined by nationality but rather by more individual and specific concerns.

The unexpected ways we ended up relating to the issue of binationality have required each individual to search again when deciding with which group to affiliate. Clearly, in connecting with or disconnecting from others, part of what comes into play is how comfortable (or uncomfortable) one feels about sharing (or not sharing) similar values, attitudes, and approaches. As long as we are viewed as equals by our constitution, though, whether we are members of the same nationality or ethnicity has become largely irrelevant. So when our connections with others result from sharing similar moral values, we tend to group ourselves along issues-oriented lines, whether the issues are political, educational, cultural, economic, or environmental.

But actually, is this not the way things are everywhere? Is it not true that every national and ethnic group actually divides its allegiances along such lines? Is it not also a fact that members of small-scale communities and families tend to be divided in a similar manner? Does history not offer countless examples of members of the same nationality, or ethnicity, or community who have fought and killed one another because they held different values or pursued different interests?

Eleven

To Leave or to Stay

Living together and accepting one another as equals was one task we had to accomplish, but we had to deal with many other critical questions as well. For example, who are we politically? What is our stance toward the wider conflict? How could we bridge the gap between our two narratives as they relate to external public opinion? More importantly, how were we, in the light of this wider conflict, to settle upon curriculum to educate our children in the community's primary school? And how would we determine which concepts and approaches should be used in the curricula of the encounter and training programs of the School for Peace?

I believe that, had we been located somewhere else in the world, finding ways to resolve our political differences might have proved an easier task. But because we exist within this very conflicted country and because we remain close to our families, friends, and other people "on the outside," the process of resolving our political differences has been made considerably more difficult. Our members often find themselves wanting to satisfy the expectations of friends and family and demonstrate that, in spite of our choosing to live with people who have a political agenda different from ours, we are still committed to our own people's cause and culture. From time to time, mostly during the early years,

The Anteater And The Jaguar

these pressures have led most of us, as individuals, to consider giving up and leaving the place. Often, this pull to disconnect from the community arises from fatigue. We sometimes feel that we simply cannot bear the burden any longer, either socially or politically; however, leaving the community is not an easy choice either.

In the first place, quitting an intentional community, ours in particular, is not nearly as simple as quitting membership in other groups that one might initially feel drawn to but later become disaffected with. Leaving our community would necessitate moving all one's earthly belongings, and one would also have to have another place to go. Returning to one's place of origin, however, might not be a better option—in my case, at least, it would not have been. Nevertheless, some members have left over the years, though most have remained, persevering through the tough times in the hope that things would improve.

In the second place, one would have to answer this question: What alternative seems more realistic? In my case, when times were hard and I toyed with the thought of leaving, I had to ask myself, "Would I be better off living in (Arab) Nazareth five hundred meters away from the Jews in (mostly Jewish) Nazareth Illit, with no realistic possibility of engaging them in any serious talk about our common life in this land? Or am I better off staying here in our shared village, where I live five meters away from my Jewish next-door neighbors, with whom I have open discussions about virtually everything that happens on a daily basis?"

In the third place, I realized at some point that life always presents us with choices between different kinds of challenges and conflicts. Had I stayed on in Nazareth, I still would not be living a life without challenges and conflicts, for I would have challenges and conflicts in any case—regardless of whether I cared about the town in the same way I do about our community. If I were to live there, I would simply be living with another set of challenges and conflicts, and I would still be facing the kinds of issues I would have to face living anywhere else in the world. So I stuck to my decision to opt for the challenges and conflicts that Wahat Assalam presents. This option seemed more beneficial and more rewarding than any other, and I think time has proven the wisdom of my choice.

A fourth aspect of this stay-or-leave dilemma became apparent some years later when we began building our own homes here, after the pioneering period when everyone lived in rather makeshift housing. Now we put down lasting roots. We were, in fact, the first Palestinian family to build a private house in the community back in 1987. If it had not been for the help of friends such as Zakaria, Voltaire, Abdel Rahman, and many others, we could not have managed to finish the house. At the time, Dyana and I did not have enough money for it, but because friends made investments to help build a permanent residence for us to live in, our commitment to staying became that much stronger.

Fifth, we got used to the rural environment with all its benefits of open space, clean air, green nature, and freedom for our children to play outside in very safe surroundings. I had experienced this kind of child-friendly and safe environment to a certain extent during my childhood in Nazareth, but with the passing years, overcrowding, noise, pollution, and social and political tensions increasingly negated the benefits of living there.

In the sixth place, leaving this community when things get tough would mean I would simply be avoiding the challenge. If I were to leave, then I would have to relinquish my mission, too. However, if I believe in the truth of my own story and believe my mission is humane, as I do, then why would I want to run away? It would be much better for me to remain and continue sharing my story of what it means to be a Palestinian. By doing this, I can continue enabling people to know that we are sincere and good people. I can also help people understand how we have become victims of homelessness because of a political dilemma that has been internationally orchestrated, tolerated, and even condoned.

In the seventh place, I learned during my seven years of living in the United States (1975–1981) and later in the Oasis of Peace that westerners and others are generally grossly misinformed about our real narrative as Palestinians. I realized that Neve Shalom would provide me the chance to tell those visitors my story of what it means to be a Palestinian. This is another reason I have not been willing to move from this place.

Eighth, the stories of close family members forced to become refugees have strengthened my determination to remain in our community. My mother, Najla, visited us for the first time a few months after we joined here. At the time, we were still living in our original home here, a small wooden house. My mother told me this was the first time since 1948 that she was spending the night at the house of another family member outside of Nazareth. When I probed a bit further, she spoke of the many summer vacations she used to spend before 1948 with her relatives who lived in Haifa. Those relatives ended up refugees. Most fled to Lebanon, leaving behind furnished houses and other property to which they were never permitted to return. I promised her then that I would remain in our community no matter what might occur, and I assured her she could always come to stay with us whenever she liked.

The events of 1948 were very painful for my mother, especially because the outcome was that she could no longer connect with her relatives. The sense of loss and the grief were overwhelming. Her generation of Palestinians was never able to overcome the trauma inflicted on them by the events of that era. The loss of property was not the greatest part of the trauma people experienced. Far beyond the material losses suffered, people were traumatized by the loss of their whole society and the loss of familial relationships.

Ninth, Wahat Assalam was and remains the only new community founded in Israel that Palestinians and Jews can join as equals. Because of this policy, I have found it very important not only to stay in Neve Shalom but also to do everything I possibly can to help this place continue to thrive.

So much of my life has been dedicated not only to living here in this community but also to supporting its existence and development. In choosing to be dedicated in these ways, I have tried to do as much as possible to provide for other Israeli-Palestinian families a model that can help them solve the problems that stem from their living as a minority inside this country. I have tried also to provide a model of community where it is possible to live a normal life without alienation, where egalitarian schooling is provided for the children, and where youngsters can study and speak Arabic as they are able to do with complete freedom in any Arab community.

One main difference between the Arabs and the Jews in Israel is that options regarding places to live in our country are much better for Jews than for Arabs. For a Jewish person, residential possibilities in Israel include many cities, towns, and small communities all over the country from the north to the south. For Arabs, on the other hand, the possibilities are limited by political, ethnic, religious, social, and demographic differences.

In my specific case, for instance, I reached a point where I wanted to leave Nazareth but remain in the country. It was clear that my choices of other places to live were not simple. I did not want to leave Nazareth to live in another Arab village or town, because these were all too overcrowded, socially conservative, and unable to allow people adequate personal privacy. I did not wish to leave for another major city either, as these were mostly Jewish. Had I decided on this option, I would have found myself living in a society that neither spoke my language nor shared my culture.

Finally, I believe we have benefited morally from raising our kids in a mixed community like ours. I have always said that if I had had to bring up my kids in my Arab hometown of Nazareth, then I might have been less sensitive as a parent about how I expressed my opinions regarding the political conflict in our land. But here we have learned to be more particular, more careful, about what we say and how we say it, because we are bringing up Palestinian and Jewish children together here who, like all children, ask many questions and are always listening and learning—mostly from their parents. Whenever visitors ask what it's like to raise children in our community, Dyana says, "Everywhere in the world parents bring up their kids, but in our community, kids also bring up their parents."

The Anteater And The Jaguar

Next to Nazareth, Wahat Assalam was the only place I actually *could* live with my language, culture, and narrative and do so in a manner equal to my Jewish neighbors. As to my personal Nazarene culture, I have to note that one aspect of it has been provided by the daily sound of the bell ringing at our neighboring Monastery of Latroun. This is a sound I grew up with in Nazareth, where I heard it coming from all directions from the many churches near my family's house in the old part of the town. Apart from the fact that this sound has become one of the components of my cultural identity, it also continually brings back to me many happy memories from my youth.

For my wife, my children, and me, Neve Shalom has provided an ideal place to live. I could not have wished for a better one in this racially divided country.

Twelve

YESTERDAY AND TODAY

Many changes have taken place in our community over the years. Once we were a small community of only a few families. In the early days, we looked like hippies and lived a kind of hippie life in wooden huts in a community without adequate infrastructure. Today we have become a small village of sixty families living in single-family houses of brick and stone. The once-barren hill has been cultivated and transformed over time into an enormous garden filled with many kinds of birds, an abundance of flowering plants, wildflowers, and fruit trees. (My neighbor Eitan Kramer has been the moving force behind the ongoing enhancements to the community's environmental and scenic beauty.)

Along with these physical and environmental changes, structural and organizational changes were required as our community grew. One crucial structural change was the privatization process that we undertook during the mid-1990s. By that time, our community had absorbed more families. As a result, a new reality started to emerge. Most of the adults who had joined and lived in the community during the 1980s had worked within the community and received equal pay regardless of what position they filled. Those who joined during the 1990s, on the other hand, were professionals who held different kinds of jobs outside of the community, so very few of them looked for jobs on the inside. This was actually a fortunate development, because our community could no longer offer everyone a job, as it had done in the past.

So, with the influx of professionals, two groups now made up our community. The downside of this was that one group continued to be paid a community wage that was very low, while members working outside were earning much more. This new situation led to the community's privatization in order to address the complaints of people who felt that the influx of the newcomers had brought about a fundamental unfairness. Since the earlier inhabitants had done the work that made the community a suitable place to live in, they believed that their labors unfairly benefited the new members, who were quite literally, as well as figuratively, enjoying the fruits of trees they had not planted. The sense of inequity these earlier inhabitants felt was only reinforced by the fact that these newer residents made a lot more money and so could afford a better life for themselves.

After many intense and emotional discussions, and in accordance with the community's constitution, the members voted to approve privatization in a general meeting. In consequence, anger and tension arose between different members, and we faced a new crisis similar to the one that had followed the formation of the School for Peace. As a result of the privatization process, some internally employed members of the community ended up being paid twice or even three times more than what they had been paid before. Others, however, got stuck with low wages, because the salaries were adjusted to reflect the pay that their positions and occupations could be expected to command if they were employed outside the community.

My view while these things were happening is that privatization was the most serious dilemma the community had ever faced, with accordingly severe consequences. Some social relationships within the village never recovered from the arguments between those who supported the change to move toward privatization and those who did not. In addition, the pay-scale changes caused widespread disenchantment, and for many members, the effect was to diminish their level of commitment to the community and its ideal—something that also happened on numerous kibbutzim that have privatized in recent decades. Those who did not stand to benefit from the changes started asking themselves, "Why should I continue to put in as much effort as I have before, when I can never hope to benefit as much as others? Isn't everyone supposed to be invested equally in the community ideal, regardless of whether he or she is a teacher in the primary school, a gardener, or a manager? Why should people end up being paid differently?"

In hindsight, however, and given the waves of privatization occurring all around us in the larger society, I suppose there was no way we could have avoided it. As a small community then comprised of fewer than twenty families, we did not feel secure enough about the economic viability of our continued collective existence. We had never been particularly secure, financially or otherwise, because the state was never really excited about our social experiment anyway. Even after the authorities officially recognized us as a community, the interest in supporting us was never very enthusiastic. For many years, we heard talk of plans to build a new Jewish community of a few hundred families right next to us, with the idea that we would be merged into that community—effectively destroying our shared (and numerically balanced) Arab-Jewish model. But the new village never materialized, for all kinds of different reasons, bureaucratic and otherwise. Meanwhile, though, we began to realize that we needed to become a much broader community with many more families if we were to achieve recognition and respect for our independent existence. Indeed, that is what finally happened.

One reason we could debate the idea of privatization in the first place was that the basic set of egalitarian ideals animating our community did not include the creation of a social/economic alternative to existing models of collective and quasi-collective communities already available in the country. The central purpose of the kibbutz and moshav models was to provide an economic and social alternative to capitalism, while fulfilling the Zionist ideology of settling the land of Palestine with

The Anteater And The Jaguar

Jewish people (the "ingathering of the exiles"). Our main objective, on the other hand, was to propose and promote a political vision that would bring equality between Jews and Palestinians and end the kind of discrimination that existed throughout the country. And while we never intended to become a variant of the kibbutz, our communal life for some years had been based on elements of communal management and equal sharing. Since these elements had been part of the community's history, some members did not easily accept the privatization process, whatever the demonstrable economic rationale. They found it natural to argue against the move to privatization, because it had not, in their estimation, provided many favorable benefits for community life when implemented elsewhere.

My own preference was not to privatize. I believed in our original approach to community life and felt it played an important role in humanizing our relations with one another. The egalitarian earning scale, with all it implies, kept us united in our commitment to our common cause. Sharing the land and sharing our earning power are not, after all, unrelated ideas. Our cause, I believe, was purer before the change, because it had not been tainted by the vices of envy, greed, and selfishness. Today I see evidence that privatization and its aftermath have enabled these vices to flourish.

Despite the disappointments and setbacks felt very keenly by some members, what has kept the community going is that both of the camps—those who have benefited from the change and those who have not—include both Jews and Palestinians. Clearly the economic divisions among us did not align with the political divisions. This example from our small-scale community, I think, raises an important question with respect to conflicts in general and with respect to the main conflict in our country in particular. How many of our conflicts are really political, as most politicians try to make them out to be? And how many of them are economic and come about because some are exploited to the benefit of others?

In most of our group conflicts at Wahat Assalam, such as the one surrounding privatization, parties face one another as a mix of Jews and

Rayek R. Rizek

Palestinians. When there is a serious disagreement with a national-political face, however, the case is almost always different. One such crisis arose over whether we should commemorate one of our community's youngsters who died while serving in the Israeli army. Tom was killed when two helicopters, carrying more than seventy Israeli soldiers on their way to fight in Lebanon, collided in midair, killing all those aboard. This tragic event took place in the early part of 1997. Our whole community, Jews and Palestinians alike, mourned Tom's passing, but a crisis arose subsequently during deliberations about how to commemorate him. One idea, because he had been an enthusiastic basketball player, was to name our newly finished basketball court after him. There was to be a plaque commemorating him, along with a kind of artistic structure.

While most (not all) of the Jews thought there was nothing wrong with the idea, most (not all) of the Palestinians objected, because the memorial would be commemorating an Israeli soldier who died on his way to fight in southern Lebanon, where a great many displaced Palestinians live. In this specific case, there were few Palestinians and few Jews who chose to stand on the side opposite from the one most members of their group were endorsing, and the division of opinion between the two groups was very sharp. For instance, when I talked about this dilemma with a Palestinian friend of mine, he compared Tom's story to a Greek tragedy. This was a good comparison, because the reality of the situation was forcing people to choose between Tom *the soldier* and Tom *the person*.

Tom's story is indeed a sad one that attracted a great deal of attention from the media. A lot of the media attention was framed in way that seemed to challenge the very legitimacy of our community and the sincerity of its people, who had chosen to live together and face together challenges of the sort we faced with Tom's death. The Hebrew-language media wondered with disappointment why the Palestinians of Neve Shalom could not agree to honor the memory of Tom, even as a soldier, as from their point of view, there was nothing wrong with his being a soldier. The Arabic-language media, on the other hand, wondered with disappointment why the Jews who had chosen to live in Wahat Assalam had also chosen to serve in the Israeli army. Serving in the Israeli military, however, was not unusual among our Jewish members. Most of the Jewish adults who have joined the community have done army service. From the second generation, about ten boys and girls so far have not done army service but instead have opted for alternative service, known here as "national service."

Few outside observers, however, have managed to see our community in its fullest possible context. Most external criticism is not based on any real knowledge of the challenges we have found ourselves facing. Critics generally know nothing of the conditions under which the community was formed. They often assume a set of preconditions that does not pertain to us, but this assumption is completely wrong, because at its inception, our community was not based on any preconditions. There was no litmus test for joining and, as discussed earlier, no written charter. Moreover, most of the arguments, the mutual disappointments, and the anger that arose between members of the community because of the crisis over Tom's memorial actually had little to do with Tom's death in uniform. Other unresolved matters, involving the spectrum of dilemmas grounded in our underlying national conflict, lay beneath the surface of the crisis around Tom's memorial, and that sad story merely provided a convenient excuse to bring them to the surface. (I will talk about the denouement to the story of memorializing Tom a little later.)

Over time, following the meetings we held during the mid-1980s, when we were still a group of about thirty adults, it has become clear that we will continue living together even if we cannot agree with one another about our different national convictions, commitments, and narratives. We accepted this alternative as the best one available, because the other choices meant that one side would have to give in to the other. This was not possible. Alternatively, we could choose to end the project altogether. This was not possible either. Nobody was ready to leave the place where they had made their home.

As a result of what one might call a stalemate, most of the Jewish members went on to perform their army service. Meanwhile, we Palestinians learned to live with their choice to serve in the military, even though we did not agree with it. We continued to live and to build our community together. We did this though we realized and accepted that, in addition to the issue of whether to serve in the army, we could never be together when it came to commemorating Israel's independence, and we could never be together in commemorating the Palestinian *Nakba* ("catastrophe"—the Palestinian name for the war of 1948 and its aftermath). We found that we could, however, be together on any other occasion or holiday.

Though some might see these exceptions as a sign of failure, I do not view them as such. Our community is successful in many other respects. We are doing our best to hold our own in the midst of a very complex reality—one from which we cannot remove ourselves. In spite of the obstructions this reality has thrown along our path, we are still successful in charting the way forward as Jews and Palestinians, because we have faced the most realistic of our challenges in a humane way and have modeled for others the only realistic and humane solution to our conflict. This solution is one that would constitutionally guarantee the equal political, historical, religious, and civil rights for every individual, whether she or he is Jewish, Muslim, Christian, Druze, or other. I believe we have no other choice but to continue living together while accepting the fact that we will not necessarily agree on everything—just like what would happen someday in the whole country of *Falasteen/Eretz Yisrael* (the Arabic and Hebrew names, respectively, for our shared country).

It is clear that, short of solving the main conflict between the Jews and the Palestinians, each party will have to go on living with its historical and religious convictions and beliefs, for the Jews will not stop believing in their rights over this land, and the Palestinians will not stop believing in theirs. Neither does it make a difference if the rights extend back over hundreds or thousands of years. But what are mainly needed are convictions that do not lead to one group's exclusion of the other. This condition is needed not only between the two national groups but also, and more critically, within them, as the internal disagreements within these and other nations have been a major obstacle for any peace here or elsewhere.

Returning now to the story of Tom, I will describe the outcome. We reached a solution by vote after a few discussions, but the outcome was not to everyone's satisfaction: the group voted to dedicate the basketball court to his memory. His parents had the plaque inscribed with these words: "A child of peace who died in a war." Nobody planned for there to be a crisis over what we should do in commemorating him. The crisis was thrust upon us unexpectedly. At first we simply did not know how to deal with it, for it was too big a challenge for most of us even to anticipate. I did not object to the commemoration, however. I knew I was living in a politically mixed community, and I was aware that we all have been victims of this conflict, whether we happened to be on this side or that. Furthermore, I did not mind any "compromise," if it meant helping Tom's parents get through their grief. They had been my neighbors and friends, and I needed to do what I could to help them get over the pain of losing their son. I did not see that commemorating a soldier who was also a young man from our community would make me any less committed to my people's just cause.

I also happened to know Tom personally and had had close associations with him on at least two occasions. The first was some time after he came as a child to live in Wahat Assalam with his family. At the time, I had replaced Abdelsalam Najar as a teacher in our community's primary school, and I just happened to be Tom's teacher. Besides having him in regular classes, I taught him spoken Arabic, and we often practiced speaking it while walking around the school. We came to be associated a second time when Tom worked with me some years later in the dining room of the community guesthouse only a few months before he started his army service. During the time we worked there together, I occasionally heard Tom arguing with much older Jewish men, sometimes a tour guide or a bus driver, while they waited for their tour groups to come to the dining room for dinner. Tom always talked enthusiastically about his liberal convictions that Palestinians and Jews should be treated as equals. My impressions here of Tom may seem overly subjective to some, but who is not subjective when it comes to friendships? Indeed, can one ever be entirely objective when it comes to political, social, religious, and personal issues?

I suppose I should also share with you here what my thinking was when I was faced with the challenges posed by the circumstances surrounding Tom's untimely and tragic death. I had already managed to free myself psychologically from needing to convince outsiders from among my own people that my living in Neve Shalom was legitimate. It had taken some years of my living in the community to build the conviction in my own mind that I was doing the right thing. It took some time, too, to learn to trust others in the community. For many years, I was preoccupied with worries about what my people would think of decisions I had to make about my personal and collective life there. I had lived for some years with the confusion of how to reconcile my world inside the community with the reality outside. Seeing that achieving any kind of reconciliation was impossible had caused me significant emotional pain.

All the crises I have mentioned are now part of the past, though even now, some community members continue to carry the emotional pain they generated. Notwithstanding the pain these members feel, though, the population of the community has managed to double in size, and it will soon triple. Because of the influx of new people, most of the critical crises faced by residents in the past are largely irrelevant to the majority living in our village today. The general atmosphere in our community today is also more relaxed socially and politically; most of my generation, who endured those crises, are now in their late fifties and early sixties. Over time, I suppose we have become much wiser about what is and is not possible, and some of us have apologized to others about previous hurtful comments we have made and trespasses we have committed. We have realized that, in making strides toward reconciliation among ourselves, we can be ahead of the country as a whole in resolving conflicts over the issues that divide us.

By now everyone in our community has realized we cannot create an ultimate utopia. But what we *can* do is advance toward a better world,

The Anteater And The Jaguar

one step at a time. We can also instill in our children the need to take our vision further. If this vision continues, generations beyond us may take our vision further still. History is on our side, because it is filled with examples of people who once fought and hated and killed one another but who are now living in peace with their former enemies. Change has to start somewhere, though, and our Oasis of Peace is a humble beginning for a possible future where love and forgiveness will triumph over hatred and vengeance. Despite all the difficulties we have faced, this vision still affords much hope and inspiration to many, not only in our own country but throughout the world as well.

Part II: Within the Middle East

Thirteen

My Public-Relations Work

As I mentioned previously, our community, because of its uniqueness, has become a sought-after attraction for many people, both local and foreign. Countless tourist groups have designated us as a must-visit stop on their itineraries. Frequently these visiting groups will request in advance that a Palestinian member give them the talk about the community and share the Palestinian perspective on the Israeli-Palestinian conflict. This does not always sit well with Israeli tour guides accompanying such groups or with random visitors who may walk around with the tour group and listen to the explanations. I have worked hard to refine my presentation and achieve the delicate balance between tact and courtesy on the one hand and undue self-censorship on the other.

There have been occasional surprises, of course. One day, when I was still a relatively new member of the community, I chanced to be giving a talk to a German group that showed up with an Israeli-Jewish guide: a typical case when tact was called for. I was shocked to find this guide extremely outspoken and critical of official Israeli policy toward the Palestinians in general. Later, I learned his name was Reuven Moskovitz, and he was a Holocaust survivor who had played an important role in the establishment of our community during its early years and who continued to visit periodically, alone or with a group.

In speaking with visitors, members of our community typically will present a version of the story that genuinely reflects our collective community view—which differs markedly from the dominant Western narrative about the situation that puts (or used to put) most, if not all, of the blame on the Palestinians for the conflict, while exonerating the Jews. Whether the presenter who speaks on behalf of our community is Palestinian or Jewish, we have always endeavored to be as fair as possible in our portrayals of the complex matrix of reasons underlying the conflict.

In 1987, after the community used donations to pave the dusty, bumpy, one-mile road that connected our community with the closest state road, annual visitor traffic to our community increased dramatically—for the first time, the road was safe enough for tour buses to drive up the hill to visit us. However, through the mid-1980s, even before the road was paved, many visitors would arrive unannounced and expect to meet somebody who would share the story of our community. Whoever was available at the time would usually volunteer. Eventually, our approach to the task of showing visitors the community became more organized, after we opened an office to deal with visitor requests and scheduling.

Because I was not very busy in those early years, and because I knew English, I ended up being one of few members who regularly greeted visitors, gave them a guided walking tour of the village and its educational institutions, and told them about our community. From personal experience, I learned that most of these guests were not interested only in the story of the Oasis of Peace; they also wanted to learn about the presenter's background and reasons he or she had joined the community.

Answering visitors' typical questions made talking about the Israeli-Palestinian conflict inevitable. For me, speaking to visitors about politics frequently resulted from their asking a specific and common question: they wanted to know what my extended family and my people thought about my choice to live in Wahat Assalam. Most visitors seemed surprised when I told them my family and people did not mind my having chosen to live here. It would take me some time to fathom the reasons for people's surprised reaction to that answer. Eventually I understood that most of the foreign and Jewish visitors to our village thought it normal to find Jews living in Neve Shalom, but to find Palestinian Arabs living here seemed to them a bit strange—based on their assumption that only the Jews wanted peace, while the Arabs did not.

As a Palestinian, when I stand in front of groups, whether they are comprised of Israelis or Westerners, I have more often than not felt I have been prejudged as guilty before I've even uttered a word. I feel that the burden is immediately placed on me to prove my innocence. I am all too acutely aware that many of those I am addressing really do believe Palestinians are motivated by plain hatred for the Jews. At the same time, they truly believe the Jews, in turn, have done nothing wrong to the Palestinians. While these things are tumbling about in my mind, I am thinking, *But all the Palestinians have done is to defend their legitimate right to stay in the land of their ancestors.* Then the thought occurs to me that this reason is not good enough for them: they still think the Palestinians, for no rational reason, merely stood in the way of Jews wishing to return to their homeland, thus proving that the Palestinians were the ones who were wholly insensitive to their Semitic brothers' human needs.

People's assumption of my nonloyalty as an Israeli Palestinian toward the state of Israel has often been proven accurate in their eyes when they learn that I did not serve in the Israeli army, as most Israeli Jews do. (Some Arabs do serve in the Israeli military; most Druze and Circassian Israelis do so, as do some Bedouin. Apart from those groups, Arab-Muslim and Arab-Christian citizens of Israel are not subject to conscription but must volunteer in order to serve, and relatively few do so.) This is a question I have been asked many times regarding myself and my two sons. Typically, no matter what I answer, I am considered guilty as charged: somehow less loyal or more suspect due to not having joined the army. None of the moral or political reasons I may cite to explain my choice have been considered sufficient justification.

Rayek R. Rizek

But why should I even have to justify myself, considering all the human suffering and misery that wars have created all through our human history? And how could my sons or I serve in any army concerned with defending the rights of one group while denying the rights—and sometimes even the existence—of another group that happens to be, in this specific case, my own people? How could the issue of civic loyalty to the state be measured by this parameter only, regardless of the fact that I obey all the laws of the state, including that one from 1982 that funded the "Peace for Galilee campaign"? That law obliged every working Israeli citizen to pay a "Peace for Galilee" tax to help cover part of the cost of the 1982 Israeli invasion of Lebanon, where most of the victims were my people, the Palestinian refugees of Lebanon. Why should the refusal of Israel's Orthodox and ultra-Orthodox Jewish communities to serve in the army be tolerated by the establishment, while conscientious objection by secular Israelis generally lands them in a military prison? I have the greatest esteem for those Jewish communities and individuals, Orthodox or otherwise, who refuse to participate in the organized carrying and using of weapons against other human beings. I hope that someday we will all—Jews and Palestinians alike—embrace this conviction. Today, alas, we are still living in a world where many people consider the organized use of lethal weapons to be virtuous or, at a minimum, justifiable.

My lectures in English frequently have needed to be translated into other languages. When Israeli guides were translating my statements into French, Italian, or German, they routinely substituted the term *Arab* or *Israeli Arab* for the term *Palestinian*. Most foreign journalists, too, would either skip the word *Palestinian* or replace it with *Israeli Arab* when they published articles about us.

No less bewildering for me is that the right of Jews to return to the land is typically understood as a given, a privilege to which they are entitled, a right not even subject to debate; however, when someone claims for Palestinian Arabs the same right to return to the land, that person is more often than not viewed as a radical. When speaking to people who are already biased, just the suggestion that Palestinians have this right is enough to persuade them that Palestinian Arabs do not believe in peace. Some audiences even hear this claim as a kind of declaration of war. Over the last few years, Israeli politicians are often heard to say that the implementation of Palestinians' right of return will be another Holocaust for the Jews. Why?

So often, it is the Palestinians' rejection, but not the Zionist movement's acceptance, of the unrealistic partition plan of 1947—which in a very weird way sliced up the population and the small territory of Palestine into no less than seven pieces—that is cited as the reason for the outbreak of the 1948 war and all its consequences. My own belief is this war was inevitable at least as far back as 1917, when the seed was planted with the issuance of the Balfour Declaration.

(Dated 2 November 1917, the Balfour Declaration was a letter from the United Kingdom's foreign secretary Arthur James Balfour to Baron Rothschild, a leader of the British Jewish community, for transmission to the Zionist Federation of Great Britain and Ireland. The message said, "His Majesty's government views with favor the establishment in Palestine of a national home for the Jewish people, and will use their best endeavors to facilitate the achievement of this objective, it being clearly understood that nothing shall be done with which may prejudice the civil and religious rights of the existing non-Jewish communities in Palestine, or the rights and political status enjoyed by Jews in any other country.")

In my view, after the Balfour Declaration, nothing could have been done to avoid an eventual war. Palestinians' rejection of this declaration and their opposition to its implementation are frequently cited as proof of their lack of generosity and their insensitivity toward the Jews' plight. Yet little or no consideration is given to the fact that my people were not responsible for the persecution of the Jews and were not part of that history, and no one but us complains about the fact that this declaration relates to Arabs of Palestine as the "existing non-Jewish communities," whose rights were reduced to civil and religious rights only, while the Jews are to be granted their national rights. Transforming the Jews in Palestine from a tiny minority into a majority was a required condition if Palestine, or part of it, was to become a Jewish national home. But the Jews had not been turned into a majority in Palestine by 1948; could the failure to meet that target not accord greater legitimacy to Palestinian claims that their diaspora was not voluntary but rather mostly a result of forced expulsion?

I have found it deeply offensive to see how my people's struggle for their rights in their homeland was reduced to a caricature of allegedly baseless, violent resistance—without regard to other, peaceful means they employed, including strikes; protests; demonstrations; diplomacy; and their internal political, social, and cultural organizing dedicated to securing their freedom and independence. Likewise, little or no regard is paid to the excessive violence committed against them by the Jewish forces and by the British army, who also had their share of violence between them.

So often the names of Abraham, David, and Solomon are brought up to support arguments favoring one-sided claims over the land. I believe, however, that these ancestors are not an exclusive possession of any single monotheistic religion. All of us, whether Jews, Arab Christians, or Arab Muslims, are descendants of Abraham through Ishmael and Isaac. Indeed, Abraham, Solomon, and David as common spiritual ancestors are all equally recognized, appreciated, and mentioned in our prayers, whether we are Jews, Christians, or Muslims.

So as a Palestinian witness coming from a unique place such as Wahat Assalam, I have been profoundly shocked to see the depths to which Israeli public relations has often stooped in its efforts to deny and distort virtually everything that has been of valid concern to Palestinians. Equally shocking for me is the realization that most Israeli and non-Israeli Jews, as well as many Europeans and North Americans, are committed to the strict Israeli-Zionist narrative only. Some question our very humanity as Palestinians. The expression of these views has often been extremely hard for me to listen to, especially considering how we Palestinians have been mistreated and portrayed as the aggressors and how we are always the ones to blame for everything that has gone wrong in our common history. Not to assign some portion of blame and responsibility to the Jewish side seems to me biased almost to the point of absurdity.

I have always said that if the story of the Israeli-Palestinian conflict were told as a story between A and B with their true identities withheld, then it would be hard not to sympathize with the Palestinian side; however, once the story is told with the specific names plugged back in, then most Europeans and Americans apparently cannot be objective or rational about it.

Despite this, I have nevertheless been able to tolerate these kinds of claims when they have come from people who mean to say that the Jews *also* have rights in the land of Palestine. However, it is clear that many others mean something different when they cite these arguments. Their intent is to question and even to invalidate my rights as a Palestinian. Since I am not Jewish, I am questioned, even though some of the people questioning me were not even born in this land. They presume it is their right to question me, even though my family has been living here for approximately four hundred years and even longer in the general vicinity.

I wonder if anything has been left undone by now in order to build a comprehensive narrative about one side being right and moral while the other is not.

Today, after my own long experience in public relations, I do not find it hard to deal with all the arguments that have been raised in order to deny my people's rights in their homeland and to distort their character and humanity. But I prefer not to, mainly because I do not want to continually revisit situations and discourse that cause me anxiety and pain. These negative states of mind come about as a by-product of the energy I have to expend on what I recognize as a worthless struggle: trying to convince others that I am as human as they are.

I do not want to rehash all the details, arguments, and justifications for who started what, who has killed more people, who was more violent, who was more or less willing to compromise, or who was more or less humane in their treatment of their fellow human beings. As is the case in every conflict of this kind, whether that conflict is collective or personal, numerous arguments can be marshaled to prove the innocence of one side and the cruelty of the other.

The blame game, however, solves nothing and serves only to stir up the pot of troubles and sustain the conflict. Elaborate attempts at justification do nothing to resolve the conflict; they resemble shovels digging deeper and deeper holes that lead not to escape but to endless darkness and perpetual agony. I realize today that both sides have committed enough violence throughout the history of the conflict to render the argument moot. No longer does it matter who started what first, if this is even possible to determine—I believe the violence committed by both sides disqualifies each from claiming any moral high ground.

Today, when I look back at my own involvement in this game of justification, it is clear that I unconsciously fell into a trap. I was naïve enough once upon a time to believe that people in general were simply misinformed and that they were, in fact, sincere in looking for the truth of the other side. Eventually I learned that I was mostly wasting my time and energy. Regardless of what I said in defense of my story as a Palestinian, I encountered from the other side yet another question, yet another argument, and yet another doubt. I have learned over time that the issues are not purely academic. Rather, what we are dealing with here is about people who cannot, for whatever reason, afford to change their opinion. Instead, they choose consciously and unconsciously to keep playing a game of manipulation, a game of mental cat and mouse.

If we sincerely intend to find a solution that will put an end to the conflict, we should start by recognizing the present moment as it is. In 2017, the conflict will have entered its one hundredth year, if we start the count at the year 1917 with the issuance of the British Balfour Declaration. Before the beginning of the 1947–48 war, about 600,000 Jews and about 1.2 million Arabs (Muslims, Christians, Druze, and others), lived in Palestine. In 2016, more than thirteen million Arabs and Jews, who were divided about fifty-fifty, lived in the same area. These populations are still struggling with the same questions and arguments previous generations have struggled with. Both sides continue to be stuck in the cycle of violence and revenge that has characterized the region for almost a century. Each side still blames the other for being the cause of the conflict and its continuation.

If we want to advance toward a humane solution to our conflict, we need to put aside our judgments about past events that we neither created nor participated in. Nothing, after all, can change the past, though we do have the power to change our understanding of it and to learn from it.

Today, for example, we cannot relate to colonialism and slavery in the same way our ancestors did a hundred years ago. People living today should not be punished for past actions of previous generations. If we keep insisting that what happened seventy years or three thousand years ago is still relevant to us today, then why not go back ten thousand or twenty thousand years and make events that happened then relevant to us as well? We cannot afford to let the past be an albatross around our necks when the present state of progress in our world demands that all peoples everywhere deserve to live as equals, no matter who or where they are. Every argument that fails to justify humane treatment of others should therefore be repudiated. We cannot afford to use selfishly motivated arguments as pretexts for sustaining structures of inequality, injustice, and suffering.

Today, I see the story of this conflict as a story of two peoples who have sought self-determination on the same piece of land. Both have been trapped in their separate needs, convictions, and fears; both believed themselves to be right; both believed the others were wrong; and both ended up being victims. It is also clear from the evidence that the conflict was not limited to their direct involvement only. All through the years, intensive and direct intervention by many Western and Eastern powers occurred repeatedly, with many historical, religious, and geopolitical considerations informing the process. Our story, then, is not a story of one good people facing another bad people, as so many people still—regrettably—prefer to present it. When will more of us become aware of this fatally flawed attitude that has arisen repeatedly throughout history, in the context of conflicts between nations or between individuals? Isn't this the attitude too commonly followed by most of us to dehumanize and demonize the other in order to justify our story, including its more violent components? Haven't we all found ourselves justifying our story by distorting the image and character of the other? Can we not do better than that?

Throughout my life at Neve Shalom, I have learned of many people, including many Jews—secular, religious, non-Zionist, and even Zionist—who as a result of their awareness of our common humanity, our common past, and our common experiences of unjust treatment by others, have chosen to identify with our cause and our pain, rather than to use their own history of persecution as a justification for persecuting others. These people did not need to hear my story in order to recognize me as an equal human being. For them, knowing all the details about the history of the conflict was unnecessary. They chose to accept me as an equal human being despite not knowing much about this history, and indeed, they did not even care to know about it. Accepting me as a human being in their minds simply did not depend on this.

I have thus learned that either people will remain stuck at a primitive level of understanding, in which they will endlessly put forth arguments for why they are right and those on the opposite side are wrong, or they will mature to the point where they recognize that our common humanity must be affirmed despite all that has happened. Talk that perpetuates the conflict is a waste of time and energy; it is also mentally painful and physically harmful. I believe there is wisdom and blessing in refraining from engaging in that discourse.

Fourteen

About Geography

Those Israelis and others who feel compelled to minimize the Palestinian tragedy of expulsion and dispersion commonly assert that *there is no such thing as a Palestinian people*. They maintain that Palestinians invented a fiction to justify their claims to a land they do not in fact belong to. They hold that the claims of Palestinians are false, despite the fact that Palestinians were born in this land. They also maintain that the Palestinians, by asserting their own claims, are trying to negate the claims of the Jews, who *do*, in fact, belong to this land and regardless of where they came from.

I would agree that up until the beginning of the First World War, there was no Palestinian nation-state as such. Despite this fact, there were at the time Arabs living in a strip of land that had no borders between it and those countries known today as Lebanon, Syria, Jordan, and Egypt. The global power players simply had not yet imposed their arbitrary boundaries upon this strip of land. When they did impose them, though, they did so without the consent of the people living there. Because boundaries were arbitrarily imposed without consent from the land's inhabitants, they must not in any way be viewed as a legitimate excuse to negate or eliminate those inhabitants' rights. These same power players' decision to disenfranchise the native inhabitants of Palestine by taking their rights away was wholly arbitrary.

Generally speaking, the penchant for recognizing nation-states is something relatively new and can be traced back to nineteenth-century developments in world politics. Even in the case of the Israeli Jewish state, it is clear that Jews who share their life together in modern Israel have formed a new kind of identity that differs markedly from the identities of all other previously and presently existing Jewish communities in the world. Before the Zionist idea was proposed in the late 1890s, the historical "people of Israel" was not a political entity but a biblical one. The small Jewish community that lived in Palestine could hardly have been called a separate people in a political sense, for most of this native Jewish community shared its identity with the other groups in the land at the time.

When it comes to assessing how identities are built and what measures are taken to justify these identities, certain factors must therefore be considered. Sometimes identities are built through processes in which people freely choose to embark on common experiences. This is certainly the case with the formation of the United States, where self-determination was the main factor—except not, of course, for the Native American tribal peoples or for imported and American-born African slaves. Identities are often forced upon populations without their consent and to their detriment. Such has been the case for many Jews in the diaspora and likewise for the Palestinians, who did not choose the conflict they are now embroiled in. Instead, they had it forced upon them simply because they happened to live inside artificially drawn borders that the British and French colonial powers imposed.

Now we shall take a look at some of the geography and history behind the dilemma of Palestine/Israel, from a Palestinian standpoint.

A book published in 1924 by Reverend Asad Mansour, entitled *The History of Nazareth from its Ancient Times Till our Present Days*, sheds light upon the fact that various Arab communities have lived in the land that formerly was called Palestine for many centuries. Reverend Mansour was from a small Palestinian town just north of Nazareth by the name of

The Anteater And The Jaguar

Shefa-Amr (*Shfar'am* in Hebrew). The book was printed in Egypt by Dar Al-Hilal Publishing House, and it's worth mentioning that this institution started as a publisher of *Al-Hilal* (the *Crescent*), a monthly Egyptian cultural and literary magazine. *Al-Hilal*, launched in 1892, was one of the first magazines dealing with arts in the contemporary Arab world. It was founded by Jurji Zaydan, a prominent Arab-Christian Lebanese writer, novelist, journalist, editor, and teacher who had come to Egypt in the 1880s.

In the second half of his book on the history of Nazareth, Mansour traced the origin and family tree of every Christian and Muslim extended family living in Nazareth, the population of which at the time numbered about ten thousand. He acquired the information from elderly inhabitants then living in the town and from written records. As to the latter, Mansour mentions two in particular: a book published in 1850 by Yakub Farah, who happens to be my maternal great-great-grandfather (the grandfather of my mother's father), and the written records of the Fahoum family. The Fahoums were an Arab-Muslim family whose roots go back to Al-Hejaz (today's Saudi Arabia). It is mentioned that one branch of the family settled in Nazareth around the end of the eighteenth century. This work documents the arrival of my own family in Nazareth during the third decade of the seventeenth century. They moved there from a village by the name of Sakhra (*rock*, in Arabic) in the area of the Ajloun Mountains, east of the Jordan River in what is now Jordan. Prior to their arrival in Nazareth, the book says, they settled first near Mount Tabor, and after that in a village by the name of Al-Shajarah (which means *the tree* in Arabic), a few kilometers northeast of Nazareth; the village of Al-Shajarah was destroyed and depopulated in 1948. A different source states that my ancestors moved to Sakhra some years before, from another village called Bosra al-Sham in the Hauran province of what is now southern Syria.[2]

---

2 This information came from *The Tree of Abdallah al-Qalazi* by Fadeel Jarjoura (Jerusalem, 1975, p.2), where Jarjoura is quoting from *East Jordan* by Frederick G. Beck (p.290). Abdallah, my ancestor who came from Sakhra, was the son of Suliman from Bosra al-Sham.

Rayek R. Rizek

Some extended families have inhabited Nazareth over an even longer period prior to my own family's arrival, while others arrived later. Mansour mentions that the origins of most of the Arab Orthodox Christian and Catholic families are in Hauran, while the origins of most of the Arab Latin and Maronite families are in Lebanon. In addition, a small community of Copts came from Egypt. Mansour's history states that the Coptic Christian community of Nazareth originated with a few young men who arrived there from Coptic communities in Minya and Asyout in central Egypt early in the nineteenth century to avoid conscription by the Egyptian army of the self-declared Khedive Muhammad Ali of Egypt and Sudan.

Nazareth and nearby towns and villages are also home to a small Protestant Christian Arab community comprised mostly of Arab Christians who converted from Catholicism and Orthodoxy. This is a relatively recent phenomenon attributable mostly to the presence of the British in Palestine through their charities and later through their occupation, the League of Nations mandate period that began in 1923 and ended in 1948. There is also a smaller Baptist community with a church and a school in Nazareth, which is likewise more recent.

It is mentioned in other sources that the roots of most of the Arab Christians of the Middle East go back to the Ghassanids and Muntherids Arab tribes that migrated from today's Yemen to the Levant and the Euphrates regions respectively. The migrations of these tribes, as well as many others, took place during the first few centuries AD as a result of the breaching and destruction of the great Marib Dam, a historical event alluded to in the Quran. The date of the first construction of this dam goes back to the eighth century BC.

The Ghassanids—called in Arabic *Al-Ghasasinah* and also *Banu Ghassan*, which means in Arabic "Sons of Ghassan"—descended from the Arab Azd tribes. Some of them merged with Greek-speaking Christian communities, converting to Byzantine Orthodox Christianity from polytheism, while others were already Christians before emigrating north to escape religious persecution. The Ghassanids generally did not accept Islam, and few became Muslim following the Islamic conquest. Most Ghassanids remained Christians and joined Melkite Syriac communities.

The Anteater And The Jaguar

As for the Muntherids, they descended from the Arab tribe Banu Lakhm and adopted Nestorian Christianity. Both of these communities of Arab Christians established flourishing kingdoms in their separate regions, and many wars were fought between them. Some of these wars resulted from territorial and tribal issues between them, while others resulted from their separate allegiances to the Byzantines and the Sassanid Persians. The Ghassanids allied with the Byzantines, and the Munthrids allied with the Persians.

As for the Muslim families, they trace their origins to similar places as well as to Iraq, Egypt, and the Hijaz region (today part of Saudi Arabia). In general, many Palestinian families could trace their origins to other areas in the region: Egypt, Syria, Lebanon, Iraq, or Jordan, and even as far as Sudan, Libya, and Morocco. Many families in those countries could similarly trace their origins to Palestine. If anything, Mansour's book illustrates the fluidity of movement of the populations across the entire region prior to the arrival of the colonial powers.

Knowing the geographic origins of families is easy in many cases, because newcomer families were commonly given the name of the region, village, or town from which they came. For example, the family name "Masri" refers to those who came from Masr, which means "Egypt" in Arabic. People named "Hijazi" are originally from Hijaz in today's Saudi Arabia. "Halabi" refers to those who came from Halab, which is Aleppo, in Syria. "Nabolsi" refers to those who came from Nablus in Palestine, while people named "Tarabulsi" originally came from Tripoli in Lebanon or Tripoli in Libya. The same is true of hundreds and maybe even thousands of other such names.

Migrations have occurred routinely throughout history, so the movement of peoples in and out of Palestine and around the region and the whole world is nothing new or unique. Isn't it a fact that, historically, we are *all* immigrants, as banners have proclaimed during recent demonstrations in Europe and America in solidarity with refugees and against xenophobia? When people move, the reasons are not obscure: they move to find better living conditions or to escape drought, famine, conflict, or oppression. I was quite young when I learned about the

Rayek R. Rizek

Armenian tragedy, because among our neighbors were some Armenian families who had taken refuge in Nazareth. Once I asked a Bedouin neighbor, Abu Abed, about his own family's origins.[3] He informed me that his great-grandfather had escaped Egypt, as many other thousands had done, to avoid the work of digging the Suez Canal. Young men were conscripted against their will and forced to work under slavery-like conditions, and some accounts state that more than one hundred thousand Egyptians died while laboring there between 1859 and 1869.

When Abu Abed's great-grandfather fled Egypt, national borders in many places were either nonexistent or very porous; in many cases, there was no need to secure official permission to travel from one place to another—even though different authorities may have been governing the areas involved.

This reality has evolved, however, over the last few hundred years, mainly as a result of the machinations of European imperial powers. As these powers fought to assert control over the non-European world they had come to dominate, territories were sliced up with artificial borders drawn on maps; different ethnicities, indigenous communities, and tribes found themselves arbitrarily separated by new boundaries that also lumped them together with groups of people with whom they shared no historical affinity or relationship. This process of arbitrary division and agglomeration was externally imposed, and the people being manipulated in this cruel way had no say in the matter. Newly delineated, newly named colonies were divided up and parceled out as the imperial European powers fought among themselves. Later, colonies turned into independent states, often perpetuating the peculiar boundaries imposed arbitrarily in an earlier era.

At the end of the First World War, the Middle East was divided territorially between France and Great Britain after their defeat of

---

3 It is more common in Arab culture to call married men and women by the name of their eldest son, as this is considered more polite. Therefore, if the eldest son's name is Abed, for example, then the father would be called Abu-Abed, and the mother would be called Om Abed, as *Om* means *mother*.

The Anteater And The Jaguar

the Ottoman Empire, which had claimed the Middle East as part of its territory for the previous four hundred years (1516–1919). When the regional map was redrawn, specific "national" borders were delineated—maybe for the first time in the region's history, and the new geographic entities carved from the erstwhile Ottoman Empire acquired new names. Countless families, communities, and tribes were divided into pieces, and their people ended up citizens of different states. Sometimes the newly drawn and often arbitrary national boundaries cut right through an existing community, whose members now found themselves living on different sides of the border. This process, while not unique to the Middle East, was particularly painful there, because the large majority of people in the region at that time were Arabs whose extended families often had large branches living in different locations that had been, until now, relatively accessible to one another. And then there were the Kurds, who ended up separated between Turkey, Iran, Iraq, and Syria.

Families, communities, and tribes even now remain spread across these arbitrarily drawn boundaries. Consider Syria, where civil war has, at this writing, driven, more than ten million civilians to seek refuge in Lebanon, Jordan, Iraq, Turkey, within Syria and beyond. Some Syrian refugees have managed to find relatives who live in the border areas of those states. A similar scenario exists in the region straddling eastern Libya and western Egypt. I learned from media coverage of the recent Libyan revolution that about ten million Egyptians, most of them residing in western Egypt, are related to Libyan tribes, from whom they became separated because of colonial divisions. The border between northern Palestine and southern Lebanon, too, is fluid in this way. The people in both places speak the same Arabic dialect and share a similar culture, and many of them are related by blood as well. This reminds me of a Lebanese friend I knew when I lived in the United States during the 1970s. We used to joke about whether his hometown of Tyre, in southern Lebanon, is really part of Palestine, making him Palestinian, or whether my hometown of Nazareth, in northern Palestine, is really part of Lebanon, making me Lebanese. Likewise, the Arabs of the eastern part of Palestine share these kinds of similarities with the Arabs who live on the other side of the Jordan River. And in the southern part of Palestine, people share many similarities with the inhabitants of the eastern part of the Sinai Peninsula. These cross-border affinities do not, I hasten to add, "prove" that there is no Palestinian identity or Palestinian people or that Palestinians don't deserve their own national independence; the phenomenon rather points to the cruel nature of the denouement when national boundaries are arbitrarily imposed from without.

In my own family, I frequently heard my father and uncles talking about the past. They would reminisce about life under the Ottomans and under British rule—mentioning places such as Damascus (Syria), Amman (Jordan), Beirut (Lebanon), and Baghdad (Iraq), which they visited regularly for pleasure or business up until 1948. I also heard them mention names of relatives living in Jordanian towns such as Irbid and Al Hosn, which are opposite Nazareth across the Jordan River. Many of these cousins descend from members of my family who decided to go back to the area of the Ajloun Mountains three or four hundred years ago, while others chose to remain in Nazareth. This is typical of many Palestinian families with related branches in the region—in Palestine, Lebanon, Syria, and Jordan—and in some cases beyond, after separations dating back hundreds of years.

Often my father and uncles talked about their regular visits to the Lebanese town of Zahle, which is famous for its beautiful natural surroundings, riverside restaurants, and homemade Arak. In addition, two of my aunts, Olga and Jorjeit, were originally from Damascus, and a third aunt, Jenny, was originally from Beirut. Olga was married to my paternal uncle Hanna; Jorjeit and Jenny were married to my maternal uncles Jurji and Faheem, respectively. After 1948, all three of these aunts ended up being cut off permanently from their families in Syria and Lebanon. Even within my own family's experience, I can see how arbitrary the geographic boundaries imposed from without are.

The Anteater And The Jaguar

Long years of separation have not, however, totally disconnected previously interrelated families and tribes from one another. This is true despite the fact that, within these new states with their different names, it has become normal over time for people to develop new commitments to these states and affiliations with them. Unique challenges faced by each new state, and the different regimes ruling over them, have predictably led to these developments. As a result, people in the region today identify as Lebanese, Syrian, Iraqi, Jordanian, and Palestinian. Indeed, these identities can be very strong. In 1978 I met my aunt Saleemi, my father's only sister, for the first time when my parents and I visited her home in Jamesburg, New Jersey. She had left Nazareth in 1920 as the newlywed bride of her cousin Saeed, who had already lived in the Dominican Republic for some years. Aunt Saleemi, who was in her late seventies when I met her, still referred to herself as a Syrian from Nazareth. Why Syrian? Because in those days, Greater Syria encompassed what is now Syria, Lebanon, Palestine/Israel, and Jordan.

In my view, it is regrettable that some internal Arab forces have promoted the adoption of these "national" identities as though they have always existed and as though they refer indisputably to entirely different nations containing unrelated peoples. Some of these states, instead of annulling these artificially imposed borders after the withdrawal of the British and the French military forces from the region, have gone to war with one another over boundaries inherited from colonial powers. Some, in fact, still have not reached a final settlement on border issues, even now.

Nonetheless, the vast majority of inhabitants of the regions we are discussing here are Arabs who share a common history; despite the political lines drawn between them, most of them still consider the borders artificial ones that someday should and shall be removed. The European Union has provided an example of what is possible on a regional basis. The European nations have managed to come together regionally, even though the peoples of the European Union speak more than twenty different languages. It thus seems strange that the Arab people, an overwhelming majority of whom speak the same Arabic language and share a long and common cultural history, should remain divided into twenty-one states when the European nations, originally responsible for dividing them up, are now (mostly) united!

I keep mentioning the example of Europe, although people often object that Europe cannot be compared to the Middle East. But really, on what grounds is this objection voiced? Have the Europeans always been as civilized as they are now? What of their long history of violence, which led to the slaughter of tens of millions? Who would have ever thought it possible, especially following the horrors of the Second World War, that the Germans and the rest of the Europeans, would achieve the level of relations and unity they share today? Furthermore, is it really true that the people of the Middle East have been fighting and killing one another since time immemorial? Did they not rather provide one of the best examples of coexistence among so many different communities throughout most of their history?

I agree that the present reality in our region does not look promising. But it remains clear that the recent upheaval (termed, for a while, the Arab Spring) had its start in peaceful demonstrations against tyranny and corruption and in the quest to establish democracies that respect human rights and practice transparency in governance. During the first few months of 2011, right after the successful and surprising revolution of the Tunisians against their tyrant in December 2010, we saw Arab crowds demonstrating peacefully for the same purpose in Egypt, Libya, Yemen, Syria, Iraq, Saudi Arabia, Morocco, Algeria, Bahrain, Oman, Jordan, Lebanon, Sudan, and Mauritania. This was the first Pan-Arab revolt in history, and it has shown that most Arabs share the same pain and the same hopes.

I have to admit I have been living these last few years with many mixed feelings of joy, confusion, anxiety, and sadness: joy when I see all those millions of Arabs demonstrating peacefully despite the great risks; confusion, because the situation is so ambiguous; anxiety, due to my fear that this chaos will continue for years; and sadness for all those suffering and dying in these upheavals, which take place under the shadow of such disappointing political developments, in which material interests and rigid ideologies are given precedence over human rights. I also feel sad when I compare the current reality to the new day that seemed to be dawning with such high hopes in 2011, with a civilized and peaceful revolution that inspired the admiration of hundreds of millions of people all over the world.

Nothing describes what has happened in many Arab countries in these last few years better than what President John Kennedy once said: "Those who make peaceful revolutions impossible will make violent revolutions inevitable." But in spite of everything, I still like to believe that this is just a temporary phase until democracy finally prevails in the Middle East, the cradle of civilizations, as has happened in many other parts of our world.

When all is said and done, we must realize that every situation has its peculiar set of dynamics. Some situations and scenarios bring out the best in us, while others bring out the worst. A scenario in which conflicts remain unresolved is fertile ground for moral degradation and strained relations between people. Protracted unresolved conflict perpetuates divisions and subdivisions even among like-minded people, as they adopt different opinions regarding the roots of the conflict and the best approach to its resolution. In these circumstances, each individual's peace of mind is difficult to achieve; nearly everyone, whether more involved and concerned or more withdrawn, becomes mired in stress, which produces impatience, outbursts of anger, and aggression over even the most trivial issues.

This state of affairs is, unfortunately, the one being played out in my own country, and it affects everyone. It is quite hard to imagine any social encounter today in my country that does not include painful arguments about the political conflict. I have come to feel that our present state of existence is like a curse I would not wish on anybody. What I do wish for is some kind of breakthrough into a new and brighter reality, where political conflicts are resolved and where everyone rises to participation in the most humane kind of relationships possible. Once this is achieved, then everything else seems possible as well.

Let us return to the community of Wahat Assalam/Neve Shalom. I have noticed, time after time, that its effect on visitors is often quite remarkable. When others see how we choose to live, they, too, become more relaxed and open to the idea of a dignified and egalitarian coexistence as we are modeling. Considering the profound effect our small community has on people, I wonder what would happen if another fifty communities like ours were to pop up all over the country. But why should we wait for another Bruno to start them? It would seem past time for influential public and political figures to step forward and initiate similar projects—or at least to view them sympathetically when they are proposed by others and to refrain from setting obstacles in their way. I believe many Jews and Palestinians would be willing to take up this challenge and to live in mixed communities as different but equal partners, were the opportunity only made available to them.

At the same time, I do not propose that the way to resolve the conflict between the Jews and Palestinians in this land is to have them all live in mixed neighborhoods as we do in our community. I remain aware of the fact that there are many legitimate cultural, religious, and socioeconomic differences that deter this possibility, not only between the nationally separate communities but also within them. But think of how different things would be if only some substantial minority of citizens were to choose the path that we in our little village have followed now for more than thirty-five years.

Fifteen

About Religion

The Middle East is known in some circles as the cradle of civilization. It has also been the most active region on Planet Earth throughout recorded human history. Geographically, it connects the continents of Africa, Asia, and Europe, so every empire that has emerged in the region and beyond has seen the need to control it. Over thousands of years, intensive and continuous movements of people have also traversed this space. Some have stayed, while others eventually returned to their places of origin. Such movements have occurred from the time of the pharaohs of ancient Egypt. Vast empires have come and gone in succession, too, including the Assyrians, the Babylonians, the Persians, the Macedonians, the Romans, the Byzantines, the Arab Muslims, the Crusaders, the Moguls, the Ottomans, and the British and French.

As a result of this continuous movement of peoples, a very complex social and ethnic reality has been created in this part of the world that demonstrates a relatively high level of tolerance toward differences and strangers. The communities that evolved here are richly diverse; in many cities, towns, and villages all across the Middle East, distinct ethnicities and cultures continue to share their unique cultures and ways of life as they have done for hundreds and thousands of years. Lebanon, Syria, and Iraq alone are each inhabited by at least eighteen different Arab and non-Arab ethnic and religious groups, with many of them sharing the towns and villages in common as neighbors. Some of the non-Arab communities in the Middle East are the Kurds, the Armenians, the Assyrians, the Circassians, the Chechens, the Gypsies, the Turkmen, and the Yazidis, and there are others. Some of these communities ended up living in the Middle East after escaping persecution in their previous homelands. Not too long ago, the Jews also were included in this pluralistic mix.

In the Galilee area in the northernmost part of Israel/Palestine, many Arab communities in villages and towns still include both Muslim residents and Christians who are affiliated with various church traditions. In addition, Druze are to be found in some of these communities. These groups have resided in this area for hundreds of years. Even though all are Arabs, all speak Arabic, and mostly share the same culture, intermarriage is not common and also not very accepted among them. There have been very few cases of intermarriages within this country between men and women from the different Arab communities and also between Arabs and Jews. And of those few, hardly any took place without causing conflicts with and between families and communities; the wedding ceremonies generally took place abroad, in Europe or in North America, because the option of civil marriage still does not exist in this country, so that a religiously mixed couple has no one to officiate at their wedding. Conversion (of one partner or the other), moreover, is typically not considered necessary by most of these couples, since their love for each other is independent of religious affiliation, and they do not subject themselves to the relevant religious restrictions.[4]

---

[4] If this subject interests you, I can recommend an excellent film by the Palestinian-Israeli screenwriter and director Michel Khleifi, *Forbidden Marriages in the Holy Land* (*al-Zawaj al-Mukhtalit fi al-Ard al-Muqaddasa*, 1995), which documents the story of a few mixed couples and the difficulties and challenges they faced throughout their lives as a result of their uncommon choice. Nazareth-born Khleifi relocated to Belgium in 1970.

The Anteater And The Jaguar

I trust that this background helps to clarify the issue of intermarriage for people who wonder or worry that our life together, featuring Jews and Palestinians (Christians and Muslims) living side by side in Wahat Assalam, might promote intermarriage. Not only is intermarriage between Jews and Arabs in this part of the world very rare, however, the same can be said of intermarriage between people from two different Arab faith communities. Whether the community is Muslim, Christian, or Druze, interfaith marriage is mostly considered taboo and can even cause violent conflicts or result in a family or community rejecting any female who marries someone from the outside. Not long ago, my father told me that intermarriage between Arab Orthodox Christians and Arab Catholic Christians in Nazareth was uncommon because it created problems for families if someone was expected to give up attending one church and begin attending another. Were Shakespeare alive today and living in my country, he could have written many more tales like *Romeo and Juliet*.

As for Neve Shalom, there has been only one interreligious, interethnic marriage here since the community was founded. This young couple, recently married, are a son and a daughter of two interreligious families. One's parents are a secular Palestinian Muslim and a Palestinian Christian. And the other's parents are also secular, a Palestinian Muslim and an Israeli Jew. Like their parents before them, the two young people were obliged to travel abroad (they chose Switzerland) for their civil marriage ceremony with the participation and the blessings of their families. As a result of their choice of partners, their shared family identity will include all three monotheistic religions.

Among the village's longtime residents, apart from the above mentioned parents, there are another three secular couples comprising partners of different religions and/or nationalities; all were already married when they joined our community.

Of the second generation of Jewish and Arab girls and boys in Neve Shalom who have been married thus far—about fifteen—each of them chose a partner from somewhere outside our community. When I explain this reality to Israeli Jewish visitors, they tend to respond, "Just like on a kibbutz." Apparently, very few kibbutz children marry others from their own kibbutz, even though they are all Jews; there is said to be something almost sibling-like about the relationship among kibbutz youngsters that discourages pairing off among themselves.

In the part of the world where I live, religious origin is an ineradicable component of identity; even people who may be religiously nonpracticing, atheist, or antireligious are still identified as Muslim, Christian, Jewish, Druze, or by some other religious designation. Asking others about their religion is a fairly common and socially acceptable thing to do here, evidently more so than in other countries. Elsewhere, many people consider the question of one's religious affiliation to be a very personal matter, and when someone asks about another's religion, the question is customarily softened with some polite excuse for having asked it in the first place.

In my country, however, the manner and import of inquiring about another person's religion is quite different. To begin with, a person's name is frequently a strong clue as to what their religion is, as some names are typically Muslim, Christian, or Jewish, but this marker is not infallible. If a person's name fails to provide an unambiguous clue, then people are more likely than not simply to ask others, forthrightly and without excuses, "What is your religion?" This question is considered no more intrusive or personal than to ask someone what kind of food he likes or what her favorite color is. Though often people are simply curious, sometimes the motive is deeper: They are asking in order to determine if the other person is one of "us" or one of "them." In Palestine and Israel, a question about religion may also be essentially a political question.

The religious question is important to many in my land because of historical arguments having to do with religious holy sites. Arab Christians, who may have disagreements among themselves about Christian holy sites, rarely have such arguments with Muslims or with Jews. However, religious arguments over holy sites do exist between Jews and Muslims, even though some sites that these communities claim as theirs were also home to churches during the Byzantine and the Crusaders periods. Two

The Anteater And The Jaguar

sites in particular are very important topics of debate: The first, and perhaps most important, is the site of the Al-Aqsa Mosque in Jerusalem (called by Muslims also *Al-Haram Al-Sharif*, the Noble Sanctuary), which Jews believe to be the site of the Temple of King Solomon and which Muslims believe to be the site visited by the Prophet Muhammad before he ascended to heaven on the heavenly steed called Al-Buraq (*lightning* in Arabic). The second site is the Cave of the Patriarchs (*Alharam Al-Ibrahimi* in Arabic and *Me'arat Hamakhpela* in Hebrew) in Hebron/Al-Khalil, where it is believed that Abraham; Isaac; Jacob; and their wives, Sarah, Rebecca, and Leah, are buried. During the fourth century, the Byzantine Christians built many churches in the Holy Land, including a church on the site of the Temple Mount and another on the site of the Tombs of the Patriarchs.

Resolving the complex disagreements concerning these and other holy sites is a considered a precondition for achieving a political solution to the Israeli-Palestinian conflict. Some people are persuaded that no resolution of these Jewish-Muslim religious issues is possible; there are historical precedents, however, that may foster some degree of hope.

Historical accounts suggest that different Muslim leaders have related to religious disagreements and to the rights of non-Muslim minorities with different levels of tolerance. Although Jews today can and do argue that Islamic rule was not always fair to their ancestors, Islam in general was more tolerant toward Jews and Judaism than were the Romans, the Byzantines, and the Crusaders, to mention just a few. Under Islamic rule, Jewish communities enjoyed considerably more freedom to live as Jews, to flourish, and to practice their religion than under any other rule. Both Jews and Christians are said to have welcomed the invading Arab Muslim armies when, in the seventh century, they conquered the Syria region (then under Byzantine rule) and the Iraq region (then under Persian rule), for example.

Early in the history of Islam, it was the second Muslim Arab caliph, Omar ibn al-Khattab, who allowed the Jews to return, hundreds of years after their expulsion by earlier rulers, to Jerusalem/Al-Quds and to Hebron/Al-Khalil.[5] It is also mentioned that Caliph Omar allowed the Jews to build a small synagogue on the site of the Tombs of the Patriarchs.[6] This occurred during the visit of Caliph Omar to those two places in 637 AD, after the Arab Muslims captured the region from the Byzantines. This act of recognition and generosity was repeated more than six hundred years later by Salah Aldeen (Saladin), the Kurdish Muslim leader who ruled from Cairo[7] after taking control of most of the region, including Jerusalem and Hebron, from the Crusaders. He ordered the reopening not only of the mosques but of the synagogues and churches as well, thus granting free worship to all. By contrast, when the Crusaders occupied Palestine, they massacred not only Muslims but also the Christian Arabs and the Jews.[8] Similarly, Ottoman Caliph Selim/Saleem the First[9] welcomed into his mostly Arab empire many of the Jews expelled from Spain in 1492, together with Muslims who were also expelled. Many of the Jews of the Arabian Peninsula (Saudi Arabia and Yemen today), before Islam, are thought to have been Jewish refugees who escaped the Roman and Byzantine persecution in the Levant (the Eastern Mediterranean).

---

5 The Islamic Caliphate lasted for 1,290 years, beginning with Arab Caliph Abu Bakr al-Siddiq on 8 June 632 AD, right after the death of Prophet Muhammad on the same day, and ending with the Ottoman Caliph Mehmed/Mohammad VI on 1 November 1922. Some Muslims believe today that the caliphate system should be restored.

6 Caliph Omar built a small mosque on the site of the Temple Mount after he ordered the cleansing of the site, which had been turned into a garbage dump by the Byzantines. Jews believe the Muslim structure was built on top of the ruins of the Second Jewish Temple that was destroyed by the Romans in 70 AD. Caliph Omar also ordered the building of a mosque over the site of the Cave of the Patriarchs after the previous Herodian castle, with its Byzantine church, was destroyed by the Sassanid Persians in 614 AD.

7 The most famous and influential Jewish scholar of that era, Rabbi Moshe Ben Maimon-Maimonides (known as the *Rambam* in Hebrew and as *Musa Ibn Maymoon* in Arabic), who lived from 1138 to 1204 AD, was also one of the private physicians of Salah Aldeen (Saladin) in Cairo.

8 For more on this, read Amin Maalouf's *The Crusades Through Arab Eyes*, published in English translation (from the original French) in 1986.

9 This Ottoman caliph is also known for having massacred thousands of Alawites, a Shia sect.

The Anteater And The Jaguar

The son of Selim/Saleem the First, Caliph Suleiman the Magnificent, granted Jews the right to worship at the Western Wall after it was uncovered and cleansed with rosewater.

Again, I would point out that Judaism and Islam remain very close to each other in many regards. The followers of both religions claim to pray to and believe in the same God, the God of Abraham, Isaac, Ishmael, and Jacob/Israel (or Israeel, as he is referred to in the Quran). In addition, both claim Abraham/Ibrahim as their father; Judaism considers him the first Jewish ancestor, and Islam considers him the first Muslim. Tradition holds that Moses is a direct descendent of Isaac, and the Prophet Muhammad is a direct descendent of Ishmael.

Both Islam and Judaism forbid the consumption of pork and espouse other similar dietary restrictions under Halal and Kashrut laws, respectively. Both practice circumcision of male children—first practiced, it is said, by Abraham. (This particular tradition gave rise to an unusual, not to say miraculous, partnership recently, when Jews and Muslims jointly protested and demonstrated against the passing of a law in Germany that would have forbidden ritual circumcision.) Both follow the ritual of washing before prayer. The more traditionally religious women of both communities wear a head covering (or, in some Jewish traditions, a wig) to cover their hair. Both traditions require separation of men and women during prayer.[10] Both follow a lunar calendar, because both religions emerged originally from the deserts of Sinai and the Arabian Peninsula respectively, where it is possible to see the moon and stars every night of the year. And it was the extreme desert heat that led to a requirement in both religions that the dead be buried as quickly as possible; both Muslims and Jews also bury their dead wrapped

---

10 This issue, among others, has been a cause of contention between Orthodox and more liberal streams of Judaism (reform, conservative, and reconstructionist). Many non-Orthodox Jews pray in mixed groups, because they believe in equality between men and women. This conflict has made headlines regularly at the Western Wall. The Israeli government, amid controversy and despite the fierce opposition of the Orthodox establishment, finally adopted a negotiated settlement allocating the reform and conservative movements a special space for gender-mixed prayer next to the Western Wall, but the government began backtracking from the agreement not long after it was announced.

in a white linen shroud without a casket. The Jews have their Hebrew Scripture, and the Muslim Arabs have their Arabic Quran, where both languages have a similar alphabet and are written from right to left with thousands of similar vocabulary words, as both originate from the same extinct Semitic language. I should not fail to mention the common suffering and persecution of the Jews and the Muslims during the Spanish Inquisition that took place from the end of the fifteenth century until the beginning of the nineteenth century AD. This period of repression by a Catholic regime followed one of the most glorious eras in Jewish history under the rule of the Muslim Arabs in Andalusia, commonly referred to as a Golden Age (*Idan Hazahav* in Hebrew and *Al Asser Al-thahaby* in Arabic).[11]

On the basis of such a wealth of shared convictions, customs, experiences, and history, a compromise between the Jews and the Muslims in our land would seem much easier to achieve than, say, between Hindus and Muslims or even between Jews and Christians. This compromise might be assisted if honesty were maintained on all sides and if the whole story, with its ups and downs and within its wider historical context, were passed on to everyone in as much of an unbiased way as possible. Another useful project would be to explore, dispassionately, the degree to which the various rules regarding the holy sites, which many believe to be strictly in accordance with the word of God and the prophets, may accord mainly with the leanings (not to say biases) of certain religious figures, academics, and politicians. Finally, I have great faith that a harmonious sharing of the holy sites would be best facilitated through a fair political solution to the Israeli-Palestinian conflict—one

---

11 Philip Hitti mentions in his book, *The History of the Arabs*, that the Jews of the Iberian Peninsula (today's Spain) cooperated with the invading army of Berber and Arab Muslim forces, because of the oppression visited on the Jews under Catholic rule. This army, incidentally, was led by the Berber Tariq Ibn Ziad, whose name was given to the large rocky promontory dominating the narrow sea passage linking the Atlantic Ocean and the western Mediterranean: *Jabal Tareq* in Arabic (*Jabal* means *mountain*). In English, Jabal Tareq became Gibraltar.

that promises equal personal and collective rights for all inhabitants of our common land.

Me, My Religion, and Others

Despite the tendency of those living in my region to want to know other people's religious affiliations, I have found it difficult to talk with people about my own religious beliefs—for several reasons.

To begin with, my religion is a very personal matter to me. Dwelling on the external trappings of my religion is not something I have found terribly fruitful in helping me connect with others. Plus, telling others what religion I belong to fails to communicate enough about me, certainly not everything about me I would wish to communicate. Just knowing the name of someone's religion cannot possibly convey an exhaustive understanding of who that person is. And finally, I have never cared to probe or pry into the lives of others to find out what *their* religions are; I have learned instead that the kind of person someone is, good or bad, may not have anything to do with his or her religion. People who ask others about their religions may, in fact, be more concerned with bolstering division than with connecting with others. My religious affiliation is not something I want to use to draw borders that separate me from believers belonging to other religions; I prefer that religion help me draw closer to others who are different from me. I believe all the prophets and spiritual teachers whose messages have aided in the advancement of humankind, including those of the Far East, proclaimed a similar, simple message: love for others what you love for yourself, and do unto others as you would have them do unto you.

A maxim from Jainism, an ancient spiritual tradition of India, says, "Harmlessness is the only religion." In my opinion, this principle is an indispensable ingredient of what all religion should entail. I believe the more superficial details of religious practice that concern what one should wear; how, where, and how often one should pray; how long one's beard should be; and so forth are much less relevant. If one's religious identity is entirely dependent upon such external markers, then one's religion (or one's understanding of it) suffers from impoverishment.

Apart from defining what my own religious identity is and is not, during most of my life, I've been obliged to deal with definitions of what it means to be an Arab, what it means to be a Palestinian, and what it means to be an Israeli. At some point, I understood that all these comprise different aspects of my own identity—and that's not all. I lived in America from the age of nineteen until I was twenty-six, and my experiences there are also an important part of my identity. My admiration for other religious traditions, notably Buddhism and Confucianism, has also influenced my identity, as I have adopted some of their values and teachings into my own worldview.

Islam, of course, has never been alien to me, as I grew up with and have lived alongside Arab Muslims all my life. I always thought of them as Arabs just like me, even though they professed a different religion. In any case, an Arab cannot distance herself or himself from Islam, which is such a major part of Arab history; Islam necessarily remains part of my identity, despite the fact that my own religion is Christianity. And as a Christian Arab, I see no problem in recognizing the contribution of Islam and the Prophet Muhammad to my culture and my identity.

Judaism is also close to me, because I, in keeping with the official doctrine of Arab Orthodox Christianity, recognize the authority of the Hebrew Scriptures. Our priests, too, when performing wedding ceremonies, ask God to bless the bridegroom and the bride, as Abraham and Sarah, Isaac and Rebecca, Jacob and Joseph, and their descendants were blessed. I have shared a major portion of my life with Israeli Jews over the years; I know their language, and I understand a good deal about their outlook, religious traditions, history, and culture.

Then there is the question of "Arab Jews"—a phrase foreigners may find confusing, but bear with me. Most Israeli Jews are descendants of Arabian Jews, who, until quite recently, had shared their life with Arab Muslims, Arab Christians, and others in mixed cities, towns, and villages throughout the lands where Arab culture was prominent or dominant

The Anteater And The Jaguar

for hundreds and even thousands of years. The Jews who came to Israel from those lands, however long ago, and their children and grandchildren are very much Arabs like me. This is true even though most of the younger generation does not speak the Arabic of their parents and grandparents. However, we still do share a similar mind-set, as well as many similar traditions and customs. Many of us also share similar tastes in food and in music, among other common realms. (I'm thinking of Om Kalthoum, Fareed Alatrash, Abdelwahab, Laila Mourad, and many other iconic Arab performers of the twentieth century.) We often share a similar physical appearance, too: "Arab Arabs" are often mistaken for "Jewish Arabs" and vice versa. In fact, this happens to me regularly. An Arab Arab might come into my gift shop/café, think I am Jewish, and start speaking Hebrew to me. I would then start talking Arabic to let him or her know I am an Arab Arab and not a Jewish Arab. Or I might speak Arabic to someone on the assumption that he or she is an Arab Arab, only to learn he or she turns out to be a Jewish Arab. Many among the younger generation of Arab Jews in Israel are beginning to reclaim this heritage with new pride.

As for the other residents of Neve Shalom, I believe most relate to other religions in more or less the same way I do. A very common question asked by visitors is this: "Are there religious people in your community?" Indeed there are, but perhaps they are more inclined to recognize and respect other religions than is true in general of people outside our community. Some among us practice prayer, both Jews and Palestinians; some practice meditation and other spiritual activities; and others engage in neither. Most of us celebrate our different religious holidays. Some do this as a result of religious convictions, while others do it as part of their cultural identity. Many of us celebrate holidays with our families in our various hometowns. We regularly wish one another happy holidays and also tend to get together around some of them in the community. This happens despite the fact that some of them result from convictions not recognized by the other religions. For example, Judaism does not recognize the birth of Jesus as the son of God (Christmas), and Islam does not recognize Jesus's crucifixion, death, and resurrection (Good Friday and Easter). Mutual acceptance, tolerance, and love all factor into the religious dimension of life in our community.

Our community not only fosters among ourselves acceptance and appreciation of diverse religious perspectives but also hosts workshops and conferences where such matters are addressed. Every year, at our guesthouse, we host dozens of very diverse groups, both local and foreign, who choose our community specifically as the venue for their gatherings, to which they bring many varied spiritual and religious activities and convictions. The conferences we host often bring internationally known teachers, lecturers, and practitioners from all over the world. Groups choose our community because they perceive Wahat Assalam to be an inspirational place: a community that, thanks to its ideals, practices, and people, radiates a tranquil and positive energy.

Ideally, and to be truly effective, actions taken toward reconciliation should be mutual. Recognizing the legitimacy of others' religions, in spite of religious and historical disagreements, should never be considered blasphemous, especially in our region, where all those involved are Semites. They are descendants of the same father, Abraham, and they all claim to worship the same God he worshiped. Nevertheless, those whose religious beliefs influence them to seek retribution for past wrongs or present grievances must never stoop so low as to burn or desecrate mosques, synagogues, or churches. I believe the worst thing we can do to hurt our own religion is to use it to justify acts of aggression and violence toward others who do not adopt our convictions. How can we claim to be loved by God if we commit such hateful acts? The followers of virtually every religion claim that their religion mainly promotes peace and fosters goodwill toward all people. Most of us, however, still fall short of proving this through our actions.

At some point during his life, the founder of our community, Father Bruno Hussar, suggested a house of prayer be built that would serve the followers of the three monotheistic religions. Bruno's original plans called for the building to be a triangular structure, with one corner set aside for each religion. After deliberation, however, he agreed to build a dome-shaped worship center. This center is known as the Place of Silence (*Doumia* in Hebrew and *Sakinah* in Arabic). Structurally, it is modeled on Fuller's geodesic dome. It is a revered place of prayer, contemplation, and meditation for our entire community and for the whole spectrum of students, lecturers, activists, workshop participants, friends, and guests who visit our community during all seasons.

Some years ago, I heard about a beautiful and generous act by a British community somewhere in the United Kingdom, whose people offered an unused church building to their Muslim neighbors to use as a mosque. In my opinion, our world is in need of more of these humane kinds of acts, instead of the violent arguments over whose rights have precedence at a specific site, ending too often with people killing one another. We can believe in the right of people of different religions to worship as they choose. We can believe in people's right to pray in different ways using different languages. The truth remains, however, that the intention of all who pray or meditate is to connect with the one whom they understand their creator or deity to be.

Sixteen

ABOUT PEOPLE

The communities of the Middle East have had their peaceful times throughout most of their history, but they've also had their share of ethnic and political conflicts. When political conflicts erupt as struggles over power and control, or parity, political upheaval too readily becomes ethnic strife. Some people begin murdering others because of their communal, religious, or ethnic affiliation, as happened during the Lebanese civil war (1975–1990), more recently in Iraq and Syria, and even in our country. It is all too easy for people to revive incidents and stories from the past to fuel their enmity toward one another. Regrettably, they fail to realize that the renewed violence they are waging against one another will soon become just one more chapter in an already dense catalog of numberless grievances. These, in turn, will trigger escalation and more conflict, and so it continues.

The intervention of external powers deserves a significant share of the blame, of course, but this is only part of the picture. The sad reality is that those who have been leading in our region have been unable or maybe unwilling to reach a formula that would help them accommodate one another's differences and guarantee equality and fair sharing for their peoples. This inability was exacerbated following the end of the

The Anteater And The Jaguar

First World War, when these groups were stacked together into the separate states that the British and the French empires imposed. I believe many of our politicians, religious leaders, and people still have much to learn from Nelson Mandela, the outstanding South African leader who achieved greatness by rejecting all calls for revenge, notwithstanding what his people had endured for centuries under a racist apartheid regime. That Mandela himself spent twenty-seven years in prison makes his record in support of peace, reconciliation, and universal human rights all the more remarkable.

The record of the relationship between Christianity, Islam, and Judaism offers many examples of deliberate distortions apparently motivated by the desire to create and sustain separation between their respective adherents. Judaism, historically, emerged as a religion long before both Christianity and Islam and recognizes neither of them. Christianity, which appeared next, recognizes the Old Testament, the Scriptures of the Jewish people, but it does not recognize the Quran, the holy book of Islam. Islam, the latest of these three monotheistic religions to emerge, recognizes the followers of Judaism and Christianity as the "Peoples of the Book," though it considers the Holy Quran as the clear revelation that serves to replace both the Christian and Hebrew Scriptures, which Muslims believe have been corrupted over the centuries.

In the annals of Christianity, one major reason sometimes offered to justify persecution of Jews has been the belief held by some that "the Jews" crucified Jesus, whereas the people responsible for this event were a relatively small and corrupt Jewish elite in collaboration with Rome (which had to authorize any execution by crucifixion). Moreover, the first historical records of this collaboration were written by Jews, not gentiles. This caricature of Jews as the murderers of Jesus (repudiated in the Roman Catholic Church in the early 1960s) has never existed theologically within Islam, since the Quran says of Jesus (*Issa*, in Arabic) that he was neither crucified nor killed but rather ascended to heaven without suffering death. (The Quran also mentions that Jesus spoke as an infant to those who doubted the story of Mary, who also happens to be the only woman mentioned by name in the Quran.) Islam thus does not accuse the Jewish people of any crimes concerning Jesus.

Another important fact is that the Prophet Muhammad and the first Muslims were mainly Arabs and therefore Semites. The same is true of Arab Christians. Most Arab Muslims and Arab Christians can thus be recognized officially as lineal descendants of Abraham.

I have always found it difficult to agree with people who claim the Jews have suffered the same persecution under Arab Muslim rule as they have in other places. The Jews of the Middle East and the Arab world in general were just another community, one more among many, who shared their life as close neighbors. In Arab lands, the Jews never lived in ghettos. Indeed, when it comes to the issue of mistreatment, it is a fact that Islamic caliphate rule of more than thirteen centuries had in general exercised much greater tolerance toward the followers of Judaism, Christianity, and many other communities than it did toward other Muslim sects and their offshoots. Sunni Islam, for example, considers Shia Islam with its many branches and subbranches to be heretical.[12] Some of these communities have suffered their share of persecution and discrimination as a result of adopting or promoting a type of Islam that did not accord with mainstream Sunni conviction, which the majority of Muslims follow. This can be loosely compared to the history of persecution and harassment of some Christians by others (Roman Catholics against Protestants, and so on) when there were doctrinal schisms.

From my perspective, and attempting to be objective, the Jewish experience of intolerance and persecution need not be singled out as unique in this part of the world. Needless to say, no one should ever minimize any group's experience of persecution, but at the same time, there would seem little value in a competition over which group deserves greater sympathy on account of the degree of their suffering. If anything,

---

12 Some sects of Shia became extinct; among those that still exist are the Twelver, the Zaidi, the Alawites, the Ismaili, and the Druze as one of its offshoots. The schism of Islam into Sunni and Shia took place about fourteen hundred years ago.

the experience of suffering should give people a reason to find solidarity with all who suffer, so that all human suffering is believed by all human beings to be deplorable.

As to the breakdown in Jewish-Arab relations in the Arab countries around the end of the first half of the twentieth century, it must be seen as a phenomenon directly connected to political events taking place in Palestine at the time when British interference at its most acute set Jews and Arabs in opposition to each other.

The Arabs did, in fact, consider Britain and France to be their enemies for many years before the appearance of the Zionist movement. Arab attitudes toward these European powers resulted from the history of brutal imperial invasions, occupations of major parts of the Arab lands of North Africa, and the oppression of its people during the nineteenth century. Nonetheless, the Arabs of the Middle East agreed to fight with Great Britain against the Ottomans during the Great War (later renamed the First World War), because the Arabs had been promised independence. This promise was given by the then British high commissioner in Egypt, Lord McMahon, to Sharif Hussein of Mecca during 1915–16 through the now-famous correspondence between them. But when the Great War ended, the Arabs were shocked to learn the British had already closed a secret agreement with France, known as the Sykes-Picot agreement, which proposed dividing the Middle East and other lands of the disintegrating Ottoman Empire into a number of separate territories and entities. This secret agreement reached between France, Great Britain, and Russia during 1915–16 was exposed by the Bolsheviks on November 23, 1917, in the wake of the Russian Revolution in October. Meanwhile, on November 2, 1917, the Balfour Declaration was made public.

To make things even worse from the Arabs' perspective, British Field Marshal Edmund Allenby remarked during his reception speech after entering Jerusalem on December 11, 1917, "The Crusades are over." This pronouncement caused the Palestinian delegation of both Muslims and Christians to withdraw from the reception in protest. For Palestinians, Allenby's use of the term *Crusades* was deeply insulting, evoking the history of Crusades to the Holy Land, seen by Palestinians purely as foreign and brutal occupations.

One can only too easily see why the Arab people did not find themselves in a position to approve of or tolerate Zionist cooperation with the British or the French—or with any other party, for that matter. Such cooperation was, after all, opposed to their own interests.

Despite the conundrum that the British and French intervention in the region created, not everyone in the Middle East made clear connections between the different Jewish scenarios and their own circumstances; more than likely, people did not fully understand everything that this political jockeying might accomplish. The Jews in Iraq and in other Arab regions, for example, did not consider themselves responsible for what other Jews, mostly European Jews, were doing in Palestine. Likewise, the Palestinians did not consider themselves responsible for injuries to Jews that occurred elsewhere in the world.

I find it really sad to read about how the interference of Western powers led to the abrupt end of the long-established and mostly positive relations between Arabs and Jews in Arab countries—after hundreds and, in some cases, even thousands of years. Human history, however, is full of examples of angry regimes or populations exacting revenge against the wrong people simply because they happen to be a convenient target. No group has proven immune to the temptation to act inhumanely toward others. Persuasive reasons can always be marshaled for the purpose of inciting inhuman and even heinous acts. There are always leaders who are swift to incite such acts against innocent people. There are always frustrated followers who are willing to carry out atrocities against blameless people. There are always looters, rioters, and mischief-makers who use tumultuous occasions as convenient opportunities to inflict more misery on those who are already savagely victimized; however, on the bright side, there are also always those who refuse to take part in the frenzies that evil people incite. There are always those who take enormous risks upon themselves by opposing injustice and by making efforts to rescue the victimized, even to the extent of hiding them in their own houses. In fact, we are making plans for a Museum of the Righteous in our community to commemorate these many courageous people from all over the world and from our own region, including Arabs and Jews. The museum will also allow us to commemorate numerous ignored and forgotten peacemakers.

True, examples do exist of the mistreatment of Jews under Arab rule; Jews who are indigenous to the region, however, including Arab Jews who came to Israel after 1948, are among the few Jews anywhere who still talk about a relatively good life alongside Arabs and good relations with their Arab neighbors. Such comments are rarely heard from European Jews. The same is true on the whole regarding Palestine, both before and after 1948. Most people talk a lot about the violent conflict, but less is said explicitly about the tapestry of normal life between Jews and Arabs of the region—and there *is* such a thing as normal life together here, make no mistake. Jews and Arabs have engaged in commerce together and have shared life as neighbors in numerous towns and cities of Palestine. Both have mutually benefited from each other, too; this, more often than not, characterizes the present moment. There is the political conflict, of course, but daily life also goes on as normal. On a daily basis, one can find Jews visiting, doing business, and shopping in Arab communities. Likewise, Palestinian Arabs go to Jewish communities and markets for the same purpose. Many Palestinians and Jews are friends, whose families share happy and sad occasions with one another. There are still, as in the past, disagreements, but who says the only solution is violent military confrontation? Competitors, even adversaries, need not be viewed as enemies and can be viewed as potential partners instead; indeed, building sustainable communities frequently requires cooperation across political, religious, ethnic, linguistic, and other divides, defining common interests while setting differences aside.[13]

One of our problems is that we tend to generalize too much. We cannot really talk sensibly about Islam, Christianity, Judaism, any other

---

[13] This is the main thesis of the book *No More Enemies* (2011) by Deb Reich.

religion, or any other nation or community as if it were one thing only. Within every religion, nation, or community, many different divisions can be found. Every one of these larger groups has its liberals, conservatives, fanatics, and moral and immoral. It is entirely wrong to judge a whole group that could count tens or hundreds of millions based upon the practices of a few. In spite of these obvious simple facts, too many devious politicians, intellectuals, and religious leaders tend to talk of Islam, Christianity, Judaism, and assorted nations in terms of categories that, when an accurate picture emerges, can be seen for what they are: erroneous and overly simplistic caricatures of these religions and peoples. Regrettably, too many people tend to believe these caricatures and proceed to endlessly recirculate the same inaccurate conclusions.

I fail to understand why people so often insist on dividing us into racial and religious groups as a template for viewing our shared reality. We all know that, within these groups, we are different individuals who have different attitudes and take different approaches. Many times we have little in common with others who, by label alone, technically belong to our own group. Why this insistence on dividing us into rigid categories persists is hard to fathom, unless it is merely for the purpose of stirring things up and keeping conflicts alive. Perhaps the material interests and psychological needs of some people are served by fostering division and discord. Some people, after all, seem to feed on negative energy.

The prospects for peace with equal justice for all, on the other hand, will improve only when we recognize that many of the people from communities and ethnic groups not our own share with us similar values, approaches, and attitudes. I have learned that it is a better and more moral choice to relate to all other human beings one at a time, each as a unique individual, rather than as a stereotyped copy of some general group image. This is one of the powerful yet simple epiphanies I have experienced through living in Wahat Assalam, according me a kind of understanding that transcends artificial barriers and protects and elevates my own humanity.

Part III: Life Experiences

Seventeen

My Parents

When I was a child, my father, Rafeek, was working as a bus driver for a local company in Nazareth. Before 1948, under the British Mandate, he was an instructor who trained truck drivers. But the war of 1948 changed everything. Drastically. My father, like many other Palestinians, suddenly found himself in a new reality, a citizen of a new political entity, the new state of Israel. If he was to have any chance of continuing the work he'd been doing, he was going to have to learn Hebrew. I believe, however, that the language barrier may have been one of the less daunting aspects of the challenge people like my father faced. In the wake of the catastrophe that had befallen my father, his family, his community, and his people, the new circumstances demanded that he make a massive and rapid adaptation, in both practical and emotional terms. And this was not the first such upheaval for him. My father was part of a generation that had experienced life in Palestine under three consecutive foreign regimes: the Ottomans, the British, and then the Israeli Jews—over a period of less than fifty years.

Until 1953, my father was unemployed. When he began driving a bus, a lot of joy came into my young life. Suddenly—because of the bus—I was given many more opportunities than other children to travel around and visit lots of interesting places, at a time when scarcely anyone owned a private car. During my school vacations, I often joined my father on his regular daily route between Nazareth and the nearby Arab villages along the route to *Tabariyyah* (Tiberias), and later between Nazareth and Haifa. These nearby villages, which at the time seemed quite distant and exotic to me, included Reineh, Mash'had, Kafar Kanna, and Tor'an. He also took me along on chartered trips with various groups of adults and schoolchildren to all kinds of other destinations. Some of these trips were truly exciting, such as when I went with him to ferry Nazareth's leading hometown soccer team to their away matches with teams from the nearby Jewish towns.

Besides filling my life with the adventure of travel and the fun of going along with my father when he was working, his new occupation continually made me feel proud to be his son. During the twenty-five years he drove a bus, my father became a very well-known and beloved person not only in our own town but also in the surrounding Arab villages. Whenever I walked with him in Nazareth, I saw the warm way he was greeted by many people of different ages. Later, after his retirement, I might ask him about somebody who greeted him as Abu Basheer (Basheer is my eldest brother's name), and generally he knew the person's name; if he didn't, he always said, "I do not remember, but he must have been one of my passengers." Quite a few men would tell me, after greeting him, "You should know it was thanks to your father that I got my driving license."

My father liked to reminisce, in later years, about one particular British driving test examiner. During road tests, this examiner would place a matchbox behind a rear wheel of the truck when it was parked on a hill. As the candidate pulled the truck out of the parking space going uphill, the slightest reverse motion would crush the matchbox, and the examiner would promptly flunk the candidate. My father appealed on behalf of many an aspiring truck driver, asking the examiner to show some leniency, especially toward otherwise well-qualified candidates who had failed the road test more than once thanks to the matchbox.

The Anteater And The Jaguar

In those days, obtaining a trucker's license was a significant accomplishment for many young men, guaranteeing them a well-paying job transporting goods within Palestine and between Palestine and Lebanon, Syria, Jordan, and Iraq.

My father was also very popular within smaller circles of friends and family for his love of singing. He knew many old and rare songs that have their roots in a musical culture known as *Halabeiat* (from *Halab* [*Aleppo* in English], in northwestern Syria). Halab/Aleppo was a regional hub, and its music, cuisine, and other cultural traditions have an illustrious history in the Middle East, going back thousands of years. Much of the surrounding region (including Nazareth) can trace its own traditions back to Aleppo.

My father learned *Halabeiat* from the Syrian-Arab wife of one of his Palestinian friends. This couple lived in Haifa before 1948, and my father visited them regularly for some years. During those visits, there was always time set aside for the women of the family to play the *oud* (a traditional Middle Eastern instrument similar to a lute) and sing; her singing, my father remembered, was very beautiful. I saw, at our own family weddings and various other social gatherings of friends, how people always waited impatiently and responded enthusiastically when my father began singing. I could not fail to be impressed by the joy and laughter evoked by my father's rendition of those traditional folk songs of love and longing with their often humorous lyrics. He was indeed a performer possessed of great charisma and a beautiful soul.

My father rarely talked of politics, but most of the time, I could guess his feelings and opinions from his facial expressions during news broadcasts. I remember him lying on his bed after work and listening to the afternoon news on the radio. There were four stations he listened to regularly: the BBC in Arabic, Cairo, Amman, and Israel in Arabic. Most important was Radio Amman, broadcasting from Jordan, which sometimes brought him news of his dispersed family, some of whom had been separated from the rest of the family in the chaos after 1948 and ended up in Jordan, along with others who had gone to live in Jordan later for various reasons. Both the Jordanian and Israeli-Arabic radio stations, located on either side of the Israeli-Jordanian border, provided a valuable special service for Palestinians who had no other means of communicating with one another across the divide. One program was called *Ab'ath Salami* ("I send my regards"), which offered individual Palestinians an appointed time slot when they could send their regards to their relatives, ask them about relatives on the other side, and relay to them the family news from this side. Then, at the end of their newscasts, these stations would read aloud the names of people who recently had passed away. This service was provided at the behest of families whose loved ones had died. My father was not unique in obtaining news of his family in this way. Many others did the same.

My mother, Najla Farah, always talked about her life in Palestine as it had been in the past. She would speak often of the relatives scattered among distant locations, and her palpable longing to see them was obviously incredibly painful. She was always recounting memories of the good old days when they had all been together—something I imagine was quite common among the women of her generation in Palestine. Yet my mother was different in one way from other women I knew during my childhood: she was a very politically outspoken and nationalistic Arab. This came as a result of an experience she'd had in her youth before she married my father in 1944.

During her teens, my mother took care of her maternal grandfather, Wasef, who lived to be very old. Besides attending to his physical care, she used to read the newspaper to him every day. This was during the 1930s and 1940s. Reading daily about politics was uncommon for most girls of her age and generation. Of course, everybody was knowledgeable to some degree about events generally and in Palestine particularly during that time; it was impossible not to be involved to some degree. That was a period when schools often went on strike, for example, and pupils and teachers took part in demonstrations protesting British policies in Palestine.

In my mother's case, her reading aloud to her grandfather every day provided her with an ongoing education in political affairs beyond what

The Anteater And The Jaguar

was typical for most women of that era. She witnessed firsthand what was taking place in Palestine, while at the same time, she acquired a broader context in which to interpret her own observations and experiences. Newspapers were almost the only source of official information in those days; televisions were not yet available, and even radios were very scarce—but my mother's father owned a radio, which expanded her horizons still further. Neighbors would come to the house and sit around the radio, listening to the news and entertainment programs.

Thus, unlike most of her female peers, my mother nearly always had something to say about what was taking place politically. Always evident as she talked was her keen awareness of the international collusion that had culminated in the victimization of the Palestinian people. Because my parents were both very devout people, however, they never lost or doubted their faith in God, despite all the things their people had endured. Watching the attention that my mother and father devoted to the news every day, I learned to do likewise, in the hope that we might eventually learn of some breakthrough or hear some statement that might offer hope for a solution to the Palestinian question. I have often dreamed of what such a statement, coming from an American president or an Israeli leader, might sound like: *Listen—we have not been really honest about the situation of the Palestinian people, who have been suffering so unnecessarily for such a long time. Therefore, it is time for us to face the truth and give them justice.* Unfortunately, no such statement has ever been forthcoming.

The Palestinian question has always received more news coverage than do other political issues. Attempting to promote a resolution, summits of local and world leaders, in addition to local and international conferences, have been held repeatedly. Presidents, prime ministers, special envoys, and other delegations and diplomats have visited the region time and again. All the activities in which they engaged were for the purpose of finding a solution to the Palestinian question. For countless people, like my parents, the hopes and dreams they continued to nurture ensured they would go on listening to the news, expecting that surely some real breakthrough might just come out of this particular meeting or that special conference. I feel sometimes that I am continuing with the same charade, since these conferences and visits are still going on with no results at all, except to give false hope that the dismal situation might finally change.

During the early 1980s, after I had returned home from my time living in the United States, I worked at my cousin Ramzy's bookstore in Nazareth. During the workday, I generally had a chance to glance at most of the daily newspapers. One of them, *Alquds*, was published in Jerusalem. (*Alquds* is the Arabic name of Jerusalem.) In addition to all the other important local and world news this daily Arab newspaper endeavored to cover, an item entitled "Twenty Years Ago" always appeared in a small box on the front page. Invariably, when I read the item, it was about some conference or visit by some dignitary who had traveled to our region to discuss or propose some approach to solving the Palestinian question.

Reading this twenty-year-old news always made me feel as if time had come to a standstill—another conference, another summit, another visit by this diplomat or that delegation or some newly appointed envoy. After so many years, I can't help but wonder: How long will this charade go on? How much patience does the world expect the Palestinians to have?

I often express how much I wish I could reach a point, as many other people on this planet have done, where my people's story will stop being a political headline. I yearn to see the day when the interest others have in me has nothing to do with my being someone whose people *have a problem*. I yearn to reach the point when the interest others have in me will not be prompted by their doubts about my humanity. I fervently wish the verdict people come to, about me and my people, didn't revolve around the notion that all we are intent on being is the nemesis of the Jews—and for no rational or logical reason. I wish all those people, communities, and governments that have been participating directly or indirectly in perpetuating our agony only because we are Palestinians could really ask themselves why they are doing so. Have we been found guilty of some terrible original sin that makes us deserve to be ignored and punished forever? Or have we been a handy scapegoat for the many sinful mistakes visited by other people on some other population, near or far away, in recent history or in more remote times? Haven't there been many people on our planet who at one time or another tasted of the same calamity, and for similar reasons?

Finally, I have an aspiration not to have a connection with, or receive any support from, any country or regime that routinely violates people's human rights, domestically or abroad. I furthermore wish that people who, for whatever reason, choose to side with the Israelis in a partisan manner would not blindly cast my people as their enemies. I wish people who choose to sympathize with our cause, the Palestinian cause, would not do so for reasons involving prejudice against Jews or issues with Judaism. I do not subscribe to the old win-lose dictum that "the enemy of my enemy is my friend." This kind of thinking will not take us where we want to go. If you were to live for thirty years in a shared village with people you have been encouraged to think of as your enemies, as Dyana and I have done, striving always to interact with them on the basis of mutual respect, equality, and dignity, you would eventually come to a similar conclusion.

Eighteen

IN JERUSALEM AND THE WEST BANK

Growing up as an Israeli-Palestinian Arab in Nazareth, I, like the rest of my people, was isolated after 1948 from Palestinians living elsewhere. However, this situation changed after the 1967 war, during which Israeli forces occupied the West Bank and the Gaza Strip. When that war ended, both Israeli-Palestinian Arabs and Israeli Jews flooded the streets and markets of Gaza City and the major cities in the West Bank—mainly East Jerusalem, Nablus, Al-Khalil, and Ramallah. Many Palestinians visited relatives they had not seen since 1948. Others renewed contact with friends. Still others went to shop, because goods were much cheaper in these places than in Israel. Since Palestinians in Israel mostly traveled by bus for those visits, my family and I also had the opportunity to visit these places with groups my father accompanied as a bus driver.

Meanwhile, for Arab politics generally, the Israeli occupation was nothing short of catastrophic: After defeating the armies of Egypt, Syria, and Jordan, Israel occupied the remainder of Palestine, the Egyptian Sinai Peninsula (since returned to Egypt), and the Syrian Golan heights (still under Israeli rule today). However, since Palestinians who happened to be from Israel, from the West Bank, or from the Gaza Strip were not directly responsible for the war and had no part in waging it, they

The Anteater And The Jaguar

benefited initially from the greater freedom the outcome gave them to travel among these areas. This was true despite the painful defeat of the Arab armies and despite the fact that the '67 war had created another wave of Palestinian refugees, who crossed the Jordan River into Jordan.

I was about twelve years old at the time, but I still have vivid memories of those first visits to the West Bank and the Gaza Strip. For me, these visits were entirely new experiences, but for my parents and their generation, the West Bank and Gaza were familiar, even after nineteen years when visiting them had been impossible. I still remember the excitement and happy faces of my parents and the other adults around me; the atmosphere during each such visit was like a big family reunion. The next few years were a happy interlude for so many reunited groups of Palestinians who had been separated since 1948.

And there were other visits. In 1965, when I was ten, I was finally deemed old enough to join the rest of my family on their annual visit to East Jerusalem at Christmas time. The Kingdom of Jordan, which governed the West Bank between 1948 and 1967, allowed Christian Palestinians from Israel to visit East Jerusalem as pilgrims for four days each Christmas. I recall that Christmas visit in 1965 as a shocking and confusing experience, and the memories are still vivid in my mind. When we departed Nazareth very early in the morning on a rainy day in early January, I knew only that we were going to Alquds (Jerusalem). I did not know how long a journey it would be, exactly where we were going, or what to expect. Later, I discovered that my parents were making this journey not mainly for religious reasons (although it is true they were very religious). Rather, like most other Israeli Palestinians who joined them on that trip, the dominant motive was to meet those relatives they had not seen for almost two decades.

We entered East Jerusalem through two adjacent, separate rooms inside a barracks. The place was called the Mandelbaum Gate (*Mandelbaum* is German for "almond tree"). Today, that crossing point stands near the entrance to the old city through one of the main gates in the Old City wall, known as the Al-Khalil (Hebron) gate and also as the Jaffa gate. I remember that Israeli officers sat inside one of the two rooms and Jordanian officers inside the other. My father presented them with our papers. After verifying that the documents were authentic and in order, they stamped them.

Next, we exited into a large square. At its far end, I saw a line of people who had been standing and waiting. After only a few seconds, the people at the opposite ends of the square recognized their relatives and started running toward one another. A flood of emotions was apparent in the people around me, all of whom were hugging and kissing one another and crying. These emotional displays continued throughout the encounter and went on for a while afterward, too. My parents hoped to meet relatives who had come to Jerusalem from Amman, Damascus, and Beirut. The brevity of the family reunion only amplified the level of emotion, and the happiness of the occasion was tainted by the dismal awareness that everyone would have to return to the state of forced separation that had existed among family members since 1948.

Nobody knew in advance who would arrive in Jerusalem to celebrate Christmas that year and enjoy the longed-for family reunion. Young people today might find it hard to believe, but in those days, there was no way to let people on the other side know who might be coming for the holiday, or when. Hardly anyone had a telephone, and in any case, you would not have been able to connect by telephone from Israel to someone in a neighboring Arab country, or vice versa. E-mail, Internet, and cell phones were still a few decades in the future, and there wasn't even direct mail service between Israel and Arab countries. The separation was complete.

Thus, who would or would not happen to show up was a mystery. People traveled long distances nonetheless, some even traveling from as far away as Kuwait, where some of my mother's relatives had ended up living. All who made the journey hoped they might by chance find some of their relatives in Jerusalem, but there was no guarantee this would happen. The more fortunate, of course, were overjoyed to meet their kinfolk, but others suffered crushing disappointment when their relatives did not appear.

The Anteater And The Jaguar

Israel's regime of direct military rule over Palestinian communities inside Israel between 1949 and 1966 did not guarantee either that everyone would be able to obtain permission to cross over to the Jordanian side of Alquds/Jerusalem. People had to *apply* for permission, and persons who were considered a "security threat," along with their close family members, were barred from crossing. When it came to traveling to East Jerusalem, however, my parents were very lucky. Unlike others, they were able to take the trip almost yearly. This became possible with the help of my uncle Moeen, who just happened to be a good friend of a Jewish man from Tiberias, whom we knew as Meeno. Their friendship went back to the years prior to 1948, when my uncle had worked as a truck driver at a transportation company owned by Meeno's father. Meeno, fortunately, was very well connected during the period of military rule. During that time, Israeli Palestinians were required to secure permits of all kinds from military officers who were stationed in every Arab town or village. Through his friendship with Meeno, however, my uncle managed to bypass the military officer and obtain a permit for almost anything Meeno requested for him. Those requests were rarely for my uncle personally: More often than not, they were for others who had asked my uncle for assistance. Through Meeno, my uncle often obtained permission for others to visit East Jerusalem, even for some who had previously been rejected. He also helped find employment for would-be teachers and government employees, whose access to jobs was contingent on obtaining security clearance. Sometimes people also approached him to help with travel permits when they wished to attend a family reunion in some other town or when they wanted a hunting license.

After my visit to East Jerusalem in January 1965, I began for the first time to ask questions that had what might be called a "political" dimension, although in hindsight, I wouldn't say I thought of them that way. Mainly I asked my mother questions such as these: Why can't our relatives come to visit us in Nazareth? Why do we have to cross a border between the two parts of Jerusalem in order to see them? Why is there an Arab Jerusalem and a Jewish Jerusalem? Why are the two parts of

Jerusalem separated by a fence? What caused your relatives to lose their homes in Haifa? Why can't they return to their homes?

Like other Palestinians, my parents were extremely cautious when answering my questions or telling anyone about our identity and our past. My father never talked about such things at all. I spent more time with my mother, however, because she was always at home—and she did answer my questions. Quietly. She always warned me, though, never to talk about these things with anybody. Indeed, throughout the remainder of her life, she repeatedly warned me to be careful about what I shared with other people. This continued even after Dyana and I moved to the Oasis of Peace, because my mother knew I gave political talks there to all kinds of people who visited the village, and she was afraid for me. (I mentioned this once to my neighbor Coral Ahron, who was forty years my elder. My parents, I told her, always warned us not to mention outside our house what we heard inside it and not to trust anybody by sharing our political views. To my surprise, Coral said this was the same thing she remembered from her own childhood as a Jewish girl growing up in England.)

My mother's answers to my questions gave me my first important lessons in history and politics. In consequence, I began to comprehend the circumstances in which I was living. I learned that the circumstances during my own childhood were quite different from what my parents had experienced growing up long before 1948, when Palestine was all one piece, and all their relatives lived around them. Then, travel from Palestine to the nearby Arab states of Lebanon, Syria, Jordan, and Egypt was easy, because there were no border complications. During the 1948 war, though, their relatives, like many others, had hastily left their houses and businesses behind to seek safer ground. They left believing that, in a matter of a few days or weeks, the fighting would end, and they would be able to return to their homes. Some of them had done the same thing during previous eruptions of violence before 1948. They had no idea that what they believed to be only a temporary remedy, as on previous occasions, would in fact become a lifelong exile.

The Anteater And The Jaguar

During the first years the new state of Israel was in existence, many laws were passed with regard to the expelled Palestinians. One law allowed the confiscation of their properties, whether lands, buildings, savings, or anything else left behind. Another law disallowed Palestinians who took refuge in nearby countries from returning to their homes. Even the many Palestinians who simply were not present in Palestine during the war—because they were away studying, on business, working, receiving medical treatment, and so forth—were not permitted to come back after the end of the war. Among them were my aunt Zbaydi, my mother's sister, and aunt Zbaydi's husband, Uncle George, who were living in New York, as I mentioned earlier. When Israel signed a peace treaty with Jordan in 1994, Israeli nationals—Jewish or Arab—could visit Jordan legally for the first time since 1948. When I visited Aunt Zbaydi in Amman in 1998, she told me Uncle George had refused to become an American citizen, saying, "Do you want me to exchange Palestine for a piece of paper?"

My parents spoke about the thousands who had left villages and towns surrounding Nazareth to take refuge in the town during the war. These refugees, and many others who sought refuge in other nearby towns and villages, were later granted Israeli citizenship, but they were defined under Israeli law as *internally* displaced and were not allowed to return to their homes or to reclaim property they had left behind. Numerous Palestinians were denied the right to reclaim their property, because they were classified as absentees, which means simply that they were not present in the town where they had their home or their business when the Jewish forces took control of it during the 1948 war. Among them was my father-in-law, Fayez, who lost his electrical parts and equipment shop in the town of Beesan (Beit She'an) near Nazareth. Another was my great-uncle Elia, a maternal uncle of my mother's. She told me he had owned a modern mill in Haifa, but sometime during the war, he shuttered its doors and went back to Nazareth for the duration. Then, when the war ended and he traveled to Haifa to check on his mill, he found one of his Jewish workers operating the machines as an employee of the state. The mill had been declared state property after Elia was declared an absentee. This worker said the only thing he could do to help was try to help Elia get a job alongside him. A few weeks later, Uncle Elia decided to accept the offer, understanding he would be unable to get his business back, because he had a family to support, and jobs were very scarce.

I have heard and read so many stories about Palestinians who were killed while trying to cross the border to return to their homes in Palestine. One of the few who successfully made that journey in the chaos that followed the 1948 war was a child who grew up to become the renowned Palestinian poet Mahmoud Darwish. He was seven years old when he and his family fled their village of Albirwa in northern Palestine after it came under attack by Israeli forces in June 1948. The family spent a short time as refugees in Lebanon, then made their way back on foot. Albirwa, however, had already been razed to the ground to prevent anyone's returning to live there. Young Mahmoud Darwish and his family went to live in another Arab village called Deir al-Asad, which did not experience what many other villages had experienced of expulsion and erasing. Darwish, who died a few years ago, is considered the Palestinian national poet, and his work is read all over the world in Arabic and in translation.

The vast majority of Palestinians who were exiled in 1948, however, were not as fortunate. Some died walking long distances to the north or east, seeking refuge. Some drowned in the sea on overloaded boats that sailed from Jaffa or Haifa and sank. Others died of broken hearts after losing everything. Still others lost their sanity or spent the remainder of their life in a state of chronic depression.

Most of the survivors of this catastrophic upheaval and displacement ended up spending the rest of their lives in tent camps, where they were obliged to endure many a burning summer and many a freezing winter. They survived somehow, without any infrastructure or facilities that might have protected their dignity and honor. I have often wondered how those people managed to survive at all. What did they eat? Where

The Anteater And The Jaguar

and how did they cook? How did they manage to sleep in such crowded conditions? How did they attend to their physical needs? What unnecessary punishment and suffering for human beings to go through, just because they are who they are!

Wars, of course, happen all the time, and people who are victims of them often leave for safer places temporarily. Still, most intend to return home when things quiet down. True, many a war has kept refugees from returning to their homes, and the argument is often heard that Palestinians are not unique in this regard. Indeed, one common Israeli argument proceeds as follows: Just as Arabs were expelled from Palestine, so were Jews expelled from the Arab countries. Thus, when it comes to comparing their plight, the Jews and Palestinians are even.

I, however, do not think this argument is helpful at all. Throughout my time living at Neve Shalom, I have had the chance to meet and listen both to Arab Jews and to Arab Palestinians, who have shared their stories about the pain of expulsion, the pain of having to leave their homeland forever, and the pain of being disconnected from loved ones. I have not been able to detect any significant difference between their agonies. For this reason, I do not wish to compare them and say, "Yes, but…"

All are victims. Most had nothing to do with the politics or issues that altered their circumstances in this manner; they cannot be blamed and should not be told that what they have suffered is just hard luck. The *pain* of every individual should be acknowledged, and the *rights* of every individual should be respected. I only hope the day will come when these issues will be dealt with fairly and humanely and no longer excused or rationalized, on whatever grounds.

If we wish to try to compare the Middle Eastern Jewish refugee crisis with the Palestinian refugee crisis, one important difference is clear: Most Arab Jews ended up living together in Israel as one entity. On the other hand, most Palestinian Arabs lost their common life, ended up being disconnected from one another, and were dispersed across the entire globe. It is as though the Jewish and Palestinian peoples have exchanged places. As the Jewish diaspora seems to have drawn officially to a close with the founding of Israel, the Palestinian diaspora has begun and shows no signs of abating. The tragedy of the Palestinians did not end at the close of 1948, and they are still being chased away, denied, disparaged, delegitimized, and dispersed by Israeli, Western, and Arab politics—even now, today.

Later, these dispersed Palestinians became a problem for Jordan and Lebanon, where at various times they were massacred and expelled. Later still, hundreds of thousands of them were expelled from Kuwait after it was liberated from the Iraqi occupation in 1991. The expulsion of innocent Palestinians was the revenge of the Kuwaiti leadership against the Palestinian leadership, who had irresponsibly sided with Iraq in the conflict. Furthermore, after the fall of the regime of Saddam Hussein in Iraq, Palestinians there were killed or expelled.

Some Palestinians who escaped Iraq found refuge in Syria, Jordan, and other Arab and non-Arab countries. Others became stuck at the borders between countries they were not allowed to enter. As a result, four new refugee camps, consisting of a few hundred families, were erected in the middle of the desert between the western Iraqi border and the borders of Syria and Jordan. This refugee situation remains ongoing, some sixty-seven years after the first expulsion from Palestine.

When and how will the Palestinian tragedy ever end? Sometimes it seems to me that the Palestinians should be dislodged from this planet and sucked out into some far-off galaxy. We remain one of the few peoples on Earth who live dispersed and vulnerable lives with the common experience of being unwanted everywhere. Everybody, it seems, wants to get rid of us or, at least, to subjugate us. To put it simply, what the Palestinians need is a secure place where they can be free from harassment, physical harm, and expulsion. This is no different from what the Jews have always wanted. It is not right, however, that a people or a government chooses to ease its qualms of conscience with the conviction that the Palestinians alone are to blame for what they have had to endure. No one today would accept as valid the similar verdict that some applied to the Jews during the time of their diaspora.

The Anteater And The Jaguar

What is long overdue, in Palestine and Israel, is the need for us to understand our common responsibility to one another as human beings, if reconciliation between our two peoples is ever to be achieved. Meanwhile, we continue believing we are right and have been victims of conspiracies; we feel not so much *defeated* as we do *cheated*. With few choices, we will go on with our story, and we will continue passing it from one generation to another until we achieve self-determination in our homeland.

Nineteen

Between Nazareth and the Americas

In 1975, when I was nineteen, my long-held dream of going to America was fulfilled. The desire to visit America had been in my mind since 1968, when I was in the sixth grade. My eldest brother, Basheer, had traveled there that year, so I believed it was only fair that I would get to go, too. When I shared my vision with my parents, more seriously after finishing high school, they were not terribly excited. I argued with them repeatedly about it, but they wanted to keep me close. "It is enough," they would tell me, "that Basheer is there." I failed to see the logic in their answer. I know now what their real worry was: they were afraid I would not return to Nazareth, and their fears had some justification. They had many relatives who had moved to the Americas toward the end of the nineteenth century or early in the twentieth century, never to return.

To get some idea of how serious and even traumatic the fear harbored by my parents and the rest of my family was, picture the bus full of people—fifty of my uncles, aunts, and cousins—who came to the airport to see me off. The same thing had happened when Basheer had left for the United States seven years earlier and when my maternal cousin Jeryis had departed for Canada in 1966.

The Anteater And The Jaguar

I still remember how hard it was for me to leave everyone: first I had an emotional parting from my grandmother Meladi in Nazareth, and then later at the airport from all the others, where I had to hug, kiss, and bid farewell to every single person in my family individually before I left them to board my flight. Thank God, however, after seven years I came back, and after twenty-seven years there, so did Basheer.

Of the generation of early emigrants from my mother's and my father's families (about fifteen from each side), only two came back to visit us in Nazareth in the 1960s. A few of their children and grandchildren, from the second and third generations in North and South America, also came to visit, and I have met some of them. I was able to meet a few more in the United States while I was there: my aunt Saleemi's sons James/Fouzi and Ernest/Faheem and a few other members of their families, plus another cousin I met through Basheer a few days after my arrival in Texas in January 1975. This cousin's name was Richard Rizek, and there's a good story about how we came to be in touch with him.

My brother had decided at some point in the early 1970s to continue his studies at A&M University in College Station, Texas. While there, he became acquainted with a few other Arab students—from Iraq, Syria, Lebanon, Libya, Tunisia, and Egypt—and also with a few other Palestinians who had come there from all over the map. This group had a weekly social gathering at some hall in the university. On one of those occasions, a stranger came in and introduced himself as Richard Rizek, noting that he had heard about the gathering and just wanted to meet the people attending, since he also had Arab roots. Asked to elaborate, he told them his father had emigrated from Nazareth to the United States just before the First World War. He added that he was born in Syracuse, New York, and was now teaching oceanography at A&M University. My brother, who was present at that meeting, had only to hear the word *Syracuse* and to see how much the young man resembled our uncle Faddool from Nazareth. He asked, "Is your father's name Habeeb?" Surprised, Richard said yes, and my brother told Richard they were cousins. Though we had never met the majority of those first emigrants, we all grew up hearing their names mentioned quite often by our parents and other relatives.

When I began working on this book, I looked into my family's roots a little more thoroughly than I had yet done. I was fortunate to have a copy of the book *The History of Nazareth* by Reverend Asad Mansour, which provided the family trees of both of my parents nine generations back, along with a wealth of other information.

Dozens of Palestinian-Arab Christian families, Rizeks and others, from Nazareth and from elsewhere in Palestine, the nearby region, and the Americas could trace their ancestry to an eighteenth-century Eastern Orthodox priest named Khleif, about whom more will be recounted shortly. Some of this information is mentioned in Mansour's book, while more detailed and updated information is found in Jarjoura's book (which I mentioned in an earlier chapter). Jarjoura's family is related to mine through that same Priest Khleif, son of Abdallah, grandson of Suliman.

The Rizek who is my family's ancestor was one of Priest Khleif's sons. Incidentally, about fifteen years ago, when I was reading the memoir *Out of Place* by the late Edward Said, I learned that Said, too, is a descendant of Priest Khleif. Said's father, Wadie, appears in the Khleif family tree as depicted by Mansour. My own direct line of ancestry from my father's side can be traced back through eight generations to the early decades of the seventeenth century: Rayek > Rafeek > Saleem > Nasser > Yakub > Rizek > Khleif > Abdullah > Suleiman. I can trace my mother's line of ancestry back ten generations: Rayek > Najla (my mother)> Jeryis > Saleh > Elias > Yakub > Ibrahim > Elias > Farah > Nicola > Suleiman. Both families descend from the same Suleiman.

By the late nineteenth century and on into the early twentieth century, thousands of Arabs were emigrating from the Middle East, their destination somewhere in the Americas. The impetus was mainly economic, as people looked for a way to escape the poverty that became more widespread during the final years of Ottoman rule. The opportunities available in the Americas beckoned.

The Anteater And The Jaguar

Then, just before the beginning of the First World War, another wave of emigration ensued as people fled conscription into the Ottoman army. Stories abound of young men from across the Ottoman Empire—Muslims, Christian, Jews, and others—who never returned from what was known at the time as the Great War. The few who survived the fighting until the war ended, or who had deserted partway through, had to walk hundreds, even thousands, of miles to get back to their homes.

Once, a Palestinian with whom I became friends during my time in the United States shared with me a story about his grandfather, who came from southern Palestine. As a young man, the grandfather was conscripted by the Ottomans and fought in the Balkan Wars of 1912–1913. He went AWOL and managed to take refuge in a monastery for a few years. When the First World War ended, the grandfather walked all the way back from somewhere in the Balkans to his village in Palestine.

More than fifty years later, this man (my friend's grandfather), who had become a refugee in Jordan after 1948, visited his grown son, who lived in one of the Arab Gulf Emirates. During that visit, the old man was taken to see a musical competition being filmed at the state TV studio. During an interlude, he grew curious about a piano sitting in one corner of the studio and asked his son if he might be permitted to approach it. The son said yes. The old man walked over to the piano, sat down on the stool, and began playing a classical composition that could have been for Beethoven, or maybe Tchaikovsky.

The old man's son, dazzled by this impromptu performance, had had no idea that his father even knew how to play the piano. Everyone present, seeing this elderly, traditionally dressed Palestinian man sit down at the keyboard and play a classical piano piece in that manner, was dazzled. When the son asked his father how he had learned to play, the old man shared with him for the first time how a monk at the monastery where he took refuge during the war had given him piano lessons. The old man had not seen a piano in many decades, and now he had finally found one to play.

Rayek R. Rizek

Another unwilling conscript was Ameen, one of my mother's uncles, who fought in the first Balkan War. Knowing that another, bigger war was going to start soon, his father, Priest Saleh, urged Ameen to take his two younger brothers, Farah and Beshara, and emigrate to North America, lest the younger boys find themselves in the Ottoman army before long. The three of them left Nazareth in 1913, just about a year before the outbreak of the Great War in July 1914.

I remember both of my parents speaking very proudly of their migrant uncles. My father spoke of his uncle Shibly, who had studied at the German Schneller School of Agriculture and at the Russian Seminary, from which he graduated with honors. Later, early in the twentieth century, he immigrated to Argentina. There Shibly and another friend from Nazareth pursued careers in journalism, publishing an Arabic literary monthly. *Cordoba*, as it was called, was first released in Buenos Aires and later in the city of Córdoba, where it also covered local news of the Arab immigrant community. My father told me that when his uncle Shibly left Nazareth, he left behind many books. One, perhaps the only one still extant, is in my possession. A red, hardbound book, *Sacred History for the Orthodox Primary Schools,* has Uncle Shibly's name duly stamped on it: *Shibly Rizek 1893.* The flyleaf says that this edition was translated into Arabic from Russian and printed in Beirut (second edition) in 1889.

My mother spoke of her uncles a lot, too, telling me different stories she had heard about them from her parents and grandparents. She was very proud of her uncle Ameen, who before he emigrated had been a high-ranking officer in the Ottoman army and spoke several languages fluently. She liked to tell me about how astonished everyone in his family was when his first letter mailed from New York contained the startling news that there were wagons in America that traveled without horses. No one had yet seen an automobile in Palestine. Even when my aunt Saleemi, my father's sister, left for America in 1920, she was taken from Nazareth to Haifa (a distance of about thirty miles) by a horse-drawn wagon, according to my father, who was ten years old at the time. Her uncle Farah, my mother told me, was a career soldier in the US Marines.

The Anteater And The Jaguar

He had stopped sending letters home after 1948, because he could not bring himself to write "Israel" instead of "Palestine" on an envelope. In fact, I, too, have always had an emotional and ethical difficulty in using the name *Israel*, as I've always considered saying *Israel* a unilateral concession: recognition of a state established at the expense of my people. A calamity! Furthermore, saying *Israel* as an answer to where I come from does not really convey much about my historic, ethnic, and cultural affiliations. I always need to add that I am a Palestinian Arab and sometimes to mention my religious affiliation, which I am asked about often. Most of the time, of course, I do not have much choice, especially when I address letters and when I complete all kinds of different forms. But when it comes to conversations and questions, it has always been a different case. Whenever I am asked where I come from, my answer is always *Palestine*, and like all other Palestinians, I add the necessary extra clarification about where exactly in Palestine. Is it from the part known as Israel, or the West Bank, or the Gaza Strip? Or the diaspora? After I moved to the Oasis of Peace, and as a result of my search for balance between narratives, identities, and languages—as the ongoing challenge has demanded—I started using both names, Palestine and Israel, in addition to the Arabic and Hebrew names of my community or of any other place in our common land. To those in my audiences who get annoyed, especially when I say Palestine/Israel or Israel/Palestine, I always explain, "This is not a denial or a concession, but rather a recognition that is a mutual necessity if we are to attain a humane, ethical, and balanced peace."

The large majority of those young immigrants from Greater Syria to the Americas before and after the turn of the twentieth century were Arab Christians. Apart from factors already mentioned, their immigration was likely facilitated by the fact that they generally had access to a better education than had most of their Muslim compatriots. This superior education was provided by the monastery schools, convent schools, and other religious schools built and administered during the late nineteenth and early twentieth centuries by different European, Russian, and

American missionaries. Most of these institutions offered free education to children of the various Arab Christian communities of that region, as well as to some Arab Muslims. This schooling was simply not generally available to most of the Muslim population, because the schools most Muslims attended, established under Ottoman rule, were limited both in number and in curriculum. Some sources also suggest that Arab Christian immigration to North America during that period was easier, because given the prejudices underlying American immigration policy, they had an easier time obtaining American visas than did their Muslim counterparts.

(As an aside, since we are talking about church initiatives in education in the region at that time, let us mention that it was American missionaries who founded the prominent American University of Beirut in 1866. The proposal by W. M. Thomson to the American Board of Commissioners for Foreign Missions in 1862 was for a college of higher education that would include medical training, and Thomson nominated Dr. Daniel Bliss to serve as its president. In 1863, while Dr. Bliss was raising money in the United States and England for the new college, the state of New York granted a charter for the Syrian Protestant College (its original name). The college opened with a class of sixteen students in December 1866. Dr. Bliss, its first president, served until 1902. Most of the first generations of Palestinian physicians studied at this university, which was renamed the American University of Beirut in 1920 and grew into one of the most respected institutions of higher learning in the region.)

When I think about those young men in their late teens or early twenties setting out to find their future in the Americas, a century or more ago, I cannot help but wonder at their courage. Courage was certainly necessary for these emigrants who chose to travel to the other side of the planet, over land and by ship, leaving their families behind and with very little assurance that they would ever see them again. Generally, they embarked by sea from Haifa or Beirut to Alexandria or to Port Said in Egypt, where they continued again by ship to the Americas. The

The Anteater And The Jaguar

journey involved more than a month at sea, in addition to a few more weeks spent in other seaports along the route, when the ship called in to collect other passengers. From what I have read, many of these young fellows were able to cover the cost of their travel by doing menial work on the ships. In any case, travel on the ships of those days was uncomfortable and exhausting, as documented in many written accounts and testified to by my aunt Saleemi. Nearly everyone was seasick from the rolling and rocking motions of the vessels, since the ships of that era were much less stable than are their more modern counterparts.

The immigration of these young Arab men brings to mind a beautiful and wise saying uttered by the fourth Muslim caliph, Ali Ibn Abi Taleb: "Poverty in our homeland transforms it into a place strange to us, while wealth in a strange country turns it into a home." Has not this prospect motivated millions of people throughout history to leave their homes and venture to more promising places?

While their journeys naturally have much in common, each of these emigrants has his own story. Once, about fifteen years ago, when one of my American first cousins, Earnest/Faheem, was visiting me, I asked him to tell me the story of how his own father, Saeed, had ended up in America. Earnest told me his grandfather, Suliman Rizek, first journeyed to the Americas in 1898. He had actually left Nazareth with the intention of looking for work in Egypt and embarked by ship from Haifa to Alexandria. While walking through the streets of Alexandria, he saw a man he knew from Nazareth. After they had greeted each other, Suliman discovered that this acquaintance was waiting in Alexandria for a ship that would take him to the Dominican Republic. Earnest's grandfather asked why the man had chosen such a destination. "Because," the friend replied, "I have heard there are plenty of opportunities to make good money there." Earnest's grandfather decided on the spot to join this man on his voyage to Central America. Suliman's story turned out well, for he started a business doing cocoa farming (he may have been a graduate of the German Schneller School of Agriculture in Nazareth), and his descendants today run and manage an international company of cacao farming and produce in the Dominican Republic under the name of *Rizek Cacao*.

Most of those early immigrants evidently succeeded financially in South and North America, and their success inspired their brothers and other relatives to follow. Moreover, a number of their descendants went into politics, and some have been elected to high office, including a few presidents of different South American countries. Others got involved in armed resistance to tyrannical military regimes. Of the latter, perhaps most prominent was Shafik George Handal of El Salvador, the son of an Arab-Palestinian immigrant from Bethlehem, who had a major role in transforming the regime of El Salvador from a military dictatorship to a democracy through his leadership in an armed political struggle.

One less prominent person who took the revolutionary road in the Americas was a relative of mine, a grandson of Suleiman Rizek named Saturnino Teofilo (Tawfeek) Rizek. This is his story, as I have been able to learn it from online sources and a personal account given to me by my cousin Ninoska Rizek, Saturnino Teofilo Rizek's only daughter. Nino, as he was known, was born in the Dominican Republic and, together with ten friends, helped to recruit some two hundred Dominican volunteers in an attempt to topple the regime of the notorious Dominican dictator Rafael Trujillo. In June 1959, they traveled by air and sea to the Dominican Republic to launch the planned rebellion. Many died fighting the dictator's army, and the rest, including Nino, who had joined the group from his refuge in New York, were captured, tortured, and executed. Nino Rizek was thirty-two years old when he gave his life for the revolution. His only brother, Carlos, who had not left the Dominican Republic, was also arrested and tortured. He was released, only to be executed later in the street, not for having taken part in the revolution but simply for being Nino's brother.

The Palestinian and Arab migration to the Americas continues through the present day. The fact that these early pioneers established a presence also helps explain why it has been more common for Christian Arabs than for their Muslim counterparts to emigrate there from the

The Anteater And The Jaguar

Middle East. The descendants of the early Christian emigrants from Greater Syria now comprise communities in Central, South, and North America that number in the tens of millions. This makes me wonder about what the character and demography of the Middle East might have been today, if those Arab Christians had not left the region. When I consider the fact that just when so many Arab Christians were leaving Palestine, the pioneers of the Zionist movement were arriving, I can't help but wonder if that was just a strange coincidence.

Twenty

MORE STORIES ABOUT NAZARETH

The inhabitants of Nazareth have been very fortunate, because of the town's historical and religious importance for Christianity. Nazareth, along with *Beit Lahem* (Bethlehem), Jerusalem, and a few other villages, have long been the main focuses of Christian missionary work in the Holy Land. In Nazareth particularly, missionaries founded schools and clinics beginning in the mid-1800s, when the population was at most a few thousand.

Through the work of missionaries, places like Nazareth became connected with the larger world. One of the reasons I like living in Wahat Assalam is that it, too, is globally connected, like the Nazareth in which I grew up. As I have already mentioned, thousands of tourists visit our village every year. In addition to regular tourists, we always have a few European, North American, and Japanese volunteers coming on a regular basis to spend a few months with us. And many friends, fans, and supporters of our educational work and our community come to visit now and then, so guests are always arriving.

Very few of the smaller areas on the planet are like our little community, where despite its modest size, one can meet foreign people and hear different languages almost every day. Oddly, it is only recently that

The Anteater And The Jaguar

I have realized how similar my experiences in our community are to the years of my childhood in my hometown: In Nazareth, it is also quite common to see foreigners and hear different languages every day. So many foreign nuns, monks, and priests come to live in Nazareth or to spend some period of time in one of the many and varied missionary institutions. Likewise, at the town's several hospitals, it is also commonplace (less recently) to find foreign physicians and nurses at work.

When I was growing up, I was exposed to foreign visitors more than most youngsters my age for another reason, too. Until I turned twelve years old in 1967, my parents, siblings, and I shared one big house with my uncle Moeen, my father's only brother, and Moeen's wife, Basmi. Uncle Moeen and Aunt Basmi, who were childless, loved us very much and related to my siblings and me as if we were their own children. I was indeed doubly blessed, growing up with essentially two sets of parents.

Once upon a time, Uncle Moeen owned a restaurant in Alhamma (called *Hamat Gader* in Hebrew), a Galilee resort with hot springs within what used to be a small Palestinian village. His restaurant was another casualty of the 1948 war, when the area became part of a demilitarized zone between Syria and Israel and remained thus until the war of 1967, when it came under Israeli control. So Uncle Moeen opened a new restaurant in Nazareth. Growing up, I spent many of my school vacations helping out in the restaurant, where the clientele included lots of tourists from all over the world.

Actually, I was third in line, after my two eldest brothers, Basheer and Bassam, to help at Uncle Moeen's restaurant. I must confess that, as a youngster, I was not always enthusiastic about spending my free days there; I would have preferred to be outside playing with the other kids in my neighborhood. I had no way of knowing at the time how much this early experience in the restaurant business was going to benefit me later in life, when I opened my own café.

My uncle's new restaurant in Nazareth was located in a prime spot in the center of town, just below the main Albishara (Annunciation) Basilica of the Arab Catholic community. This impressive basilica was constructed

Rayek R. Rizek

between 1960 and 1969 above an old Byzantine church and was dedicated by Pope Paul VI when he visited Nazareth in 1964. I remember that papal visit and the big gathering of people near the site of the church. I also remember the construction of the basilica, the progress of which I followed during my four daily walks past the site on weekends and vacations. In the morning, I would walk down with my uncle from our shared house in the old part of the town to his restaurant downtown, a walk of twenty minutes. Later, around noon, I would walk up to the house again to fetch my uncle's lunch, prepared by Aunt Basmi, and carry it back to the restaurant to my uncle. (It never occurred to me to wonder why he did not just eat the food served in the restaurant; Aunt Basmi probably took pleasure in having him eat the food she herself cooked.) Then in the evening, Uncle Moeen and I would walk home together.

There is a smaller and older Annunciation Church about a kilometer from the Annunciation Basilica that belongs to the Christian Arab Orthodox community. This church was built in 1763, also on the site of an old Byzantine church, by Priest Khleif, my early ancestor, whose tomb is located inside the church. This church is about fifty meters away from Mary's well (called *Ain Al-Adra* in Arabic, meaning the *Well of the Virgin*) and fed by a spring that for thousands of years has been the main source of water for Nazarenes; visitors to the church can see the water flowing underneath the altar to this day. Priest Khleif was granted a permit to build the church by Sheikh Zahir al-Umar, who at his peak in 1774 governed the whole region from Beirut to Gaza, in addition to the Ajloon Mountains of what is now Jordan. Al-Umar, an Arab Muslim whose roots go back to Al-Hijaz (Saudi Arabia today), was known for maintaining good relations with the Arab Christians in general, the Orthodox Christians in particular, and the Jews. He is said to have ordered the restoration of an old Jewish synagogue in the town of Shefa-Amr (*Shfar'am*, in Hebrew), which was then and still is an Arab town of Muslims, Christians, and Druze.

I must tell you a story that began in Nazareth during my childhood and ended in Neve Shalom many years later. One day, walking down to

The Anteater And The Jaguar

my uncle's restaurant, I saw from a distance a crowd of people standing at the bottom of Casanova Street below the Annunciation Basilica and the Casanova Hospice—right outside the entrance of the most famous restaurant in Nazareth at the time, the Abu Nassar Restaurant. When I got there, I saw that the crowd was listening to and cheering for two men who stood on a table just inside the restaurant. One of the two was a familiar man from Nazareth by the name of Abdel Aziz Zouabi (1926–1974), who was a member of the Israeli Knesset from the leftist Mapam party from 1965 until his sudden death in 1974. I did not recognize the other man right away, but then his host, Mr. Zouabi, mentioned his name—Abie Nathan—and it was instant recognition, because he had recently become a celebrity. Abie Nathan, some weeks previously, had flown a small private plane from Israel to Egypt in February 1966 on a "peace flight," as he called it. His intent was to deliver a petition to Egyptian president Gamal Abdel Nasser, asking on behalf of Israelis for peace between Egypt and Israel. He was refused access to Nasser and deported back to Israel, where he was promptly detained and interrogated for having left the country by an illegal route. Abie became something of a folk hero overnight. An Arab Jew, he had been born in Abadan, Persia (now Iran), in 1927 and grew up in India. His bold foray by air into international politics led him to pursue a series of humanitarian projects in Israel and beyond until his death in 2008. The best known of these was probably the Voice of Peace radio station (1973–1993), transmitting from a ship outside Israeli territorial waters, which he bought with John Lennon's help. The station broadcast twenty-four hours a day, mostly English-language programs that mainly included popular music and promoted Nathan's political agenda. He was also involved with disaster relief in different countries. Abie Nathan was one of the first few Israelis who held meetings with PLO officials beginning in the early 1980s. He met with PLO Chairman Yasser Arafat on a few occasions at his Tunis headquarters and, in consequence, was jailed in Israel for six months in 1991, after the Israeli government officially outlawed meetings with PLO-affiliated figures.

Rayek R. Rizek

One day, in November 1999, while I was serving as mayor of Wahat Assalam, I received a phone call from someone identifying himself as a friend of Abie Nathan's. He was calling to tell me Nathan's friends would be holding a ceremony to unveil a plaque in Nathan's honor to be mounted on a boulder at the entrance to the forest bordering Neve Shalom. He added that Mr. Nathan would be present and asked whether our community would agree to participate in the ceremony. Without any hesitation, I said yes, and I helped arrange the participation of a few of our members, along with a group of twenty children and some teachers from our primary school.

At the ceremony, there were a few short speeches, and then the children played some pieces on their flutes with Mela, their music teacher. Abie Nathan was confined to a wheelchair at that point in his life, following a stroke that had left him partially paralyzed. He was not able to talk but was very emotional during the ceremony, crying openly, especially when the children played their music and again when they gathered around him at the end. I was glad Abie Nathan was being recognized in this way and honored to participate with my community in showing appreciation for this unique humanitarian and peace activist. I found it sad, and very moving, to see this special man wanting so much to say something but physically unable to speak. It was a strange coincidence to have him come to Wahat Assalam thirty-three years after I first had seen him in person in Nazareth at the Abu Nassar Restaurant. Whether coincidence or destiny, it felt like the closing of a circle.

Finally, I must mention that, at the time of the ceremony, I did not know about Nathan's early military career as a combat pilot. I found it very painful later on when I learned he had taken part in dropping bombs on some Palestinian villages during the war of 1948. Apart from causing the needless deaths of a number of Palestinian civilians, those actions—and the widespread fear they generated—have also been a central factor in the depopulation of many Palestinian villages. This new information about Nathan's life prompted me to ponder for a while about the rightness of my participation, back in 1999, in the ceremony

The Anteater And The Jaguar

held in his honor near my community. Should I (I wondered) now regret my participation in that ceremony, or should I still consider it an appropriate act of appreciation for the courageous and humane outlook he had come to embrace later in his life? After all, how can we repair our world and move beyond wars and suffering if we do not reconsider the attitudes that underlie such phenomena? Isn't it a fact that peacemakers oftentimes evolve from a personal history of violence?

To return now to my stories about Nazareth: There were many aspects to the services provided in Nazareth by nuns and monks from all over Europe. In addition to schools for boys and girls, they also founded and ran nurseries, orphanages, and shelters for the elderly. Some nuns gave private lessons to young women, teaching them foreign languages, basic nursing, piano, needlework, and painting. Besides the many regular schools, there is also a French Salesian vocational school; Ecole Jésus Adolescent (the School of Jesus the Adolescent), which originally taught carpentry, shoemaking, tailoring, and later other crafts; and the Schneller School, a German vocational and agricultural school. A Russian school offered a seminary for teachers. Reverend Mansour, in his *History of Nazareth*, wrote that the Russian complex was constructed in 1904 to serve the needs of Russian pilgrims by the Palestinian Orthodox Imperial Society, founded in 1882 by Prince Sergei Alexandrovich, brother of Russian Tsar Alexander III. It was named after the prince, but the local population nicknamed it the *Muskubiya* (from "Moscow"). This was a substantial institution, with sleeping accommodations for some 1,500 Russian pilgrims at a time; a dining room; a hospital; a pharmacy; and two day schools, one for boys and one for girls; in addition to a boarding school. When the British occupied Palestine during the First World War, the Muskubiya became a headquarters for the British authorities after it had served as a headquarter for the German army during the war. After 1948, it began serving the Israeli government as a police station (among other functions, such as a post office and a court).

Some of these schools closed down after many years of operation, while others are still operating to this day. Other missionaries opened private medical clinics that over time became hospitals. These are today the French, the Italian (previously Austrian), and the English Hospitals. The English Hospital was later renamed the Nazareth Hospital and celebrated its 150th anniversary in 2012.

For more than 150 years now, thanks to the educational and medical services Nazareth has offered, it has been an important hub for most of the Arabs living in the villages in its vicinity. Its markets have supplied a diverse range of products and services provided by Nazarene carpenters, blacksmiths, coppersmiths, tinsmiths, goldsmiths, saddlers, shoemakers, tailors, potters, and more. I remember many of these workshops quite well, because many of them survived into the late 1960s.

Our elderly were always proud to mention that the famous Lebanese author and poet Mikhail Naimy, author of *The Book of Mirdad,* had studied at the Russian Teachers Institute in Nazareth (Muskubiya) during the early years of the twentieth century. He later immigrated to America. There, with another famous writer, poet, painter, and philosopher Jubran Khalil Jubran (generally known in the West as Kahlil Gibran, author of the immensely popular book *The Prophet*) and other Syrian writers, he formed a movement for the rebirth and propagation of Arabic literature. This movement came to be known as the New York Pen League.

Clearly, then, if we look back to the last few decades of the nineteenth century and the beginning of the twentieth, there were many highly educated young Arab Christian men and women in what was then Greater Syria. Many of these young people later became known for their role in the Arab renaissance that began in the late 1800s: writers; authors; poets; educators; lawyers; physicians; artists; politicians; and translators of foreign books, which included much of European, American, and Russian literature. For example, the most famous Arabic newspaper, *Al-Ahram* (*the Pyramids*), published in Egypt, was founded in Alexandria in 1875 by two Arab Christian Lebanese brothers, Beshara and Saleem Takla.

Another outstanding name is that of poet, essayist, and translator May Ziade, the pen name of Marie Elias Ziade, who was born in Nazareth in 1896. Her mother was Palestinian and her father Lebanese; as a girl, she attended school in Nazareth and later went to a French convent school

The Anteater And The Jaguar

in Lebanon. Ziade was an important literary figure in the turn-of-the-century Arab renaissance and is described today as an "early Palestinian feminist" and a "pioneer of Oriental feminism." Ziade corresponded for nearly twenty years with Kahlil Gibran and is credited for introducing his work to the local public.

And there were others, some of whom were influential beyond the Middle East, such as Kulthum Odeh, a writer, translator, and professor who was born in Nazareth in 1892. She studied in the Russian school for girls in Nazareth and later in the Russian Seminary for girls in Beit Jala, a small town of mostly Christian Palestinians near Bethlehem. Odeh married a Russian physician she met while working as a teacher in the Russian school in Nazareth and afterward lived most of her life in Russia. In addition to being a prolific Russian-Arabic translator herself, Odeh also authored a series of books for teaching Arabic to Russian speakers, and she taught Arabic at the University of Leningrad. Her students included many prominent Russian Orientalists and politicians, some of whom may have been among the prominent intellectuals who intervened to have her released from prison after Stalin had her jailed for her outspoken opposition to the Soviet recognition of the state of Israel in 1948.

History, like our own personal lives, is full of odd coincidences, as I am reminded quite often whenever I think of my uncle's restaurant in Nazareth, where I served reluctantly while unwittingly soaking up the know-how that would stand me in such good stead many years later at Wahat Assalam. Uncle Moeen's prime downtown location was adjacent to the spot where all the tourist buses stopped to drop off their passengers. About forty years later, I, like my uncle, ended up opening a café right next to a main square where the tourist buses stop to drop off their passengers. At the Oasis of Peace these days, tourists often enter my place because of its convenient location, just as my uncle's customers did back in the day. And even in my little gift shop/café, it is very common to hear five languages being spoken at once. This made me think at one point that maybe Dyana and I should change the name of our cafe from *Ahlan*, which means "welcome" in Arabic, to *Babel*. But we never did.

Twenty-One

Aliens on our Own Planet

In 1975 I joined the stream of young Palestinians journeying to the Americas in search of a different future for themselves. My own goals were not all that well-defined; I was unsure what the outcome of my travel to the United States would be, and I was unsure about what to expect from my time spent there. But my main intention, like that of my brother, was to continue my studies. Naturally, I was also extremely curious about the country and its culture, especially after all that had happened there during the 1960s, so I wanted very much to go. Atypically, perhaps, making money was not one of my purposes.

In total, I spent about seven years in the United States studying, working, and traveling before returning to Nazareth. Those years, despite some financial and psychological challenges I faced, were the most exciting of my life. I had some very intense experiences, as I was learning so much and becoming knowledgeable about so many new things.

Apart from the excitement of experiencing American life firsthand, another development I had not considered ahead of time contributed greatly to my evolving perspective. In the United States, I met many other Palestinian students of my generation from the West Bank, Gaza, Jordan, Lebanon, and Kuwait. This was the first time I had spent much time with

The Anteater And The Jaguar

Palestinians, and also with other Arabs, outside of Nazareth. My unanticipated encounters with other Palestinians helped me to strengthen and clarify my identity. These encounters, however, also increased my sense of anger, because through hearing of other Palestinians' experiences, I began to realize the real extent of my people's tragedy and the enormous price they were paying for defending their rights in their homeland. I saw, too, how much alike we all were, despite our being born and raised in different parts of the Middle East. We had all gone through similar experiences of feeling unwelcome. We had all been subjected to harassment wherever we had lived. We were all similarly ignorant about one another's circumstances and fates. We all had problems connecting with our relatives, who were scattered throughout the Middle East—a by-product of the bad relationships that existed between the various states of the region and the fact that we were Palestinians. Virtually none of the Palestinians I met felt at home in the country of their birth and upbringing, and this was especially true of those who were born and raised outside Palestine. I could readily relate to their pain. Every time we wished to cross a border, we were treated with hostility, humiliation, and suspicion. Many times we endured long hours of interrogation. Some even had experienced imprisonment. These inhumane experiences were common to us all, so there is little wonder that these experiences also became one of the most common topics of conversation among us.

In his book *Palestinian Identity* (Columbia University Press, 1997), Rashid Khalidi recounts some truly dramatic cases of what Palestinians experience in crossing borders. He tells the story of one Palestinian "who was shuttled back and forth on airliners between an Arab Gulf state and Lebanon for three weeks in 1991 because his identity documents were not satisfactory to the authorities at either end of his trajectory. In September 1991, Gaza Strip Palestinians carrying Egyptian travel papers who were expelled from Kuwait spent twelve days sleeping in Cairo airport because they did not have the proper documents to enter Egypt or the Israeli-occupied Gaza Strip, to go back to Kuwait, or to go anywhere else" (p. 2).

Rayek R. Rizek

This issue of proper documents remains, to this day, a common dilemma for many Palestinians. They are among the unfortunate people trying to live a normal life in the twenty-first century without a valid national passport. I cannot stop wondering why no one has yet devised an internationally recognized solution for this category of people. Isn't it enough that they have lost their homeland and their right to go home again? Should they be further punished by being turned into some kind of illegal alien? What could justify this situation today, which cruelly punishes so many people who are morally and in practical terms innocent of any responsibility for the causes and outcome of the conflict that has rendered them stateless?

I once read that Steven Spielberg's film *The Terminal*, starring Tom Hanks, was based on the true story of an Iranian who spent seventeen years (from 1988 to 2004) living in Charles de Gaulle Airport in Paris as a result of problems with his documents—although in the Iranian's case, he was free to leave the airport and return to it at any time, unlike Hanks's character. The situation depicted in the film could easily have featured a Palestinian who got stuck in an airport.

In my case, I am an Israeli-Palestinian-Arab citizen in possession of an official Israeli passport. Ironically, this fact makes me an object of envy on the part of some passport-less Palestinians, since it eases my travel and defines me as a legal citizen of this planet. Its possession does not, however—not by a long shot—guarantee me treatment similar to what is accorded to most Israeli or even foreign Jews when traveling through Ben Gurion Airport.

Some people justify airport passenger profiling simply for security reasons, and the argument is not without merit. But this fact alone does not necessarily help me understand and accept it. The experience of being negatively profiled and treated as a security risk causes me much anxiety and leads me to feel as though I do not belong to the country in which I happened to have been born. I am made to feel different. I am made to feel like a stranger. This is where I connect with all other Palestinians. This is what makes me realize how wrong, how abnormal, the reality in which I live is. This is why I continue to wish and work for a brighter reality beyond these conflicts that will guarantee my people and me normal treatment on an equal basis with others.

Leaving America

Once Palestinians settle in America, they generally stay there. People have often asked me why I chose to leave America and return to my home in Nazareth. Partly it was because I had reached a point where I was unsure about continuing my studies, especially since I was unable to make up my mind about which subject to major in. Moreover, I felt that life in the United States had started to become, for me, too normal. I had made many American friends and had learned a great deal. I also appreciated and adopted as my own many values from American culture and society. I sensed that, as a young man coming from a small town such as Nazareth to America, I had already had my quota of novel experiences in the new environment. What had been a really enjoyable period of my life there (between the ages of nineteen and twenty-six) seemed to be tapering off, and I felt the time had come to move on.

And then there was my increasing political awareness. An additional aspect of this awareness emerged during the last few months of my stay in the United States, when I was ready for a change. I happened to watch two reports about my country on the famous CBS program *Sixty Minutes*. They included interviews with new American-Jewish settlers, recent immigrants to Israel, who talked about Israel as their homeland but with scant sensitivity to or consideration of the rights of Palestinian Arabs also living there. Watching them, listening to them, I began wondering about myself. I wondered what I was still doing in America when those people had left America and gone to my country, driven by their convictions.

Among all my Palestinians friends, acquaintances, and fellow students in Texas, I was one of the few who had the option of returning to Palestine. When my Palestinian friends came to bid me farewell, we were all a bit sad. There was, as yet, nothing like the Internet, Skype, or affordable telephone communication to help people stay in touch, and we were not sure we would ever meet again. I also felt that they envied me, because I was able to return to the place most of them had only heard and dreamed about.

It has been more than thirty years now since I parted from the friends who came to bid me farewell back then, and I have not seen them since. There were many other friends, too, whom I had come to know over my seven-year stay in America, and I have not seen them either. This has been one uniquely painful loss I have had to live with; we Palestinians are still some of the relatively few people on this planet who do not have a collective home to return to. (Recently, I have been able to reconnect with a few of my Palestinian friends from that era through Facebook, thanks to Mark Zuckerberg, after I opened a Facebook page of my own about two years ago.) Despite all the obstacles and difficulties, I continue hoping a day will finally come when these displaced friends will be able to come home. Meanwhile, I have learned not to regard myself as an unlucky person because I do not have my own country.

Throughout my life, it has become clearer to me that all the situations we live in and all the positions we occupy have their advantages and disadvantages. Once, I was listening to one of my Jewish neighbors talk about how much he wished for peace, so that his eldest child of ten years old would not be required to do army service when he reached the age of eighteen. Suddenly, I realized I did not have the same worry. Because my sons and I were Arabs, we were not required to do army service. This made me feel luckier than my Jewish neighbor, even though I'd always thought I should be envious of him because he had his own independent state. Could it be that I was freer than all those people who had to kill and be killed for their country? Could it be that I was freer than they, because I did not have to honor commitments such as serving in the army, saluting my flag, or standing for my national anthem? Why did I need those invented symbols to make me feel special and different when they ran contrary to my yearning for world peace? (In these musings, my thinking has been complemented by, among many other resources, a book written by Avinadav Begin, grandson of former Israeli Prime Minister Menachem Begin, entitled *The End of the Conflict*.)

So I ask myself: How can we hope to change the world if most of us are stuck with attitudes and ideals that others conceived hundreds or even thousands of years ago? Are the reasons for their emergence then still valid today? How long and how often must we be fooled by the conviction that it is an honor to die for our country or to sacrifice our life for our flag when this conviction merely camouflages a host of dishonorable secrets and malicious motives that remain obstacles to peace?

Twenty-Two

The Gaza Experience

One day, about three years after I began living in Wahat Assalam, a Swedish journalist named Lena whom I had met once before stopped by and asked if I would be willing to join her for a visit to the Gaza Strip, along with a group of Swedish tourists she was leading. When I agreed to go with them, I had no premonition whatsoever that this trip was going to cause me terrible personal pain for many years to come.

On the trip to Gaza, we visited different sectors around the Strip, including Rafah, a town at its southernmost end. At the border, a broad ditch separated Gaza from the land on the other side—Egypt's Sinai Peninsula. There was barbed-wire fencing along both the near and far sides of this ditch, and an armed Israeli soldier sat in a high guard tower, keeping an eye on the entire area. When we arrived, we witnessed dozens of Palestinian men and women on either side of this border shouting toward one another across a distance of perhaps a hundred meters. One or two used megaphones. As I listened, I figured out that these people were relatives trying to share their family news with people on the other side: who had recently died, who had given birth, who was sick, and who was to be married. The scene we saw resulted from Rafah's having been divided between the Gaza Strip and the Sinai Peninsula.

The Anteater And The Jaguar

This took place after Israel withdrew from Sinai in accordance with the Camp David Peace Treaty between Israel and Egypt in 1978. US President Jimmy Carter had midwifed that treaty, which was signed by then Egyptian President Anwar Sadat and then Israeli Prime Minister Menachem Begin.

Rafah was originally a Palestinian town that hosted one of the approximately fifty Palestinian refugee camps erected by the United Nations after the 1948 war concluded. (These camps were set up within Palestine and in Jordan, Syria, and Lebanon.) Through the years, the town of Rafah and the camp it hosted expanded toward the Egyptian territory of Sinai. Before the 1967 war, the Gaza Strip was under Egyptian control, but this territory, together with the Sinai Peninsula, came under Israeli control immediately following the 1967 war.

When the international border between Israel and Egypt was redrawn as part of the 1978 Camp David Peace Accord, however, the newly demarcated border cut Rafah in two, with one part on the Israeli side and the other on the Egyptian side. As a result, some families—brothers, sisters, and cousins—ended up being separated between the two countries. This division was the original impetus for the famous tunnels of Rafah. Initially, the tunnels were simple, and their use was limited. Later, however, as a result of the Israeli and Egyptian siege of the Gaza Strip, these tunnels were used to bring numerous basic necessities, such as food, medicine, and gasoline from Egypt to the Strip's inhabitants. This situation persisted until the recent destruction of all these hundreds of tunnels, in addition to most of the houses on the Egyptian side, by Egyptian authorities.

I often wonder why no other way could be found that would have avoided the division of this town, sparing its Palestinian population yet another agonized experience of separation among brothers, sisters, fathers, and mothers. This is perplexing, especially considering that the main objective of the Camp David Accord was *peace*. However, history has revealed that none of the major players really cares about the well-being of the Palestinian people when it comes to drawing borders. Whether the border is drawn as a result of war or peace, the outcome has always been the same. In addition to Rafah, at least two Palestinian villages I know of were carved up between Israel and the Jordanian-ruled West Bank in 1948, a situation that lasted until the 1967 war, when Israel occupied the West Bank. One of these villages, Barta'a, lies along both sides of the northern boundary of the West Bank. The other, Beit Safafa, is located midway between Jerusalem and Beit Lahem (Bethlehem). Some years ago, someone gave me a picture of a wedding that took place in Beit Safafa prior to 1967. The family was obliged to celebrate this wedding with one group of family members gathered on one side of the fence that separated them and a second group gathered on the other side. The line that cut those communities in two and constituted the border between Jordan and Israel, and between Egypt and Israel, was known as the *Green Line*, which was named for the color of the ink used to draw the boundary on the maps. Considering the inhumane outcome of those lines, I believe it would have been more appropriate to use black ink.

Toward the end of my visit to the Gaza Strip with Lena and her Swedish tourists in the summer of 1987, we had a conversation with the renowned Palestinian psychiatrist Dr. Eyad Sarraj at his home in the city of Gaza.[14] He talked with us about the traumatic effects on children of the presence and actions of the Israeli soldiers in the Gaza Strip. As our conversation was winding down, one of Eyad's friends, who happened to be about my age, came in. He introduced himself as Mohammad Abulnasser—or Abu Ahmad, as he preferred to be addressed. Abu Ahmad had been released from an Israeli prison two years earlier, after having spent fifteen years as a political prisoner.

When Dr. Sarraj finished talking with us, Abu Ahmad asked us if we would like to hear his story. Because the Swedish guests were with us and Abu Ahmad spoke only Arabic, I was asked if I would be willing to translate for him. I gladly agreed, and we spent another hour listening to him recount his experience of being incarcerated in several Israeli prisons.

---

14 Dr. Sarraj died in December 2013.

The Anteater And The Jaguar

We were interested to learn that he was very proud of the fact that he had been a prisoner. Though the Israelis considered Abu Ahmad a terrorist, he considered himself a freedom fighter opposing the foreign occupation of his own people's land.

Abu Ahmad had been arrested in the early 1970s when he was barely seventeen years old. This happened at the beginning of the first armed resistance to the Israeli occupation of the Gaza Strip. He was accused and sentenced to life imprisonment, but as a result of a prisoner exchange between the Palestinians and the Israelis in 1985, he was released along with another twelve hundred others.

Abu Ahmad's pride in his experiences as a prisoner was quite evident as he spoke. He explained how Palestinian prisoners were able to organize life on the inside in ways that surprised the Israeli officers and guards. Because Abu Ahmad and his fellow prisoners were members of different Palestinian factions, they formed committees among themselves with equal representation. Each committee was tasked with something specific to serve the needs of the prisoners. They organized numerous hunger strikes and revolts for the purpose of bettering their living conditions inside. They protested in order to be permitted to receive newspapers and books, extra blankets, and better food. Abu Ahmad told us how they resolved their conflicts with the prison officials through negotiations conducted by their elected committees. Specific hours were set aside for talking and for periods of silence. Times for classes and for political discussions were designated. He himself had not finished his schooling before entering prison; however, he managed to study in prison and to publish a book of short stories that he wrote while incarcerated.

After Abu Ahmed had finished talking, it was time for us to return to Neve Shalom, but before leaving, I had a short talk with him. He told me he would like to visit me, as he was very curious about my community. A week later, Abu Ahmad showed up at the community for a visit. His visits became a weekly occurrence, and they happened to be convenient for him since our village is located on the main road connecting Gaza and

Birzeit University near Ramallah. At the time, he was studying Arabic literature at Birzeit.

Just as I felt pride in Abu Ahmad and his achievements, he likewise was proud of me for what I had done in bringing attention to the plight of Palestinians. During his first visit, he told me he recognized some similarities between our different experiences. As he had succeeded in earning the respect of the Israeli prison guards, for example, I had earned the respect of my Jewish neighbors in the community. Abu Ahmad understood that I was not merely living in the community but that I had also been struggling for many years to achieve respect and recognition as a Palestinian. Though we were talking about two totally different approaches to the problem, we had a shared purpose in bringing attention to the Palestinian cause.

Twenty-Three

My First Visit to a Refugee Camp

A short while after Abu Ahmad's first few visits, I went to visit him at the Jabalia Refugee Camp, where I met his wife; his mother; and his youngest brother, Hosni. To my shame, this was my first visit ever to a Palestinian refugee camp. I had heard quite a lot about the camps in Jordan and Lebanon while living in the United States through Palestinians I had met there. But hearing about these camps is not the same as seeing them. Jabalia, the largest refugee camp within Palestine, today has a population of more than one hundred thousand. The camp covers an area of only 1.4 square kilometers (about 350 acres), making it one of the most densely populated places on Earth. It would be like putting fourteen thousand people on the fifty acres that my community owns—a space planned for 150 families.

Camps like the one at Jabalia were erected by the United Nations for Palestinian refugees immediately following the 1948 dispersion. They were made of tents organized in parallel rows, with only narrow passages between each of the rows. My first visit to Jabalia shocked me to my core. I had no idea people were living in such miserable conditions and in such dire poverty—and these just happened to be *my* people. I remember Abu Ahmad asking me, "What have we done to deserve such a life?"

Rayek R. Rizek

When the refugees first landed in the camps, they were under the mistaken perception that they would be able to return to their homes in a matter of weeks. Instead, to their disbelief, years passed, until gradually here and there a family managed to replace a tent with a tin shack or a mud-brick hovel with an asbestos roof. The camp remained mostly a tent camp for a long time, but even as the tents were replaced, the narrow passageways remained, making it impossible for two people to pass each other without one or both leaning against a wall. An open sewer, fed by small ditches running from every dwelling place, ran down the center of one passageway. An unbearable stench lingered everywhere, making the living conditions deplorable.

In his description of these humiliating conditions, Abu Ahmad also told me that, when a person dies, it is impossible for a group of men to carry the body out of the house on their shoulders and lay it on the ground in the traditional way. Someone must instead roll the body in a blanket, hoist it up, and carry it on his back. He must then maneuver through the narrow passageways until he finally manages to reach a square. Only then is there enough room to lay the body in a coffin that pallbearers can carry on their shoulders, as Arab custom requires.

I vividly remember, on that first visit, how relieved I was when I was finally able to leave the camp. After only a brief interlude of enduring the suffocating and revolting stench of sewage, I could hardly wait until I could again breathe normally. Later, I felt terribly ashamed. Like the people interned in the camp, I was a Palestinian. They were my people, and I had owned their cause. Still, while I was unable to tolerate the horrendous smell for very long, they were forced to live in this squalor all the days of their lives. I felt guilty and hypocritical. Compared to them, my life was easy.

Though my visits to the camp have continued, the emotional pain evoked each time has not lessened. Indeed, the pain has only intensified as I have gradually become better acquainted with more of the people living in the camp.

The Anteater And The Jaguar

If one looks at a camp like Jabalia from a distance, one's first impression would be that it is a dangerous and forbidding place. It looks like one of those shantytowns where crime and drugs are rife. But after having visited inside Jabalia or another camp like it, one actually comes away with a totally different impression: Though it is true that most of the camp's inhabitants are poor, they are, if anything, overly hospitable. The dignity of many remains undimmed, despite the hardships they have had to endure, and it is not uncommon to find at least one university graduate living in each house.

The refugee camps are a relatively new phenomenon on the Palestinian scene. Historically, they could be classified as anomalies, and the people living in these camps know this. They know that their parents or, for the youngest, grandparents led normal lives in normal villages and towns. These places had plenty of space, and people dwelling in them had ready access to nature. They also know that their parents and grandparents were unjustly expelled from their homes. Indeed, the elderly do not stop talking about them, and the young do not stop dreaming of them.

Many of the Palestinians expelled in 1948 from cities and towns across the region were highly educated professionals and skilled people who were able to rebuild wherever they ended up. Among them were physicians; lawyers; bankers; businesspeople; teachers; artists; and professionals of different vocations, as one finds in every city or town. Some of them even became millionaires. The great majority of those who were expelled, however, were hardworking village people whose backgrounds were mostly in farming. Working the land was what these villagers knew, and they knew it well, but they knew little else. Many of them were illiterate, and their new environments were physically and politically inhospitable.

Among the first generation of rural Palestinians displaced to these refugee camps, very few were able to find a way out, though many of the second generation have managed to leverage an escape to something better, mainly through education. I knew many of them during my university years in the United States. Others ended up joining the newly formed armed-resistance groups during the 1960s—having concluded that the only way to return to their homes and their homeland was to fight their way back, just as the Jews had done before them.

Sadly, the entrenched political conflicts in this world that have been resolved without the use of force have been rare indeed. Whether individually or collectively, if people are not strong enough to command respect, no one pays them any mind. Others may show sympathy by donating a few tents or something to eat, as has happened with the Palestinians—but people often grow weary when pleas for sympathy continue indefinitely.

Twenty-Four

THE FIRST INTIFADA BEGINS

On December 9, 1987, several months after my encounter with Abu Ahmad, the first Palestinian uprising protesting the 1967 Israeli occupation of the West Bank and the Gaza Strip broke out. The uprising, which started in the Jabalia refugee camp, was precipitated by the funeral of four Palestinian workers, who had been killed in a traffic accident as they returned to Gaza from Israel. Some claimed at the time that the vehicle that caused the accident was an Israeli army truck and that the crash was intentional.

I do not intend here to rehash the various analyses of what actually occurred. Nor will I try to identify who was responsible for the outbreak or what their motives were. This would only result in the usual table-tennis match, in which each side tries to justify itself by slamming the Ping-Pong ball of blame into its opponent's court. Whatever might be said, one thing is clear: The situation at the time—after twenty years of occupation and military rule—was like a tinderbox, and the truck accident just happened to be the spark that ignited it. All in all, the uprising was but one more chapter in the history of the Zionist-Palestinian conflict.

The sudden unfolding of these events came as an enormous shock and surprise to both Palestinians and Israelis. Nobody could explain the sudden surge of courage that Palestinians of all ages showed when they came out in thousands into the streets of every city, town, village, and refugee camp in the West Bank and the Gaza Strip. This massive wave of protest continued, despite the heavy human and material cost to the Palestinians, as Israeli policymakers wielded a crushing military response. Most of the confrontations took place within Palestinian communities, between Israeli soldiers armed with guns and clubs and Palestinian civilians, including many young people armed with stones, slingshots, and Molotov cocktails.

By way of context, note that Israel had a coalition government at that point, with the two main political parties, Likud and Labor, governing jointly. Yitzhak Shamir (Likud) was prime minister, and Yitzhak Rabin (Labor) was defense minister. Rabin adopted harsh measures to stop the demonstrations, giving orders to use force by shooting and beating the Palestinian demonstrators.

Another interesting historical footnote is the role of prominent Palestinian nonviolence activist Mubarak Awad, who had published papers and lectured on nonviolence as a technique for resisting the Israeli occupation. Awad's organizational base was the Palestinian Centre for the Study of Nonviolence, which he had established in Jerusalem in 1983. Among the tactics employed were the planting of olive trees on land slated for proposed Israeli settlements, asking people not to pay their Israeli taxes, and encouraging people to eat and drink Palestinian products. He carried on with his activities and teaching through the Intifada, until he was arrested and deported in June 1988 from the city of his birth, Jerusalem, to the United States, where he had previously acquired citizenship. The charge against him was that he broke Israeli law by inciting a "civil uprising" and by helping to write leaflets that advocated civil disobedience that were distributed by the Intifada's leadership. The disruptive potential of a tax revolt and other nonviolent approaches was very clear to the Israeli authorities, apparently, and they took no chances.

In hindsight, I know my own sense of pain and internal turmoil were intensified because of the additional suffering that the Palestinians of

The Anteater And The Jaguar

the West Bank and the Gaza Strip had to endure. By the time the uprising started, I had come to know many people from the Gaza Strip and from the West Bank. Many of these people had visited our community out of a sense of curiosity. We had made a connection with one another. And there were others whom I had come to know because they had spent time as construction workers in our community.

This situation of ongoing crisis went on for almost five years, from December 1987 until the signing of the Oslo Peace Accords in September 1993. Though I was not involved in any of the action directly, those years were the most difficult of my life. I remember crying profusely and quite often, because I simply could not handle the situation emotionally. I was in a state of shock, because it went on and on for such a long time. I kept thinking it could not continue for more than another month or two—surely some kind of international intervention would be forthcoming. But I was wrong.

When the Intifada broke out, almost every Palestinian, including me, supported and understood the motives that precipitated it. Thinking about it today, however, I believe we were mistaken. Judging from the present results, the alternative the Palestinians chose in their effort to rid themselves of Israeli occupation was not the best. I do not blame the people any more than I do the leadership figures, who were supposed to be wiser.

I think the wrong choice was made because the Palestinian people had forgotten the benefits they enjoyed after the three parts of Palestine were reconnected in 1967. I mentioned earlier that this was one good outcome of the Israeli occupation of the West Bank and the Gaza Strip following the conclusion of that war, when Palestinians inside historic Palestine were reconnected with one another again following a nineteen-year period of separation. In hindsight, which is always twenty-twenty, of course, I believe the Palestinian leadership should have thought things through more comprehensively and planned their policies more carefully to avoid any actions that would undo those benefits. Quite possibly we would have done better if, instead of struggling to form our own separate state, we had struggled to obtain equality within Israel/Palestine for everybody.

For about twenty years (1967–87), very few roadblocks or military checkpoints existed anywhere in the country. The movement of Palestinians between all parts of Palestine was easy. Families had reunited, and many marriages were made between Palestinians from the three separate sections of the country. My community overlooks the main road connecting Gaza to the West Bank, and all through those early years of my life there, I would see thousands of Palestinian-owned vehicles passing between those two parts of Palestine. Convoys of trucks ran, carrying oranges from Gaza to Jordan. On many occasions, when I decided to visit Gaza or Ramallah, I easily picked up a ride from a Palestinian taxi on the main road.

I cannot place blame for the destruction of that reality solely on the Israeli side. We Palestinians should have been wiser than to ruin the open connections we enjoyed then. Later, the possibilities for open connections would be further curtailed as a result of the building of the Separation Wall that now divides most of the West Bank from Israel. Here again I feel compelled to say that the suicide attacks carried out by Palestinians inside Israel during the Second Intifada (starting in late September 2000) were a major factor in supplying Israel with an excuse to build the wall. While a wall was excused by many on the grounds that it provided greater security to Israel, however, there was no way to rationalize its role in creating more agony for so many West Bank and Jerusalemite Palestinians. The wall separated many families and communities from their agricultural lands, their places of employment and education, and one another. I fail to understand why those who advocated the building of the wall thought it would be sustainable for Israel to take control, and sometimes ownership, of immense parcels of privately owned Palestinian agricultural land. As for Palestinian Jerusalem, the wall also tore apart many neighborhoods, imposing the separation of families from their nearby kin, businesspeople from their places of business, and children from their schools.

The Anteater And The Jaguar

Today I cannot travel to the Gaza Strip (only one hour away by car) to visit my friends, because Israelis are not allowed to go there. My last visit to Gaza was in September of 2000. This was about one week before I left for the United Kingdom to resume my studies and just prior to the beginning of the Second Intifada. I used to go to Ramallah at least once a week, but I don't go there often now either, even though it is less than an hour away. A trip to Ramallah involves the experience of nearly unbearable anxiety as one navigates the Israeli military checkpoints en route. Moreover, one can easily end up stuck for hours at these places, especially if something happens to go wrong.

Twenty-Five

The Death of Abu Ahmad

Prior to the end of the first year of the Intifada, Abu Ahmad was killed, or to put it more precisely, *executed*. A few days before his death, Israeli security sought him out for the last time. They had targeted him several times before. During the first year of the Intifada, Abu Ahmad was twice beaten unconscious. The first time, he was beaten inside his home, in front of his wife and his mother. The second time, he was beaten in the street. Abu Ahmad was targeted because the Israelis suspected him of being one of the leaders of the uprising. Once he told me that Israeli security had threatened him a few times and issued him an explicit warning: "If we find that you have any role in this uprising, we will not arrest you; we will kill you!"

Even though we were in contact most of the time prior to his death, I do not know exactly what happened in the events leading up to it. Sometime toward the end of his life, he used a pistol on two separate occasions against two Israeli security personnel in the city of Gaza, where he injured one in the shoulder and missed the other. A few days later, he was killed at an Israeli military roadblock inside the Gaza Strip. The news of his killing was the first thing to appear on the Israeli newscast that evening, and it appeared on the first page of one of the major newspapers

The Anteater And The Jaguar

the day after. Both media avenues reported that Abu Ahmad had been killed because he was a terrorist suspected of promoting the use of weapons in the uprising.

The news of Abu Ahmad's death came as no surprise to me. He had called me late one night shortly before he was killed, and his telephone call was the strangest I have ever received. Abu Ahmad had somehow learned that he was finished, so he called to say goodbye. At first, I could not understand what he was telling me, so I asked, "What do you mean, you're saying goodbye?" Then I said, "Wait. Maybe something can be done."

He, however, insisted it was over for him and that it was too late to do anything about the situation. "I just want you to know how much I have appreciated our friendship," he told me, "and how much I liked you and respected you." I told him how proud I was of our friendship and that I would never forget him. At the end of the call, he asked me to look after his mother and his wife. This request was followed by a few very long seconds of silence. Then he asked me to excuse him for having to hang up. I wanted to keep the line open, for I was hoping to hear more from him or to say something that would encourage or help him. But there was the click of the disconnection.

One unique fact about Abu Ahmad stands out in my mind: Despite all he had gone through, he bore no hatred for Israelis. On the contrary, he strongly believed and enthusiastically supported the idea of peaceful coexistence between the Jews and the Palestinians. I happen to know this was true, because he became closely connected to our community. He regularly brought his family and many friends to visit what he considered to be a utopia. He also got to know and talk to many other people in the community, including my Jewish neighbors.

I felt so much grief for Abu Ahmad's wife, Khadija, or Sana, as he liked to call her, who was left with two babies when she was only twenty-four years of age. In spite of this, she managed to finish her BA in education, as Abu Ahmad had encouraged her to do, and to begin work as a teacher to support herself and her family. I felt even more sorrow for his elderly mother, whose younger son had to leave the Gaza Strip to avoid arrest by the Israeli army, leaving her utterly alone. Two other sons had already landed in jail, because of their political activities.

Abu Ahmad was buried in a special Israeli cemetery for those designated terrorists. Only about a year later did Israel agree to release the body back to his family for a proper burial in a cemetery in the Gaza Strip. This happened as a result of an Israeli court order issued after the intervention of the prominent Israeli lawyer and human-rights activist Felicia Langer. I had a very modest role in this development by serving as a connection between the family and Felicia and by raising the money to cover the fees involved.

The situation faced by Abu Ahmad's mother was not, however, unique. In the course of my regular visits to Jabalia, I learned that most families in the refugee camps faced similar challenges. Indeed, finding even one family without at least one martyr or political prisoner was quite rare, for the majority of Palestinians who joined the different resistance groups from the mid-1960s through the present day came from the refugee camps—whether these were in Jordan, Lebanon, Syria, the West Bank, or the Gaza Strip. The number coming from the Gaza Strip, however, is by far the largest compared with any other Palestinian community in the Middle East, because more than 75 percent of Gaza's total population of about two million is comprised of refugee families.

Remember that the Gaza Strip is only about 365 square kilometers. It's a flat, sandy piece of land with no forests, mountains, valleys, natural rivers, or streams. And let's not forget that the residents of the Gaza Strip, who have been living under direct or indirect Israeli occupation since 1967, have been subjected to a cruel siege since 2007. Taking these facts into consideration is crucial for any understanding of the recent wars between Israel and the Gaza Strip—including the most recent outbreak of fighting in July 2014, which began while I was writing this book. Describing these periods of intense fighting as "wars against terrorists and terrorism" is not entirely accurate—indeed, the phrase is misleading, because these wars also have to do with the unresolved

The Anteater And The Jaguar

Palestinian-Israeli question that goes back, in its modern incarnation, about one hundred years.

Once Jabalia became such a vivid part of my life and my thoughts, it has been always with me. The death of Abu Ahmad did not end my connection with Jabalia and Gaza. Several months before his death, he introduced me to a friend who had chanced to be traveling with him to Gaza on a day when he stopped at my house for a visit. The friend's name was also Muhammad, and he was also from Jabalia, where he was working as a physician, having obtained his medical degree from an Egyptian university. After the death of Abu Ahmad, Dr. Muhammad and I became more closely connected, and we are still close friends to this day.

Some years earlier, during the First Intifada, a wealthy Austrian Jewish friend of our community donated about $30,000 for us to use for humanitarian causes in the West Bank and the Gaza Strip. When I mentioned this to Abu Ahmad, he suggested the money be used to supply needed laboratory equipment for Dr. Muhammad's private clinic in Jabalia. I approached our community administration with this idea, and they agreed to designate half of the donation for that purpose. This initial modest donation turned out to be only the beginning of a much bigger project aimed at helping refugees in Jabalia.

Throughout the First Intifada years, I kept receiving donations of a few hundred dollars here and there from various European and American friends I had come to know while living in Wahat Assalam. I forwarded all those donations to Dr. Muhammad, who spent them to supply free medicine and food for many needy people.

At some point in the early 1990s, Dyana and I, following the wise advice of Dr. Muhammad and with the assistance of his sister, Zakeia, started a project to produce and market Palestinian embroidery. Eventually we employed about fifteen women from Jabalia, and Zakeia supervised their work. For that project, I traveled to Gaza once every week or two to deliver the money and material for the work and to collect the finished embroideries for sale. Unfortunately, the project ended after four years, when Zakeia married a cousin who lived in Nablus in the

Rayek R. Rizek

West Bank and when, around the same time, the Oslo agreement went into effect, making my entry to the Gaza Strip more complicated, as I was now required to cross an official border.

Later, following the establishment of the Palestinian Authority, Dr. Muhammad took my advice and founded an official charity. This charity, over some twenty years of operation thus far, has received a few hundred thousand dollars from private donors and organizations, both foreign and Palestinian. All this money has been spent on helping refugees. Dr. Muhammad has used it not only to supply medicine and food but for other projects as well. He purchased five thousand pairs of eyeglasses for children with vision problems and helped purchase backpacks, notebooks, and other school supplies for needy children. He offered many days of free medical services to destitute patients, a service made possible through the assistance of other doctors who volunteered at Dr. Mohammad's clinic. The free medical services included general checkups and treatment for blood pressure, cholesterol, diabetes, and so on. Special days were designated for the circumcision of newborn baby boys, for medical treatment of pregnant women, for care of the elderly, and more. A more recent project launched by Dr. Muhammad, Abu Lehia is a bakery that supports thirty-five families through its paid staff of thirty-five employees. This project is run as a not-for-profit humanitarian program, offering various kinds of bread at cost.

It is undeniable that a project offering low-cost bread and supporting thirty-five families still seems like a drop in the ocean when juxtaposed with the vast amount of human suffering endured every day by so many Palestinians; on the other hand, I have found that my own personal pain has been eased somewhat by the fact that I have been instrumental in bringing relief to at least some people. I have always wished I could do more, and often I have wished I could spend more time in Jabalia, even if I could not do much in practical terms. Meanwhile, I saw, whenever I was there, that just visiting and listening to the people meant a lot to them. For me these Palestinians have become the real Palestinian cause that I wish more than anything else to remain connected to and to serve.

The Anteater And The Jaguar

I have never felt a larger meaning to my life as a Palestinian than I have experienced by being part of this specific effort.

The pain and anger I felt from seeing those miserable refugee camps was one thing, but what looms larger still is the fact that so many Palestinians elsewhere still know very little about what people stuck in the refugee camps have to go through. Sometimes I think that, were it not for my own visit when I accompanied the Swedish group to the Gaza Strip, maybe I, too, would have continued indefinitely in my ignorance.

Living at Neve Shalom and being active in community affairs here, including outreach and fundraising for our educational institutions, has given me the opportunity to travel to many regions of the United States and Europe. During some visits, I have participated in conferences and lectured about my community. During others, especially trips to the United States, I have traveled from city to city raising funds for our various projects. These fundraising tours gave me the chance to meet audiences all over the map, and many of them were Jews, Palestinians, or Arabs. One of my strongest impressions from meeting these people was that the Jews are organized, whereas the Palestinians are not. The Jews care for Israel by donating billions of dollars, but Palestinians give less. Many Palestinians, of course, have been giving to the Palestinian cause, but in the aggregate, they have not stepped up sufficiently to raise anywhere near the level of assistance that is truly needed.

Larger questions loom: Why should Palestinian refugees be left for decade after decade to endure such miserable conditions? Why can we not continue our struggle for freedom and justice, while in tandem working to create for them a more humane and healthy existence? When I used to describe the deplorable condition of the camps to many Palestinians I have met over the years, even those living in my community and in Nazareth, the common reaction was one of utter shock and disbelief. They found it hard to believe that people were living with open sewers and that they were forced to endure conditions so filthy as to endanger their physical and mental health. Dr. Muhammad told me of the different illnesses that periodically spread through the refugee camps—illnesses that can be found only in the world's most impoverished countries. Most result from contaminated water. Many children suffer from malnutrition as well. Still, the medicines most prescribed to adults are antidepressants. The United Nations (through UNRWA) provide the camps with clinics like the one my friend Dr. Muhammad works in, in addition to his private clinic. These, however, are still insufficient to provide adequate services to the camp populations, for each doctor sees an average of about one hundred patients a day.

In spite of the shock and disbelief that hearing about such conditions causes, few people suggest doing anything about them. I used to suggest that a well-to-do Palestinian, by donating a few hundred dollars a month, could undertake the support of one family or one student or even more. Donating to an individual bank account might be an option, since many claim they did donate in the past—only to learn that most of the money was siphoned off along the way, in one way or another, so that little of the original amount ever reached the people who actually needed it.

Many rich Palestinians need to do some soul-searching for sure. After all, why should we depend on foreign aid that always comes with conditions attached and sometimes verges on political blackmail, while many rich Palestinians could provide needed money? Could a legitimate Palestinian fund be created to which many Palestinian multimillionaires from all over the world could contribute? Why do Palestinians of the diaspora not form associations of friends for the different hospitals, universities, and institutions for the purpose of helping them provide better services and education for their constituents? I cannot help but feel wonder and admiration whenever I visit an Israeli hospital or university and see the many plaques honoring Jewish philanthropists who gave generously to build these and so many other institutions.

Why then is it that most Palestinians in the diaspora today are not organized politically and financially? Why do they not make their voice heard, and why are their diverse abilities not being constructively channeled to help their own people? I remember the late prominent

The Anteater And The Jaguar

Palestinian scholar and intellectual, Professor Ibrahim Abu-Lughod, who spent the last ten years of his life teaching and researching at Bir Zeit University and the Qattan Cultural Centre in Ramallah. He came to Bir Zeit University from the University of Chicago in 1991 with the intention of spending one year as a visiting professor. When that year ended, he decided to stay on at Bir Zeit. Indeed, he remained there until he passed away in 2001. I remember hearing him talk, when he visited our community on one occasion, about how surprised he was when he came to Palestine and realized a Palestinian community existed all across Palestine that constituted a sizable political, social, economic, and cultural presence. I also remember how he lamented the fact that he did not return to Palestine much earlier, when he had been most needed.

I cannot help but wonder why all those thousands of prominent Palestinian intellectuals, scientists, and physicians do not volunteer to spend some time in the West Bank and the Gaza Strip, offering their knowledge and expertise to help their people. I believe many Palestinians do not realize we have the nucleus for the formation of a state that is actually much more solid and well-established than the nucleus the Jews had before they formed their state in 1948. I believe we have all the needed qualifications and means to help facilitate the establishment of an independent state for our people, especially for those who are still being tossed from one place to another. This will not happen, however, until we all unite in taking responsibility and stop depending on others to do the work for us.

From my conversations over many years with innumerable guests of our community's guesthouse and with patrons of our own café, I have learned about the thousands of Jewish youth from all over the world who visit Israel through different programs that are funded by the state and by different Jewish organizations. The purpose of these organized visits is to raise these young people's awareness of and commitment toward the state of Israel, its agenda, and its needs. I have always wondered why the well-established Palestinian communities and leaders in the Palestinian diaspora have not put together similar programs for their young people that could connect them personally and concretely with the homeland? (In recent years, happily, a few such programs have begun to sprout, but not anything like the dimensions that are possible and needed.)

One thing I find surprising about the Jews I have known, based on my experience of living alongside Jewish members of our community, is how ably they deal with differences of opinion on the whole. From my earliest participation in community meetings in our village, I noticed how easily the Jewish members seemed able to resolve even the most heated of disagreements. Sometimes an argument between two people could turn loud and even a bit hostile; then, to my amazement, I would see the same two people walking out of the meeting room together and behaving as though nothing had happened between them that was worth ruining their whole relationship over. When we Arabs argue, however, resolving differences of opinion does not come quite so easily. It seems almost impossible for us to argue our different opinions without intensely personalizing the whole thing, and people often appear to be concerned to an unrealistic degree about issues of honor and dignity. Sometimes the accusations and counteraccusations escalate to the point that people accuse their interlocutor of treason!

My experience in the small community of Neve Shalom has taught me plenty about our human weaknesses, our failures, and the reasons for them. I have learned that in order to achieve some kind of balance with one's opponent, better organization and stronger moral conviction always win out against disarray, angry gesturing, and misdirected physical power. Moral power, unlike physical power, accrues to us when we practice honesty, humility, compassion, sincerity, and willingness to take personal responsibility.

The Anteater And The Jaguar

Dyana, the first from the left, is pictured here with her family in front of the Christmas tree in the late fifties.

My family in front of the entrance to the Orthodox
Church in Mount Tabor in the midsixties.

The Anteater And The Jaguar

My father's uncle Shibly with his sister Katrina before his immigration to Argentina. This image was taken sometime during the first decade of the twentieth century.

My maternal grandparents, Jeryis and Meladi, in their 1908 wedding photo.

My maternal grandparents with their family. My mother is pictured just behind my grandmother with my aunts and uncles. This image was taken in the midthirties.

Here I am pictured on my mother's lap in early 1956.

Priest Saleh Farah, my mother's grandfather, photographed
wearing an Arab traditional dress in the 1920s.

The bus my father drove in the early fifties. He is the first from the right, wearing the black jacket.

The Rizeks of Nazareth, spring 1958. I'm in the middle of the front row (the boy with the shaved head). My mother is behind me in the back row, carrying my younger brother, and standing to the left of my father.

Here I am pictured touring with a group of visitors in the Oasis in the mideighties, when there were no paved roads.

I am first from right with my siplings. my parents (behind me) with Aunt Basmi and Uncle Moeen, spring 1958.

The Wedding of my parents Rafeek and Najla, August 6, 1944.

The Anteater And The Jaguar

The Christian Arab Orthodox Community Annunciation or Saint Gabriel church in Nazareth. Built between 1750 and 1763 by my great ancestor priest Khleif.

Part IV: Reaching an End to Conflicts

Twenty-Six

Our Responsibility

Palestinians, I believe, are a realistic and sincere people. We talk openly about the fact that we, too, have our share of responsibility regarding the outcome of the major confrontation between the Jews and the Arabs of Palestine, which took place mostly during 1948. I have already indicated how that confrontation resulted in the loss of our shared common existence in our common homeland. Now I must talk about our responsibility for that outcome, in spite of our knowing we did not choose this conflict but had it imposed on us. I must talk about our responsibility, even though we know how some Arab regimes collaborated with both the British and the Jewish-Zionist movement against our national interests. I also must talk about our responsibility, even though we know how our people's expulsion and dispersion was, for the most part, caused by dozens of (now fully documented) massacres that the Jewish armed forces carried out in different Palestinian villages and towns, mostly during 1948.

We talk with much regret about our personal problems with disorganization and internal conflicts. Not only have these been causes of our failure, but they have also given some of us a reason to resign from the struggle and withdraw from supporting the general Palestinian cause—or even to align with the Jewish side. With much regret, I have to say this is as true now as it was in the past.

Considering our reality today, we do not seem to have changed much. As we were prior to 1948, so we are today: still full of arguments and beset by behaviors that hinder the very unity that is a precondition to our overcoming our failures. Our own failures do not diminish the fact that Israel bears a large share of the responsibility in perpetuating the sad reality that many Palestinians living inside and outside Palestine have had to endure. However, it is difficult *not* to place a major portion of the responsibility and blame on our leadership and ourselves—perhaps ourselves even more so, insofar as leadership tends to reflect the people they lead. Yet this still does not absolve our leaders from their obligation to lead by offering more exemplary role models with regard to democracy, transparency, humility, and much higher levels of tolerance to our differences.

It is embarrassing that we have so often ended up accusing and blaming one another even more than we do Israel. We cannot seem to reach a compromise, although we are supposedly one people with one cause. How can we persist in being so stubborn about our positions when many of our own people are paying such a high price by suffering poverty and humiliation? When we engage in the struggle for what we consider a just cause, then wisdom dictates that we must win to our side as many friends and supporters of that cause as possible. This effort should be directed not primarily toward our supposed adversaries, who belong to the other nation, but toward members of our own national group. How could we fail if we elicit the support of those closest to us, instead of adopting ideologies and convictions that exclude others' views and discourage meaningful dialogue with them?

We also talk about the absurd behavior of some Arab regimes and people who were instrumental in causing tens of thousands of their own country's Arab Jewish citizens to leave and to come to Israel. This happened mostly during the early 1950s, and it has helped to double the Jewish population in our country, as if the Arabs had taken a direct role in

The Anteater And The Jaguar

supporting the Zionist movement's agenda of populating Palestine with more Jews. Regrettably, as time has gone by, these Arab Jews, who were once neighbors and partners, have become strangers and opponents.

With regret, we tend to talk about the naïveté of those Palestinians who believed the Jewish forces were sincere when they asked them to leave certain villages temporarily, promising they would be allowed to return once the fight was over. Those Palestinians, of course, along with many others, were never allowed to return. Take Iqrit and Kufr Bir'im, for example—two Arab villages located near the border of Lebanon. Iqrit native Father Elias Chacour, in his book *Blood Brothers,* describes what happened in these villages, where the houses, like hundreds of others, were physically erased after the areas were depopulated.

We harbor doubts as to whether the escape and flight of some Palestinians in 1948 was justified even before the Jewish armed forces showed up. They fled in terror, because they believed the (partly real and partly exaggerated) news and rumors they had heard about atrocities, the cruelty of the Jewish fighters, and their mistreatment of Palestinian civilians. These rumors were not only spread by the Jewish side but also, regrettably, were sometimes spread by Palestinians. On April 9, 1948, a little more than a month before May 15, the official date when Britain was to leave Palestine, about one hundred people were killed in Deir Yassin, a Palestinian village near Jerusalem, during and after an attack by Jewish fighters belonging to the Irgun and Lehi groups. The civilian casualties included women, children, and elderly. These facts have since been well-documented. When reports of these events began circulating, however, some Palestinians deliberately exaggerated numbers and stories about atrocities in Deir Yassin. They claimed a higher number of pregnant women, mothers, girls, and children who were killed and added that the Jewish fighters committed acts of rape against Palestinian women, as if what had happened there was not sufficient to be considered an atrocity. Though their intention was to amplify the level of determination among Palestinians to stand fast and resist, the rumor backfired. Thousands of Palestinians from villages nearby and farther away fled in terror. Some people later confessed to having authored these exaggerations, but the damage had already been done.

Many reports were issued over the years by various sources—Palestinian, Jewish, British, and even by the International Committee of the Red Cross—concerning the massacre in Deir Yassin. Most of the accounts reported more than two hundred Palestinians killed. Long afterward, however, in 1987, a study regarded as authoritative was published by Palestinian scholar Sharif Kan'ana of Bir Zeit University. Kan'ana, after interviewing survivors, concluded that 107 Palestinians had died, with another twelve wounded. Almost all the earlier reports had also mentioned acts of rape of Palestinian women and young girls, who were then killed, but the Palestinian survivors of the massacre denied that rapes had occurred. It is also mentioned that the Irgun and Lehi fighters who committed the massacre were mostly young men and women, among them adolescents.

As to the Jewish side, various reports suggested that the Irgun and Lehi had reason to spread the atrocity narrative, because they wanted to frighten the Palestinians into fleeing. Meanwhile, the Haganah (led by Ben Gurion) had its own motivation for disseminating these reports: so as to tarnish the Irgun and Lehi, with whom they were competing for leadership.

Even my father at one time, amid the chaos and fear, suggested to my mother that they needed to leave and go to Lebanon, because it was safer there, a story my mother later would retell many times. My mother, however, refused to flee, because flight was not exactly safe either, as there was still fighting going on in nearby areas. In addition, she did not see how she could agree to leave with two young children to care for: my older brother Basheer was only eighteen months old then, and Bassam was a newborn, just three weeks old. My mother also had a very strong belief in God, which evidently persuaded her that she could not run away from death, and she explained to my father that she would prefer to die in her home than to run away.

And there was something else. My mother sometimes saw visions that, in hindsight, would turn out to have been predictive. She used these prescient visions as guides, seeking clues to things that would later come to pass, in particular within the family but also in general. During the months preceding the outbreak of war in 1948, her visions had hinted of disaster and had also cemented her reluctance to leave home despite all the chaos, confusion, and fear then prevailing. In one vision, she saw a full moon falling from the sky to the ground and understood it was a powerful portent of catastrophe; some months later, she understood her vision had been an omen about the fall of Palestine. Meanwhile, in another vision, she saw Mother Mary walking along the street in a white gown, not far from our house, a lighted lantern in her hand. She interpreted this vision as reassurance that, no matter what else might occur, nothing bad was going to happen to Nazareth, and the family could safely stay there. And, indeed, that was how my family ended up staying in Nazareth. I was born there seven years later on September 18, 1955—my parents' fourth child, following Basheer; Bassam; and my older sister, Afaf; and followed later by my youngest brother, Shibly.

I remember my mother giving voice to her pain and remorse when she learned of the tragic massacres that befell the Palestinians in Jordan in 1970, and again later in Lebanon during the 1970s and 1980s. "Look at those poor people," she would say. "They ran for their lives away from Palestine only to find death in Jordan and Lebanon. Could it have been different if they had stayed here, or is it the will of God?"

Nazareth was the only sizable town in Israeli-controlled Palestine whose inhabitants were not expelled in 1948 and its aftermath. The consensus seems to be that the town's Christian identity, and hence its importance to the Christian world, played a major role in the protection of its population from eviction. Many people remember the foreign flags that were hoisted over the twenty-five or so Christian institutions in Nazareth just before the town was surrendered to the Jewish forces by a delegation that included several religious authorities, along with the mayor, on the evening of July 16, 1948.

Another reason more Nazareth residents were not leaving town during those chaotic and horrifying summer months of 1948 was that the all-volunteer Arab Liberation Army had set up a checkpoint to prevent just that, with an armored car and some soldiers guarding the northern exit, the only remaining outlet from Nazareth for about two months before July 16. The soldiers were under orders not to allow anybody out. I was told my maternal aunt Mariam and her family were among the people turned back at the checkpoint when they tried to flee Nazareth en route to Lebanon.

Note that during 1948, about twenty thousand refugees from nearby villages and towns ended up in Nazareth, whose population at the time was only about sixteen thousand. Some refugees were hosted by their relatives or friends in the town, and others were able to rent a room in a private home, but the majority were crammed into convents, churches, schools, and the mosque—and were even lodged in Nazareth's only movie theatre, the Empire Cinema. Those who couldn't find a place in any of the designated buildings slept in improvised tents and shacks. I still have a vivid memory from my childhood of two Nazareth neighborhoods of tin barracks, though at the time I did not know they were refugee camps. One of those neighborhoods housed refugees from a depopulated village near Nazareth by the name of Safuriyye, the story of which is documented by author Adina Hoffman in her moving biography of Palestinian poet Taha Muhammad Ali, *My Happiness Bears No Relation to Happiness*. I heard and read much about the harsh conditions that the Nazarenes generally and the refugees in particular were obliged to endure at that time and for some years later: crowding, poverty, unemployment, a severe shortage of water, terrible sanitary conditions, and severely inadequate supplies of food and clothing.

The shortages of food and clothing persisted, according to many accounts, despite the help offered by the different convents, churches, and hospitals, as well as the Red Cross and UNICEF. I learned that these institutions had hosted Polish refugees during the Second World War—people released in 1941 from Soviet labor camps in Siberia and Kazakhstan, where 1.5 million Polish civilians had been incarcerated by the Soviets when they, together with Nazi Germany, invaded and divided Poland between them during September 1939. Stalin subsequently released the remainder of these prisoners as a condition of receiving help from the

The Anteater And The Jaguar

Allied Forces, mainly Great Britain and the United States, to counter the Nazi invasion of the Soviet Union in June 1941. A few thousand of these refuges ended up in Palestine, with hundreds of them in Nazareth. At various times, I had heard about the Polish refugees from my parents and others. Eventually I found a more thorough account by Dr. Elias Srouji, in his memoir entitled *Cyclamens from Galilee*, which I highly recommend for those interested in reading about life and events in Nazareth and the nearby regions of Galilee and Lebanon from the 1920s through the Palestinian catastrophe of 1948 and through the late 1960s.

All my life I have heard so many stories, related to me personally by other Palestinians, recounting what happened to them and to their families as a result of the events of 1948. I must admit that, despite everything I have heard and learned about 1948, I still find the whole subject bewildering. I cannot comprehend why three-quarters of a million Palestinian Arabs, from more than twenty cities and towns and four hundred villages, ended up displaced and dispersed inside and outside their homeland. Irrespective of whether it was planned in advance or an unintended consequence of the war, the fact remains that the vast majority of those Palestinians were simply innocent civilian victims. I am still convinced that what happened during that period was an unnecessary human tragedy and that there are still a great many details yet to emerge. I remain convinced that this saga is not a story about the "good guys" winning out against the "bad guys," but rather a story about one group of people that was victimized in order to compensate another group of people for a sin committed against them by a third party. I have yet to be convinced—in a manner not subject to distortion, manipulation, and dehumanization—that this tragedy was a "fair" outcome of a "fair" fight and a "fair" reading of "fair" historical circumstances. Nothing about this story seems very fair to me, but that is what would be required in order for me to relinquish my conviction as to the right of my people to return home to this land and their right to live here as equals. Sadly, many—too many—people are persuaded that this is precisely what we Palestinians should do in order to be considered serious partners for a just and fair peace.

Twenty-Seven

I am Responsible

Visitors to my community have often made comments along the lines of, "Wow, you must be very happy to live in such a place! It is like a paradise!"

When I used to mull over these words in my mind, I had to agree. The place where I live really is a paradise. But even living in paradise does not guarantee a person inner happiness; hence, I was not so sure the word "happy" described what I truly felt. This oft-repeated comment and my own response to it have kept me aware that something was still wrong with my life in general. And I wondered: How could I be living in such a place—the envy of many—and still not be happy? Its serene natural environment alone ought to have been enough to produce happiness. Moreover, it is close to being a utopia, for Jews and Palestinians live together here in relative peace. Nonetheless, I realized, these idyllic conditions were insufficient to make me truly happy.

Though I live in such an ideal place, people's saying I should be happy did not make it so. For one thing, my life here on the whole has not been easy, because for many years, willingly or otherwise, I have been involved in various conflicts, both ideological and administrative in nature. Social relationships have often been difficult and painful,

The Anteater And The Jaguar

and I, along with others, have suffered mental anguish that at times has become almost unbearable. Indeed, at one time, I had reached a point where I would avoid even walking around the community. I would do all I could to avoid seeing or meeting people with whom I was extremely angry. And even when I was several thousand miles away from home, I was unable to remove those people from my mind.

In September 2000, I had an opportunity to continue my studies for a master's degree in peace studies at the University of Bradford (United Kingdom) for another year. This time away from home followed three intense years, during which I had served as our community's secretary general. During that period, I had numerous unpleasant and perhaps unavoidable confrontations with various community members coming to me, in my official capacity, to express their disagreement regarding administrative concerns or ideological issues the community was facing. Many of those confrontations caused me intense mental anguish, because I fully believed that my conduct was proper and that the way I was running things was in the best interests of the community as a whole, but others seemed to be behaving very selfishly.

From the year I spent at Bradford, I remember in particular one student neighbor by the name of Adejo, who was from Nigeria. He, too, was feeling anguished about various personal experiences he had been through. More than once he asked if there was some way I could help him rid his mind of the disturbing memories of people who had harmed him. Regrettably, I could not help him, because I did not know what to do about my own very similar problem.

I suppose it is rare to meet anyone who does not carry around at least some degree of emotional pain. Disappointing social interactions and unpleasant life experiences happen to us all and guarantee that everyone will have their share of inner anguish to work through. I have come to realize, however, that living in an intentional community often gives one an extra dose of such anguish. Managing and organizing a community is harder than managing and organizing one's personal goals. In a community, one must encounter the same people—with their own unique sets of problems—day after day. When this occurs over a period of many years in a very small social space, avoiding the problems of others is not easy.

Over the years, I have made friends at kibbutzim near our community, mainly from Kibbutz Nahshon and Kibbutz Harel, and they have extended much support and help to our community, especially during its founding years. I've discovered through these friendships that, even in a kibbutz, an intentional community where with few exceptions all the residents are Jews, angry disagreements arise between members, mostly as a result of communal life. Apparently, regardless of who lives in a particular community, the same kinds of arguments and conflicts occur and make for similar patterns of social disharmony. Indeed, Israeli Jews with whom I talk nearly always want to know about the difficulties of life in our community, and when I tell them a story or two, they often exclaim in surprise, "But that's just like in a kibbutz!" I have been amazed to learn how similar such conflicts are in intentional communities generally, whether they have occurred recently or hundreds of years ago. Living in a community like ours is certainly not for the faint of heart. Over the years, a few families have left Wahat Assalam (a daunting step logistically, financially, and socially) *because* they were unable to withstand the conditions and requirements of communal life. Many Jews have left their kibbutzim for the same reasons.

Over the course of my life, meanwhile, I have also become aware that I am responsible for creating much of my own mental anguish. I have harbored some negative attitudes, reacted and responded in negative ways, and held some negative convictions. Some thoughts and judgments I have had about myself and others have been negative, too. For a long time, I managed to convince myself that there was nothing I could do about it. I came to that conclusion because I saw that I was living and acting like everybody around me and because I believed that whatever I did was a justified reaction to what they had done to me. I became convinced that I was the victim and that others were the aggressors. In order to make things right, I believed others needed to take the first step in asking my forgiveness.

The Anteater And The Jaguar

All this changed, however, after I read a book a Jewish friend named Hagit gave me about ten years ago, after she saw that I was carrying around a load of mental and emotional pain. The book was *The Golden Key to Happiness*, by Japanese author Masami Sayonji. My friend asked me to read the book and said I'd find advice there that could help me. I thanked her and then allowed the book to be buried under a lot of other books, until one day a few months later, when I was searching for something else, I discovered it sitting there. ("When the student is ready, the teacher appears.")

Through reading this book and others like it that kept coming my way—a partial list of the most notable would include books by Jiddu Krishnamurti, the Dalai Lama, Viktor Frankl, Thich Nhat Hanh, Katie Byron, and Eckhart Tolle—I began to realize for the first time that I could continue living my life without having to endure so much mental and emotional pain. Indeed, I could do this even as a Palestinian living in a complicated intentional community such as Neve Shalom. I came to realize that if I would only get rid of my mental anguish, I would be better able to solve the challenges and difficulties life presented to me. Until I arrived at this point, I knew nothing about how lessening my mental pain was possible by controlling my mind instead of letting my mind control me. I had not realized much about how mental pain results from our efforts to protect and feed our egos. I was almost completely ignorant about how certain ways that we construct our identities could cause mental pain. This is true especially if our identities are constructed in such a way that they separate us from others. Identities formed in intentional opposition to what others stand for can become sources of conflict.

I also did not know much about how living a life of regret about past things and of worry and fear over what the future holds could be a source of mental anguish. Nor did I know much about how living life in the present could relieve mental pain. I failed to realize how closely interconnected mental health is to physical health. I did not realize that living with mental pain could be a cause of the kind of stagnation that disables people from finding solutions to the problems, difficulties, and challenges in life. I did not know that, by taking responsibility, by forgiving others, and by forgiving ourselves, we could all rid ourselves of most of our mental pain. I did not realize that by forgiving others, I would be doing a favor to myself, for it is only through forgiveness that we can free ourselves from the persistent memories of those people who have hurt us. Not forgiving others guarantees they will remain lodged in our mind even after they die, and their haunting of our minds will, in turn, become for us an inexhaustible source for mental pain. Living with this mental pain could unconsciously cause us to mistreat others, both verbally and physically, whether those people are close to us or strangers who may well have had nothing to do with the original cause of our pain. Generally, when I talk about the need to practice forgiveness toward others, people tell me it is a difficult thing to do. But what I discovered to be more difficult than forgiving others is forgiving myself. And, finally, I failed to realize I could start changing my life immediately instead of (as I had always thought necessary) waiting for others to make the first move.

Suddenly I started asking myself questions: What if others did not make the first move? Would this mean I would have to spend the rest of my life in my state of continuous mental pain, waiting for an apology that might never come? And could others also be waiting for me to change, because they were equally convinced they were the victims and I was the aggressor? Have we not all adequately rehashed the same old, tired arguments, poring over trivial issues such as who acted first and who reacted in this or that way? Does not this very common scenario between Palestinians and Jews play itself out over and over again when we start arguing about things that happened today and end up arguing about things that happened hundreds and even thousands of years ago? Perpetual stalemate in such arguments will never deliver mental peace!

Thinking about these issues more deeply, I have come to see clearly how these action-reaction situations drive arguments round and round in vicious, inescapable closed circles with no absolute beginning and no hope for an end. Whether the arguments revolve around personal or collective conflicts, they still seem to go in loops with no clearly identifiable beginning and no clear destination. Today, from all my reading and searching, I have come to believe there is no exact beginning to anything "under the sun"—unless we speak of the Big Bang, which is thought to have happened fifteen billion years ago...and we are not even sure this was an *absolute* beginning.

Finding the Way Out

Relief from my mental suffering came once I learned to internalize the concept of self-responsibility. I began to understand that my inability to rid myself of the tendency to keep blaming others (and blaming myself) for my miserable situation caused most of my mental pain. I learned that blaming is not the way. Taking full and immediate responsibility for this situation was the only way to alleviate my ongoing anguish. Furthermore, talking incessantly about the past and dwelling on my feeling of victimization in no way improved my situation or lessened my mental pain. Instead, these activities merely kept me stuck in a rut, unable to find a way out. At the time, it seemed logical to me that looking for a way out was something I needed to not concern myself with, as I believed utterly that I was right and others were wrong. However, when I accepted that the present moment in my life's journey was determined to a very large degree by my own attitudes about and responses to my situation, and not only by what others had done to me, I soon started to get unstuck from my rut. Accepting the fact that I had a share in creating my present reality was a good start in internalizing the idea of self-responsibility.

Now, whenever I find myself in an argument that verges on collapsing into a closed circle, I try right away to reconnect inwardly with the concept of self-responsibility. Otherwise, I would end up trapped by an unwinnable "Which came first—the chicken or the egg?" type of argument. If I keep insisting that my reaction is right, won't I cut myself off from other viable solutions to a particular problem? Could I have reacted, for instance, in a way that could stop an argument's escalation into outright conflict? Would I be willing to confess my own error or apologize after I realized how my reaction caused greater pain and further complications, in my efforts to get my opponent to see eye to eye with me? Or would I insist on my rightness, even though doing so might literally be the death of me, rather than confess I might be wrong?

We can choose to take full responsibility, partial responsibility, or no responsibility at all for our attitudes and reactions toward those undesirable situations into which life casts us. These choices lie between two extremes: continued suffering and the alleviation of suffering. The alleviation of suffering is possible only if we take full responsibility for the negative perspectives and attitudes we ourselves have formed regarding the undesirable life situations we must face.

I could go on and on in an effort to prove how my personal and collective tragedy has resulted from others' having wronged my people and me; however, though I may have convinced myself and persuaded others that my story justifies universal outrage and sympathy, what matters most at the end of the day is whether I have gotten rid of my mental pain or have decided to continue clinging to it. What good can come, though, from staying in a spot where I keep complaining about what others did to me, unless it is to satisfy the needs of my ego to be right and to get others to feel sorry for me, a poor victim?

The feeling of victimhood is a common recourse that many people all over the world take when they are involved in social or political conflicts. In our Israeli-Palestinian case, it is so common to turn our discussion into a competition about who is the greater victim every time we discuss our conflict. I was in that place myself until I realized the position of victimhood is mainly needed to help us justify our negative acts and thoughts toward the other. The negative actions and thoughts of victims are not seen by them as aggression but rather as a response. If I am the victim, then I am allowed and right to hurt. I have also realized that the end result of proving our victimhood is achieved after we start our story from a specific, consciously chosen point. I wonder if we would reach the same result if we went with our story a bit back or forward in time. Don't most of us do that? Otherwise, how could we go on claiming, and persuading ourselves, that our physical and mental mistreatments are a justified, human reaction to "their" inhumane actions? In addition, I realized I would have to give up on victimhood if I wanted to be able to practice forgiveness.

How could we not suffer, being stuck in such a place? How could we ever become more positive and more practical, living in such a spot? And most important of all: How could we repair and heal our wounded relations with our adversaries, and even more so with our friends and family members, if we continued living in a state of victimhood? Finally, I understood I must overcome victimhood if I did not want to end up victimizing others. Isn't this our case in this land? Who has been practically and daily maintaining the victimhood of the Palestinians of the West Bank and the Gaza Strip, if not a group comprised of people who have all experienced victimhood? This situation is reflected mainly in the structure of the Israeli army. This army, as mentioned before, is mostly Jewish, but it includes within its ranks most men of the Druze and the Circassian[15]communities, in addition to some other Arabs, belonging to the Bedouin, Muslim, and Christian communities. Most of these people have a history of persecution, which functions to ease their participation in victimizing others. Therefore, it is important to consider the psychological dimension when one wants to better understand what is identified as the Israeli-Palestinian conflict. It is a political conflict that is also fed by a psychological state of mind of people who cannot let go of their victimhood. This state of mind does not only move these groups to victimize others, but it moves the Palestinians to victimize one another.

---

15 The Circassian community in Israel numbers about four thousand people. Most live in two villages in the northern part of the country, Al-Reyhaniye and Kafr Kama. The Circassians, who are Sunni Muslims, took refuge in Palestine in the 1880s during Ottoman rule. They came to Palestine and other parts of Greater Syria from the Caucasus region between Russia and Turkey. The impetus for their immigration was Russian warfare waged against that region, including wars between them and the Ottomans, over a period of one hundred years.

Taking responsibility can liberate us from the past by drawing a clear, bright line between the past and the present and between yesterday and today. Though it may be true that today is the result of yesterday and tomorrow is the result of today, if I want a brighter tomorrow, then I must start by making *today* bright. Of course, I could go on forever delineating the causes of my present reality, but since the causes are in the past, I can do nothing to change those. All I can change is the *present* moment. This can be done because the present, unlike the past, *can* be changed. Indeed, if you think about it, the present is the only real life we have anyway. Therefore, by taking full responsibility for my situation in life, I can face life's present moment without letting past pain remain an obstacle to me.

Making the Choice

I made my choice when I realized that to continue harboring my previous convictions was hurting me more than it hurt others. Being angry and complaining most of the time turned me into a negative person. Fewer and fewer people wanted to be close to me when I was in that state. It also caused me deep depression that had begun affecting my physical health. I would learn later that living with negative thoughts such as anger, hatred, envy, regret, and blame creates not only pain in our minds but illnesses in our bodies as well. Indeed, thoughts always are translated into feelings and emotions, and feelings and emotions affect our bodies. Another thing I have learned is about the effect language has not only on our social relations but also on our bodies.

But before I go on with that theme, I must share with you my mother's story of why I was named *Rayek*, which in Arabic means *serene* or *calm*. My mother told me that by the time the midwife came to our house to help her with my birth, as she had with the rest of my siblings, I was already out. The midwife just completed the procedure, and then she suggested Rayek as a name, because I had emerged so easily. My mother agreed, and afterward, I had to spend most of my life trying to become my name.

The Anteater And The Jaguar

I spent many years finding it difficult to answer the simple question, "How are you, Rayek?" I would usually answer, "Just so-so," or "I don't know," or "I could be better," when there was nothing seriously wrong with me except for some common life worries and difficulties. I did not realize what effect these words were having on my face and body until I learned about the concept that our bodies believe our words—an idea I first encountered in 1998 during one of my fundraising tours in the United States, when a woman named Barbara Hoberman Levine gave me her book, *Your Body Believes Every Word You Say*. I read it, but a few more years would pass before I really began to internalize the truth of that concept.

Health becomes very precious to a person in danger of losing it. At a certain point, when I understood I was beginning to lose mine, I decided for my own good to begin adjusting my answers to that ordinary query, "How are you?" I began replying with phrases like "Great," "Very good," and "Excellent." I decided this was best, even though I had not yet fulfilled all my wishes and dreams and even though the world I lived in was not yet perfect. As a result of this simple change, my environment, too, started changing for the better. I became more sociable, and others began to enjoy being around me. Thinking of it now, who really enjoys being around a negative person? Interestingly enough, Confucius proclaimed this truth thousands of years ago, when he held that "the rectification of society begins with rectification of language."

After I decided to take responsibility for my present moment, I realized that, for the first time, those who had hurt me were no longer living in my mind. Upon reaching that point, I started to realize I was no longer angry. I was no longer complaining. I was no longer blaming others or badmouthing them. Because I had taken responsibility for my own situation in life, I no longer felt compelled to do these things.

Living in my new reality has cleared my mind from distortions resulting from my anger, frustration, and anxiety. My relations with others, even with those whom I believed had caused my mental pain, have improved. Realizing the benefits of this change in my thinking, I have decided no longer to carry inside my mind and my heart negative feelings toward anyone or anything. I do not want to be angry anymore, and if I do find myself harboring negative thoughts that incite anger, then I do not want such thoughts to remain in my mind for long.

I cannot say I have been totally successful. I have, however, become more aware of my choices, reactions, and responses to situations and events happening around me. I have also become more aware of states of mind, attitudes, and ways of reacting to others that benefit me instead of dragging me down. I believe I have reached a point where I am in much better control of my thoughts and emotions. Now I understand that I must choose to allow others to draw me into a dynamic that produces anger and hatred or to remain faithful to my stance and sustain the hope that I can bring others to share that stance with me.

I am convinced that we always have a choice between options, whatever our circumstances may be. Regrettably, most people continue to believe that living immersed in pain, suffering, anger, spite, hatred, hurt, and insult constitutes normal human behavior. People wonder how human beings can perpetrate so much violence, so many endless wars, and such great suffering upon their fellow human beings—not to mention the damage they do to the environment. Yet the people who themselves cling to this so-called "normal" behavior rarely stop to consider their own roles in perpetrating and perpetuating suffering. They criticize other human beings for creating a hell on earth, while they are doing the same.

People in that state of mind may be fond of telling others how they should behave without rectifying their own behavior. Often, they have a staunch opinion about what is wrong and how this wrong should and could be rectified—while tending to be unaware of the fact that they have not found real answers, even for themselves. Indeed, they cannot find real answers, because they refuse to internalize their own responsibility at the same time as they continue playing the blame game. They insist that they know who is right and who is wrong. They go on preaching and telling others how to act and how to live their lives. Meanwhile, they continue to create dissension and discord.

The Anteater And The Jaguar

Many people are unaware of how creating conflict or making peace relates to their own internal state of mind. We usually reflect on the outside what we are on the inside. Thus, if we are angry and frustrated, we will most likely channel this anger and frustration in our dealings with others. On the other hand, if we are satisfied, content, and relaxed, then we will reflect this demeanor in our relations with others. If I am unhappy, I probably will not want to see anyone else happy either—misery loves company, as the old saying goes. And likewise, if I am happy, then I will want others to be happy as well.

Our internal challenge is to reach that level, first of all, where we are not living in conflict with ourselves. Our own conflicted personalities give rise to conflicts with others, for a conflicted personality not only guarantees that we will live with intense personal pain but ensures that our relationships with our closest family members, friends, and other people will be tumultuous. Everyone knows that some of the most intense conflicts and some of the highest levels of anger, hatred, and violence exist within families. Stories abound of siblings who no longer speak to one another and of domestic disputes that spin out of control and end in murder.

Responsibility and Conflicts

Throughout the years I have lived at Wahat Assalam, I have given talks and lectures to groups that come to visit our community. For a long time, my talks tended to feature my defense of my own side as a Palestinian, while I blamed the Israelis for the bad things that had happened to my people and me. Those who listened to me have, for the most part, respected me both for my knowledge and my sincerity. But something always seemed to be missing, especially when I addressed Jewish groups—because my intention, for the most part, was not merely to tell them things they did not know about us and to correct some of their misinformation. I always desired more than this: I desired to connect with them in a personal way, so something better could come from our dialogue. This desire, which has been clear to me for many years, resulted from my realization that the best possible resolution of our conflict would have to offer a solution that was good for both of us and included both of us.

A significant change occurred when I started talking to groups in a new way. I dispensed with the "I am right, and you are wrong" approach and began to speak about how we are both responsible for the present stalemate in Palestinian-Israeli relations. Because both parties were responsible, it would take nothing short of the effort of both parties to effect positive change. The positive attitude reflected in my new presentations opened up space for others, for the first time, to feel comfortable enough to admit openly that they, too, were responsible for allowing the stalemate to continue. The will to confess our own responsibility would make it easier for us all to recognize the flaws in our common humanity and even to apologize to one another.

I have finally learned to accept my own flaws and imperfections. I no longer blame and accuse others of being *this* or *that* kind of people. I took responsibility by asking myself what *I* could do to bring about change; I was no longer focused on what others should do for me. By taking responsibility, I was able to change my attitude, my language, and my tone whenever I spoke with others. I became more aware that in order to bring other people to stand alongside me, I needed to assure them that things would be better for us all. I have learned to be very careful not to appear arrogant, patronizing, or disrespectful of others' ideas and viewpoints. I have learned that my failures and my successes have nothing to do with my being either a Palestinian or a Jew, as regrettably some still believe is the case.

Taking responsibility means that, instead of taking the easy way out by blaming others, I need to check myself constantly and find ways I can change and improve my attitudes and the way I present myself. In this way, I can make it easier for others to see my point of view and agree with me. People will come over to our side to stand with us and champion our cause when they feel secure and unthreatened and see that we are also considering their interest as much as our own.

I keep hoping to hear someday an Israeli president and a Palestinian president saying in a common statement, "We are responsible, too."

Twenty-Eight

US AND THEM

While one cause of my mental pain resulted from my social interactions, a second cause has been my Palestinian origin and my Palestinian affiliations. I have witnessed the tragedy that many of my people are caught up in, a tragedy that shows no signs of abating. Sometimes I feel that a solution to the Palestinian question may never be found. This pessimism has only been reinforced by the complexity of the Palestinian question and by my realization that our world, instead of being managed according to justice, is managed to satisfy certain interests and maintain a skewed balance of power.

I have read much about the history of my people. I have also heard numerous stories from my mother and many other relatives and from others who were alive during the period prior to 1948. For the most part, what I have read or heard has evoked in me tremendous mental anguish, depression, and anger. I, too, have witnessed an inordinate share of tragedy throughout my own life, even though I was born seven years after the events of 1948.

The 1956 war in our region began one year after I was born. Britain, France, and Israel invaded Egypt after the Egyptian president at the time, Gamal Abdel Nasser, nationalized the Suez Canal. The first memory of conflict I recall, however, was of the 1967 war. I was about twelve years old when Israel occupied the Egyptian Sinai Peninsula, the Syrian Golan Heights, the West Bank, and the Gaza Strip. The next event that stands out in my memory was Black September of 1970, when thousands of Palestinians in Jordan were killed and tens of thousands made homeless. Next came the 1973 war that Egypt and Syria waged against the Israeli occupation of the Sinai Peninsula and the Golan Heights. Then came the 1975–1990 civil war in Lebanon, which resulted in the killing and murder of tens of thousands of Lebanese, Palestinians, and others. Next, from 1980 to 1988, the First Gulf War was fought between Iraq and Iran. This war had hundreds of thousands of victims. But this was not all that happened during those years: In 1982 Israeli forces invaded Lebanon, and another twenty thousand Palestinians were killed. The First Intifada (1987–1993) resulted in the death of a few thousand mostly Palestinian victims. This Palestinian uprising proceeded alongside the Second Gulf War in 1990. The latter erupted after the Iraqis occupied Kuwait. Later, in 2000, a second Palestinian Intifada began, and while it continued, another few thousand people, both Palestinian and Jewish, were killed. Then, in 2003, the Third Gulf War started when the United States invaded Iraq. The war between Israel and the Lebanese Hezbollah followed in 2006. Next came the war on Gaza in stages, beginning in 2008–09 and resuming in 2012 and again in 2014. Now, war still rages in Syria, where in addition to millions of Syrian victims, there are also Palestinian refugees, who had already been living as refugees in Syria since the events of 1948; these unfortunates were doubly victimized when they got stuck in the middle of still another war, and more of them were either killed or forced yet again to find refuge wherever they could.

Wherever they have ended up living, many of the Palestinian people have had to endure an enormous amount of suffering. This has gone on from after 1948 until the present, especially within the Middle East. I can only wonder whether this tragedy will ever end. Indeed, the more I have searched, the more I have realized the complexity of the problem. The vast amount of individual and collective pain of the Palestinians and the

The Anteater And The Jaguar

Jews has only been exacerbated by their deeply rooted tragic memories. I believe this conflict may indeed be like none other in the entire world. No other cultures have had so much history or so much religion invested in a conflict, at least not to the extent that we have tended to involve God in it. The conflict is also unlike any other, because the entire world is both focused on and divided by it. Never has a conflict had so much political intervention expended and moral involvement invested. This conflict is one of few that could ignite a global war.

Often I have thought about the case of our two peoples as being similar to a description of an encounter between the anteater and the jaguar. In his book, *Life on Earth*, David Attenborough alludes to this story as follows: "There is a tale of the bodies of a jaguar and an anteater being found out in the savannahs, locked together. The anteater had been dreadfully torn by the jaguar's teeth, but its claws were sunk in the jaguar's back" (*Life on Earth*, Fontana/Collins, 1981, 229).

I have often contemplated whether I was cursed to live my life in pain and sadness just because of who and where I am. Or was this experience something I was meant to go through so I could become a better human being? After I had internalized the issue of personal responsibility, I began to have real hope for the first time in my life that our national problem could become resolvable. Taking responsibility means the concerned individual or group must cease expecting that a solution to their problem will come from others. For when the party concerned waits in a suspended state for others to solve their problems, then their ability to think freely and creatively will be inhibited and thwarted.

Is this not our case as Palestinians? We have always waited for others to solve our problem, whether they are the Americans, the Europeans, the Israelis, the Arabs, or the United Nations. It is true that my people did not choose the challenge they now face. It is also true that others forced the challenge upon us. But is this not the way life is? Which one of us knows what to expect from tomorrow? Can we ever expect that our life will always be smooth and free of surprises and challenges, whether individually or collectively? True, the challenge came to us, and it is unfair. We tried our best to protect our rights in this land, though we did not fully succeed. So what can we do now to find our way out of this dark cave we have been cast into?

Taking responsibility in this specific situation means we must be willing to admit that, thus far, we have not made the best decisions. The reason we have not is that anger and pain have shaped most of our attitudes and behaviors. The same, however, can be said of the Israeli-Jewish people. They, too, have made many wrong decisions based on their own experience of anger and pain. Indeed, I believe that famous Israeli statement that the Arabs "never miss a chance to miss a chance" is just as true of them. Still, despite this similarity between us, the fact remains that, until this moment, the Palestinians are suffering more than Jews are within our common conflict. They are, after all, in control of every detail of our lives; when it comes to harm, they can do much more to us than we can do to them.

Therefore, changing the present reality is much more urgent for Palestinians than for Jews, and this means we should figure out the best and quickest way to bring this change to pass. To do this, we must first internalize the fact that we are alone and that only we can create the change we seek. Second, we must internalize the fact that there is no better scenario for Israeli policymakers who wish to perpetuate the status quo than to have to deal with angry and frustrated Palestinians, who, as a result of their anger and frustration, revolt every so often. These revolts provide the Israelis with the excuse to continue their policy of domination and punishment of the Palestinian people.

The Palestinians' situation, on the other hand, is close to impossible, because the international community expects them, in spite of all they have been going through, to show good intentions and demonstrate goodwill toward the Israelis. First, the United States asked the Palestinians to recognize the UN Security Council's Resolution 242. (This was passed after the 1967 war, and accepting it implied recognition of Israel). This was an American precondition to direct talks with Palestinians. The precondition was duly accepted in 1988. Next, Israel requested that Palestinians recognize the state of Israel in writing so that direct talks between them could commence. They agreed to this in 1993, and talks were initiated between the late Israeli Prime Minister Yitzhak Rabin and the late PLO chairman Yasser Arafat. Both leaders exchanged letters. As a result, Israel recognized the PLO as the representative of the Palestinians, and the PLO recognized the state of Israel.

Now the Palestinians are being asked to recognize Israel as a specifically *Jewish* state. Otherwise, they are accused of not being serious about reaching peace with Israel. Indeed, it is possible that if the Palestinians were to agree to such recognition, then they might be requested next to give up officially on their right of return by signing a document to that effect. This would logically follow, as affirming their right of return would contradict their recognizing Israel as a *Jewish* state. If they were to agree to do that, then they might be expected next to confess that they have been the aggressors all through the years of the conflict. In this case, I am afraid they would be requested to extend an apology to the state of Israel.

The Israeli officials need to explain in greater detail what they mean by a *Jewish* state. Would this mean that we, the Israeli-Palestinians (about 20 percent of the population in Israel), would be forever relegated to a second-class status simply by virtue of the fact that we are not Jews? Or would this mean that we might end up being deported to the "state of Palestine"—should that become a reality—if we were to keep complaining? Would most Israelis accept it if any country in the West were to proclaim itself a *Christian* state when considering the rights of the Jewish communities there? Indeed, have the Jews themselves resolved the questions of who is *jewish* (the subject of endless internal wrangling within Jewish society almost everywhere, my Jewish friends tell me) and what a *Jewish state* is? Furthermore, if Israel's leaders believe this request is fair, then why do they never say anything about what they are willing to give to the Palestinians in exchange for the Palestinians' recognition? Could they openly say to the Palestinians that they would grant them a fully independent state if the Palestinians recognized Israel as a Jewish state? Could they say that this recognition would guarantee the

Rayek R. Rizek

Israeli-Palestinians equal rights within Israel? I believe that what is fair and sincere is to offer our opponents something when we ask them to accept our requests. Regrettably, most of the Jews and the Palestinians who claim that all Mandatory Palestine is theirs (Eretz Yisrael or Falasteen) still stop short of asserting that their claim guarantees equal status and equal sharing for all others, too. Whether it is this or that side, basic morality requires that the dream of one side should not be the other side's nightmare.

Are today's Israeli leaders really serious when they talk about peace with the Palestinians? They might desire peace for themselves, of course, but do they fear that introducing changes that in any way might favor the Palestinians would compromise their sole political and administrative authority over the land of *Falasteen/Eretz Yisrael* and its resources? Why should Israelis consider any process that would involve their relinquishing absolute authority? Why should they consider any process that would bring an unwanted partner into their affairs? Furthermore, what would an end to the conflict look like ten, twenty, or forty years into the future? Would the dynamics of peace, for example, end up causing Israel and Palestine to become one entity? And would this reality be helpful for their idea of a separate Jewish state?

Maintaining any status quo has its cost, and it would seem, from the Israeli perspective at least, that the price the state of Israel and its people are paying to maintain the status quo in their favor must seem to them more bearable than the price they might have to "pay" if resolution and reconciliation with the Palestinians were achieved. In spite of the cost, most Israeli Jews see and believe that their life in Israel cannot be compared to their life before the state came into being, when they were (collectively, at least) so vulnerable. They are living out their Jewish life, identity, and culture like never before. They also realize that if it were not for the fact that they are an independent entity, then their voice as Jews would be marginalized.

The Jews in Israel also realize that, without their present ability to leverage power, those who hurt and persecuted them for so long

The Anteater And The Jaguar

might never have extended the apologies to them that they deserved. Furthermore, historians and Christian theologians might never have revised their accounts and theological systems to accommodate their presence on the world stage as an independent state. For the first time in their history, they have a home they can return to in case things go wrong for them elsewhere in the world. In this home, they are no longer subject to the rules and restrictions of lands in which they were a minority. Instead, they are free to determine their own destiny.

Even as a Palestinian, my feelings about this issue are mixed with relief and sadness. I am relieved that this long chapter of hatred and persecution of the Jews has ended, but I am sad my people are the ones who have had to pay the price for this existential improvement that the Jews have long deserved. I am even sadder to be placed in an impossible and unfair situation where we as Palestinians, in our present circumstances, have had to acknowledge the Jewish story with all its pain and complexity, no matter the impact of doing so on our own fate—for if we do not acknowledge it, then we are accused of not understanding them and of not being trustworthy. Here, however, I must reiterate the fact that our particular story of turbulent relations with the Jewish people is only about one hundred years old. As such, it comprises only about a 2 to 3 percent portion of their whole story (of Jewish history). This portion of the story has, moreover, not centered on persecution and anti-Semitism. It has instead mainly centered on a political conflict through which the ordinary, peaceful Arab inhabitants of Palestine have been delegitimized, dehumanized, and outlawed when, to begin with, they were simply minding their own business. This happened because, at some point, our presence in our homeland became an obstacle to the plans that the major World Powers had for the Middle East. Despite all this, I still believe a day will come when these facts will be recognized and apologies will be extended to us, too. Perhaps then, at long last, revisions will be made that portray our story in a more humane way.

One could argue, though, that *not* resolving the Palestinian question has now become a condition for Israel's continued existence as an ethnic state, for as long as the problem remains in a state of suspension, Israel appears justified in not recognizing the need for its Palestinian-Arab population to be counted as equals.

Prior to 1948, when the British Mandate was still in effect, the Jewish community of Palestine already enjoyed an independent political, economic, military, social, and cultural life. It was then that they revived the Hebrew language, founded separate schools, and established institutions of higher learning. At that time, they had their own newspapers and book publishers; their own medical institutions; their own banks and businesses; their own industrial and agricultural productions; their police force and flag, and freedom to display Jewish symbols. They also had their own military forces, which, by the way, produced and stored weapons in secret workshops located under houses at different Jewish settlements, just as the Palestinians of Gaza are doing today.

Therefore, the idea that compromise with the Palestinians would place the Jewish state under constant threat, as many Israeli officials—along with much of the Israeli public—believe, or that it would signal the end of Jewish life in Israel/Palestine, is a fallacy. Such an extreme outcome would, in any event, be impossible to achieve. On the other hand, giving up on their absolute authority and sharing it with a partner who has already been sharing the land with them for many years would seem the better option.

Considering all of the above, I do not believe it is in the best interest of the Palestinians to build on the notion that Israeli Jews are just as interested in a resolution to the conflict as the Palestinians are simply because the Israelis, too, are paying a price for the continuation of the status quo. Most Israeli Jews believe their present sacrifice is the price they must pay to protect the independence they finally gained after three thousand years. They firmly believe that any other reality would be much worse than the present one they are enduring.

We should remember, though, that a large majority of the Israeli population is comprised of simple good-hearted people like us. Like every other nation's majority, they get their knowledge of current events and politics from general newspapers, television broadcasts, and politicians, most of whom are biased and cannot see any different future apart from a linear extension of the present.

I have learned over the years that being weak physically and materially does not have to mean that we can do nothing to change our reality. This is not only a wrongheaded belief, but it is also an excuse that keeps us in a state of oppression. Life, contrary to this belief, is filled with examples where physically and materially weak people, both individually and collectively, have achieved remarkable things.

Twenty-Nine

As a Palestinian

Throughout my life, I have heard people around me, including some of our leaders, put all the blame on others for our problems. "Listen," goes the typical statement on this theme, "we cannot do anything about improving our situation, because we are an oppressed minority and because we are alone." And in general, of course, one cannot deny the fact that minorities, wherever they are in the world, have always had their share of difficulties and obstacles to overcome.

I have already alluded to my own challenges of living as a member of two minorities—as a Palestinian Arab inside the majority Jewish community of Israel and as a member of the Arab Orthodox Christian community among a Muslim Arab majority. I have realized, though, that by no means does living as a member of a minority automatically makes you some kind of loser. There is no such thing as a total loser or a total winner, no matter who you are or what you may have accomplished. I believe that my being a Palestinian and a member of a minority has made me a winner in one very important respect: I have become a much better human being, thanks to the sum total of my experiences in the role I inherited at birth. I have no regrets. I am totally satisfied with my lot in life. I am no longer angry with anybody. I do not blame anyone for anything or envy others for who they are or what they have.

At the beginning of my time living at Wahat Assalam, I thought our life revolved totally around my group, the Palestinians; I was preoccupied with how our group needed to face up to the other group, namely the Jews. I have lived to witness the results of this preoccupation, too. Many conflicts arose within our separate groups, some of which might have been avoided if we had been able to think differently. Thinking differently, however, was difficult, because we all were taught certain things and took certain things for granted as we were brought up. This was true whether we happened to be Palestinian or Jewish. Regardless of which group we belonged to, we believed we needed to agree with everything we had learned about ourselves and the other side. Indeed, anyone who believed anything that deviated from the strictly partisan views of his national or religious group ran the risk of being labeled a traitor.

At some point, however, I let go of trying to live up to these arbitrary designations and polarized divisions. After that, I started to enjoy more success in bringing about changes as an individual. As an individual, it was much easier to attract people from both groups to join me in my stance on an issue. When, on the other hand, we speak only for our specific national or religious group, we end up automatically alienating others and causing them to mistrust and fear us.

Alas, in the status quo that exists outside my community, people are still divided according to their national and religious affiliations. Outside our community, no mixed political party that includes people from all groups has been authentically successful. Even though cross sections of these various groups may share similar concepts and human values with groups that they officially disagree with, cooperating across the boundaries that define these groups has at best been short-lived. Once upon a time, for example, a small Israeli communist party, originally almost equally represented by Arabs and Jews, later became mostly Arab with only a few Jews. Attempts between Jews and Arabs to form political alliances have been sporadic. The most prominent, the Progressive

Rayek R. Rizek

List for Peace, was represented in the Israeli parliament between 1984 and 1992. The late Israeli Jewish general and peace activist Mati Peled, in concert with the Israeli Palestinian political activist and human-rights lawyer Muhammad Miari, founded this alliance, but it is now defunct. Most Jews and Palestinians are afraid to leave their circle and make alliances with people from other groups. This seems to be the case even though members of a particular national or religious group may have deep philosophical differences from others within their own group.

Because of all the mistreatment and persecution the Jews have gone through during their history, their children are brought up not to trust anyone. The Palestinians, on the other hand, think they are too weak to change their situation. It would seem that both groups are stuck in a mind-set of victimhood, which convinces them that initiating any move toward reconciliation is entirely up to the other side, when in fact, the change should be mutual.

I should nevertheless like to think that Palestinians are in a better position than Jews to initiate a change in the status quo that exists in this land. Though materially and militarily, the Israelis are more powerful than the Palestinians, still I believe, despite all the Palestinians have been going through, they do feel more secure *psychologically* than do the Israeli Jews. This has nothing to do with any genetic differences; rather, it is due to the fact that the collective experiences and memories of Palestinian Arabs have on the whole been less traumatic than collective Jewish experiences and memories.

Neither are the Israeli Jews as secure psychologically as the Palestinians, because Israel is surrounded by Arab countries. This fact may add to a greater feeling of security among Palestinians, but for the Jews, it produces tremendous insecurity. We Palestinians are, furthermore, still very deeply rooted in this land. We have no doubts about our rights to be in it or our connections to it. This is true in spite of the many arguments, theories, and convictions—both modern and ancient—that others have advanced. We know, too, that Israel cannot and will not be able to get rid of us. Another expulsion or exodus of Palestinians from this land is

The Anteater And The Jaguar

very unlikely, as the lessons of 1948 (and, to a lesser extent, 1967) have been learned.

It is nonetheless sad to hear many Israelis still putting all the blame on the Palestinians for the present conflict while demonstrating their unwillingness to acknowledge their part in its creation and perpetuation. The Zionist movement and, later, the state of Israel have always viewed us as an obstacle, and though almost one hundred years have passed, this attitude has remained largely unchanged.

The Israeli official policy in general is anti-Palestinian Arab, and this is no secret. To hear different Israeli voices openly propose some novel plan or other about how to get rid of Palestinian Arabs is not uncommon. Some still talk about forcibly transferring Palestinians to other countries, while others suggest paying them money as an incentive to leave and to go elsewhere. Conferences are held regularly, books are written, secret studies are carried out, and political decisions are made to determine ways that the demographic "threat" can be ameliorated. Some Israeli officials regularly refer to the Palestinian population in the country, and its natural growth rate, as a ticking time bomb. I often wonder whether these officials are truly able to sleep serenely at night. I suspect that some of the choices they have made regarding the Palestinian issue must, on some level, haunt them.

I am not certain whether the first Zionists foresaw the life they were passing on to their descendants or whether they had a more positive vision that just failed to materialize. As I see it, the story from one generation to the next has been one of continuous worry, fear, and anxiety; the ongoing need for military security; and wars. I therefore do not envy them—nor do I want to be in their place.

The Israelis, however, are not the only ones in the Middle East who have had to contend with the demographic issues to which I have alluded. Regrettably, Arab countries such as Jordan and Lebanon have had to deal with the problem as well. Within Jordan, many times political arguments center on the fact that Palestinian Arabs make up the majority of the population. The majority of both the Palestinian Arabs and the Jordanian Arabs are Sunni Muslims, and many of them are related. Indeed, they were a homogenous human population long before the end of the First World War, when they were divided by an artificial boundary inscribed on a regional map in green ink with the stroke of a pen wielded by foreign colonial powers.

The problem is much more complicated in Lebanon, whose overwhelmingly Arab-majority population is comprised of a tapestry of some eighteen disparate religious and ethnic communities. These are governed under a constitution that reflects the multicommunal makeup of the country: the president is supposed to be a Maronite Christian, the prime minister is a Sunni Muslim, and the speaker of the parliament is a Shia Muslim. These three major communities share the ministries with other, smaller Christian and Muslim communities. It is worth mentioning that Iraq has, since 2003, adopted a similar system where the president is Kurd, the prime minister is Shia Muslim, and the speaker of the parliament is Sunni Muslim. In both cases, the president has limited powers.

In Lebanon, in addition, there are about four hundred thousand Palestinian residents still classified as refugees. Most of these still live in camps erected following the expulsion from Palestine in 1948. An aspect of the Israeli plan to resolve the Palestinian problem calls for Lebanon to absorb these Palestinian refugees by granting them Lebanese citizenship. This would give them a place of permanent residence and eliminate any need for them to return to their original homes in what now has become the state of Israel. Again, Israel's official position has been not to allow the return of the Palestinian refugees, because the state believes this return would relegate the Jews to a minority status in Palestine/Israel.

At the same time, Lebanon refuses to consider the idea of absorbing the Palestinian refugees, because the large majority of these refugees are Sunni Muslims. The Lebanese fear that absorbing them all would alter the communal structure of their own country, upsetting the existing balance among Sunni, Shia, Christians, Druze, and others. The Palestinian refugees, too, refuse to support the idea of being absorbed into Lebanon as a solution to their problem, because they refuse to relinquish the idea

The Anteater And The Jaguar

of returning home to Palestine. Citizenship aside, I cannot understand the official Lebanese attitude toward this community of Palestinians. Their deplorable living conditions are among the worst in any of the Palestinian refugee camps in the Middle East, and the numerous restrictions imposed on them by Lebanon curtail their ability to work, infringe on their civil rights, and hamper their ability to travel.

Because of the consequences we Palestinians have suffered as a result of the ways in which the Zionist plan has been implemented, we generally tend to be furious at the lack of compassion demonstrated by some Arab regimes. This anger extends as well to many Western countries, as we believe they, too, are complicit in the creation and the perpetuation of our tragedy and ongoing agony. For the Western world to turn a blind eye to our humane and just cause while adopting the Zionist narrative in order to apologize to the Jewish people or make restitution to them for past atrocities committed against them is immoral and unacceptable. Two wrongs do not make a right! Regrettably, though, the dynamic that results in having people's rights either considered or ignored, and the decision whether to hold the oppressor responsible or instead to blame the victim, is more about the chess game of alliances than it is about a concern for justice and human dignity for the oppressed.

Besides being angry with the Arab regimes and the Western powers, we are angry with the Israelis, and they are angry with us. But with so much history of oppression in their collective memory, I fear Israeli Jews are unable to draw the distinction between this anger, resulting from our recent shared experience in Palestine, and that other anger, which has accumulated over centuries of painful experiences having nothing to do with Palestinians. This, I believe, exaggerates their anxiety and prompts their use of disproportionate force against us, which in turn complicates and hinders any attempt at reconciliation between us. The resulting state of mind on both sides is a recipe for unending violence—an inescapable, vicious circle that may go on for many years to come with further wars, more victims, and even greater pain and suffering. Both peoples are equally stuck in the suicidal situation that now exists and are unable, for different reasons, to remedy it. Our only recourse seems to be to continue this mutual dehumanization, blaming, and slaughter. Clearly, no matter what each side does, and no matter how much force each side uses, nothing will change the binational and multiethnic reality of this land or the historical and religious convictions of each side concerning their rights over it.

I think it is imperative that we dwell on the fact that most of us living today are heirs of a situation we had no hand in creating. However, by keeping the conflict going, we are preparing the next generations and our future progeny to inherit our troubles. If we Palestinians are truly sincere when we say we have nothing against the Jews per se but that our problem is with Zionism; if we do not want to just switch positions with them so that the roles of oppressed and oppressor are simply reversed; if we do not want to give up our right to return home, or cannot do so; and if we want to put an end to the seemingly endless Israeli conditions and restrictions upon us—then why can we not suggest a solution to the conflict that, by including everybody, will recognize our shared natural rights as human beings first and foremost?

Again, I do not think Zionism entails one monolithic perspective. Like all ideologies, some followers are fanatical and radical, while others are liberal and moderate. From my point of view, if Zionism is about believing in and promoting the historical and religious rights of the Jews in Palestine without excluding or diminishing our rights as Palestinian Arabs in the same land, then I have no problem with it. And if the Jews believe they have the right to return even two thousand years after they were massacred and expelled by the Romans, then they should not deny this right to my people, who have no such history vis-à-vis the Jews. We are claiming our right to go home after an interval of less than seventy years, when the memory is still alive and fresh; when many still have the keys to their houses and businesses; when they still possess deeds to their properties; and when each knows the specific name of the village, town, or even the neighborhood to which they, their parents, and grandparents belonged before 1948.

The Anteater And The Jaguar

Therefore, with regard to religious and historical claims, I do not mind anyone claiming such rights, as long as they are not exclusive of others who have similar claims. Many times I hear people arguing and claiming exclusive rights to the land of Palestine/Israel on the basis of their Jewish or Islamic religion. I end up wondering, however, where such claims leave me, because I am neither Jewish nor Muslim. Does this mean my rights are irrelevant, even though I was born here and belong to a family that has lived in this land for about four hundred years?

I cannot understand how anyone can claim exclusive rights on the basis of religion. Does saying "I am Jewish," "I am Christian," or "I am Muslim" in any way guarantee such exclusive rights, without regard to how authentically religious a person is or how he or she practices that faith? If someone is a thief, a criminal, or a liar, can that person still claim to be a pure Jew, a pure Christian, or a pure Muslim? Moreover, for those who say, "But our holy book says God gave us this land," I believe—as various commentators have frequently stated—that God's bequest of the land to his people is conditional upon their *not oppressing, not killing, and not expelling* those who are deemed to be strangers in the land. Should we not all fear the God who will judge us according to our deeds? Surely, since Jews, Christians, and Muslims alike believe in a God who will one day judge the world, we should all be wary of committing the sin of presumption. No one can claim they are God's fortunate favorites simply because of who they are, how they pray, how much they pray, or how they dress. Rather, it is the condition of the heart that God will be concerned with on the Day of Judgment.

Thirty

To Divide Or Not To Divide

The question of dividing up historical Palestine has been argued back and forth over many years. Even today, various interested parties and observers argue that some form of geographic partition is the only viable option, while others insist it is not. What is clear by now, though, is that territorial division, far from ending the conflict, has only exacerbated it, and both peoples have had to pay dearly in consequence, both in bloodshed and in tears. As concerns the no-division option, clearly we are living it in reality right now and have been doing so since June 1967. By the end of the 1948 war, the area of Mandatory Palestine had been dissected into three pieces as follows: Israel, with 78 percent of the land; the Gaza strip under Egypt's control, with 1.6 percent of the land; and the West Bank (so called because it is west of the Jordan River) under Jordan's control, with about 20 percent of the land. Nearly two decades thereafter, as a result of the 1967 war, the fractured land was reunified to encompass both its Jewish and Palestinian populations (excluding refugees living elsewhere, of course). The question of partition or no partition thus came to the fore once again.

Exhaustive efforts, both locally and internationally, have been invested in attempting to reach a solution to the Israeli-Palestinian conflict. These

The Anteater And The Jaguar

efforts have become more intensive and more direct between the Israelis and the Palestinians recently, specifically since the agreements known as the Oslo Accords, signed in Washington, DC, in September 1993 (Oslo I) and in Taba, Egypt, in 1995 (Oslo II). Nonetheless, thousands more on both sides have been killed during the twenty-three years since the signatures were affixed to Oslo I, and achieving a resolution to the conflict based on a two-state solution has never seemed more complicated than it does today. I myself have begun to wonder if this solution remains viable at all, especially if we consider all the tangible changes Israel has managed to introduce on the ground, both in Jerusalem and across the entire West Bank. In light of these actions, the two-state solution seems more and more impractical with every passing day. Perhaps we ought to be asking ourselves, given that the division of the land was not exactly a success during 1948, how some form of partition could possibly work today, now that circumstances have become infinitely messier and much more complicated.

Before 1948, the majority of those within the Zionist movement were unwilling to consider any solution apart from an independent Jewish national home in Palestine, which they viewed as the only viable solution for the question of Jewish statehood, more so following the horrors of the Holocaust. However, the Palestinians at that time were unwilling to accept this idea; they opposed partition, because they deemed it impossible to implement without causing drastic harm to numerous existing Palestinian-Arab communities scattered throughout the land. By the end of the 1948 war, tragically, that tapestry of communities had suffered damage even more disastrous than the proposed partition plan had been expected to cause.

Moreover, the two-state solution can address only part of the lingering Palestinian question. What of the right of return for Palestinian refugees? This right, which immediately following 1948 was secured (by UN General Assembly Resolution No. 194) for the purpose of guaranteeing the return of more than seven hundred thousand refugees, is cited now as the basis for the right of more than four million Palestinians in the diaspora to return home to Palestine. The majority of Palestinians refuse to relinquish this right, whereas the majority of Israeli Jews refuse to accept it as legitimate.

Could there, after all that has changed, be two separate states now? If so, then how would we draw the lines? Could there also be a separation between the two peoples, and if so, how would this separation be accomplished? Or could we coexist in the same land as equals? If coexistence won't work, why not? What then could the solution be?

An Undivided Land

My idea is simple: unite our efforts as Palestinians within the space of Mandatory Palestine and act through a civil-rights movement to bring equality and fair sharing in one entity for all its people. To succeed, however, we must become much better organized. At the moment, the Palestinians are divided into three entities—those living in the Gaza Strip, those living in the West Bank, and those living inside Israel. In addition, there are the Palestinians of the diaspora.

There is no reason we cannot become unified in our effort. We are one people with a common history, literature, and culture, so why can we not unite? Are we really that different from one another, in the Israeli-Zionist point of view? Aren't we all considered a demographic threat for the Jewish state, whether we are living inside Israel, in the West Bank, or in the Gaza Strip?

Why is it that the Israeli Palestinians have never been represented in the Palestinian National Council (the parliament in exile), as has been the case with the rest of the Palestinians? Is it too late to convene a new parliament that will represent the interests of all Palestinians—as the Zionist movement managed to do for Jews more than a hundred years ago? At that time, Jews collectively were hardly a unified voice, for they were citizens of many different countries and spoke many different languages. I believe that if we Palestinians were to face the world and the Israelis with a unified purpose, then the political situation would be totally different from what it is now. We would be requesting a solution for all Palestinians and all Jews without wasting time, energy, and more lives trying to implement partial solutions for this group and that, because the most substantial problem began not in 1967 but in 1948.

If the Israelis would reject a solution that divides them geographically and politically within this land, then should not we Palestinians likewise reject any solution that would divide *us* again within this land? Regrettably, it seems to me that many of us have accepted our being partitioned into West Bank, Israeli, and Gaza Palestinians.

Some Palestinian families from East Jerusalem have petitioned the Neve Shalom community to live in our village, but some of our own Palestinian members, to the surprise and disbelief of our Jewish members, have rejected those petitions. They base their rejection on their conviction that accepting Jerusalemite families would somehow legitimize the Israeli annexation of East Jerusalem, which was enacted right after the 1967 war.

An official from the Palestinian Authority in Ramallah told me personally once that we should not accept such families. At the time, I questioned why every Jewish person could apply to live in our community and have the potential to be accepted regardless of his or her place of birth, while certain Palestinians could not, simply because they had been born in occupied East Jerusalem. How could we expect the Israelis to recognize us as one people when we did not recognize ourselves as such? Furthermore, who has the authority to say we Palestinians must accept the artificial borders that now divide us?

The fact remains that there are more than six million Palestinian Arabs living inside historical Palestine who are subject to Israeli rule (including military rule), alongside an almost similar number of Jews (all subject to Israeli civil law). The Palestinians, however, are treated as second-class citizens or worse—for Israel assigns them to one class that is Israeli, a second class that is East Jerusalemite, a third class that lives in the West Bank, or a fourth class that inhabits the Gaza Strip. Even the West Bank Palestinian population is subdivided based on three different administrative divisions into areas A, B, and C. This last fragmentation dates to the Oslo Accords (Oslo II), under which areas A and B include the major West Bank Palestinian cities and their nearby villages, together representing an area of less than 30 percent of the total land area of the West Bank under joint Palestinian and Israeli administration. Meanwhile, area C, which comprises more than 70 percent of the area of the West Bank, is under full Israeli administration (run by something called the Civil Administration, a perfectly Orwellian term, since it reports to the Israeli Ministry of Defense).

No matter what excuses Israel's leadership keeps offering for this state of affairs, they are not absolved of their moral responsibility to search for a humane overall solution to this problem. From my point of view, taking moral responsibility should not be only political; it should also be Jewish, as Israel considers itself not just another state but a *Jewish* state, whose founders, quoting the Bible, promised it would be "a light unto the nations."

I have talked about the idea of an undivided land for the past few years, even though I am acutely aware of the complexity of the conflict. I know many arguments could be made against this possibility. Just as many arguments, however, can be made against a partition solution. Yet while arguments can be proffered that cast doubt on any possible solution, examples can also be offered in favor of those kinds of solutions—including some that have been implemented, in more or less parallel form, elsewhere. There will always be pessimists who look at the glass as half-empty and optimists who see the glass as half-full. Although there will always be doubters and believers, I choose to wager on the side of the believers. I think I am right in making this wager, because doubt and fear have never produced human progress. Only an optimistic faith that casts away fear and doubt can do that.

Not only should we wager on an optimistic faith, but compassion both divine and human should also motivate us to arrive at solutions that will alleviate suffering for everybody. Removing people from hearth and home can hardly alleviate suffering. However, efforts to keep the country in one piece can help to ease it. If the Jews cannot, for whatever reasons, find a way to inaugurate this change, then I as an individual will attempt to move things ahead in that direction, and I will encourage others to do the same. I will do this because I do not want any of us to have to opt for a life of constant anxiety and worry, which is the kind of atmosphere we are living in now.

I believe some Palestinians would respond positively to my suggestion that the solution to the problem is to grant equal citizenship to everyone living within the borders of Eretz Yisrael/Falasteen. Some, of course, will balk at the suggestion and say, "Do you think the Jews will accept such a solution?" But my reply is this: "Why not?" If we agree, first of all, that the Israeli Jews, like us and like people in every other nation, are not copies of one another and, second of all, that our intention is not to deceive them or to displace them, then *why not*? Sometimes I wonder how the Israelis would react if we raise their flag with ours in the course of a movement for equality and peace. I really wonder about the immense power that such symbols have on our psychology.

It should be clear that a viable solution would be just as much about liberating them as it is about liberating ourselves. After all, we are all victims of the present situation, whether we happen to be the oppressed or the oppressors. As the African American singer Marian Anderson once said, "As long as you keep a person down, some part of you has to be down there to hold him down, so it means you cannot soar as you otherwise might." This is so very true.

The great civil-rights leader Martin Luther King Jr. had many reasons to be angry and to speak out in anger about the oppression his people had endured for centuries. However, realizing that the liberation of the oppressor must be a prerequisite for achieving the liberation of the oppressed, the dream he talked about was intended to include everybody: *my children and your children*.

We must therefore be willing to declare that we have no problem with the presence of Jews in our homeland, as long as their Zionism does not exclude us and recognizes us as equals. We must be willing as well to omit from any existing or proposed Palestinian constitution all words that would contradict our recognition of them as equals. If full equality is our ultimate aim, then I do not see any more humane way to achieve it between our two peoples than this. We must not, however, wait any longer for them to take the first step, for the situation is much more urgent and critical for us than it is for them.

I say that we Palestinians need to be inclusive of Jews and recognize their equal rights, even though I know the state of Israel and its founders did not proclaim anything regarding our rights in Palestine, nor did they fulfill their promises of full equality toward us as Israeli Palestinians, as these promises were affirmed in the Israeli Declaration of Independence of 1948.

I make the above statements because the challenge in life is not to become like others you are critical of; rather, the challenge is to bring others over to your side and help them see that your claims are moral, just, and sincere. This can be achieved through speech that is not angry and that does not frighten others. Angry words spoken in a fit of rage are only "good" for the ego that likes to think of itself as always right.

I find it sad that so many still cling to wishful and unrealistic thoughts that total separation between the two peoples in this land is achievable. Some still think the country should be emptied of the other people; some still think universal equality is more dangerous than subjugation of the other. These ways of thinking, however, have led only to stalemate and dead ends. Working toward a solution that allows our two peoples to coexist in one country on an equal basis would be a better way forward. We could consider a kind of confederation. We could have two separate parliaments and an additional joint intermediary one. We could have a high court of justice with equal representation for Jews and Palestinians representing all the different communities. We could even have two presidents and two governments. Or there could be a kind of rotation in some positions, like what we had once in our own little community of Wahat Assalam, until enhanced mutual trust made it less relevant. We could also have two different flags, or we could make a new one

The Anteater And The Jaguar

that would include the Star of David, the cross, and the crescent. We could also keep the two names of Israel and Palestine, or we might go to the original name, the Land of Canaan—since Canaan was, after all, a grandson of Noah and hence a common ancestor—or we could call the land by the name it will deserve someday in reality: the Holy Land. And if our different communal and religious affiliations within our own Arab-Palestinian community were to prove a cause for disagreements, then we could suggest a system that would allow rotation between the Muslims, the Christians, and the Druze over the three main positions of the presidency, the premiership, and the chairing of the parliament. We could also formulate other ideas to further guarantee that diverse material, political, and psychological needs are addressed to the full satisfaction of everybody.

Why can't any Palestinian, whether living in Israel, the West Bank, or the Gaza Strip become a member of the same Palestinian Parliament, when any Israeli Jew can run for the Israeli parliament without regard to where he or she is living, whether within Israel, the West Bank, or even the Syrian Golan Heights?

From many examples coming to us from all over our world, we can learn of societies where social and ethnic tensions and conflicts were even more complicated than ours. Many of these have found formulas that satisfy everyone, enabling their people to live in peace, while others remain stuck in conflicts and wars. In our case, all the formulas tried so far have been a shared failure. They have failed despite the fact that both sides have highly qualified people. Counting inside and outside of Falasteen/Eretz Yisrael, our combined population of Jews and Palestinians worldwide is only about twenty-five million, and we really do have plenty of room for everyone. Just for comparison, the area of what was Mandatory Palestine is about thirty-two thousand square kilometers, with a present population of a bit more than thirteen million Jews and Arabs; compare that to Hong Kong, with over seven million people living on only 1,104 square kilometers, or Singapore, with about 5.5 million people living on just 716 square kilometers. With all our knowledge and qualifications, with all our good hearts united, and with our common love for this land, I believe the Palestinians and the Jews together could create a miracle here. I believe there is a place for everybody and that the right to return—the right to come home to the shared homeland—should not remain limited to the Jews (who have it now) or to the Palestinians (who do not yet have it) but should be granted to everyone equally.

I believe this right is much more in the nature of a moral right and a human right than it is a political issue. And I believe that through living under a constitution that says we are all equal, we will end up sharing a reality that will transcend national and ethnic lines, and we will end up divided and united around common economic interests, moral values, and issues, just like what our life in the Oasis of Peace has become. Personally, when Israel recognizes and proclaims these rights—the right to come home and to live here in equality—for my people, too, I will not hesitate for a moment to raise the Israeli flag on the roof of my house.

A Divided Land

So far, Israel's approach to democracy has managed to keep all power in the hands of the Jewish majority. Partly because they are so few in number and partly due to politics, the Palestinian-Arab-Israelis in Israel's legislature, the Knesset, have been able to provide meaningful solutions for very few of the problems of real concern to the Arab minority within Israel, most but not all of them budget-related: lack of infrastructure, barriers to adequate city planning (despite competent local initiatives that are mostly ignored), housing shortages, environmental threats, equal access to high-quality health care, equal investment in education, and the refusal by government to recognize and regularize existing Arab communities long relegated to the Orwellian limbo of "unrecognized."

Every time efforts are made to organize a coalition to form a new government, the Arab legislators are excluded. Indeed, if they are accorded any consideration (rare), it is only as shadow partners and not real ones.

The Anteater And The Jaguar

Their participation as elected members of the Knesset makes for good propaganda (Look! Arabs serve in the Knesset!), but since they are routinely dealt out of the political poker game before it begins, their mere presence is not operationally very significant.

When the late Israeli Prime Minister Yitzhak Rabin undertook to form his coalition in 1992 and to endorse the Oslo agreement in the legislature in 1993, he managed to obtain a majority only with the support of the five Arab members who at the time represented two Arab parties. In return for this favor, they were promised that some of their sector's ongoing problems would be solved. Even then, however, the opposition criticized Rabin, because his majority was not all Jewish.

It is true that most Palestinian Israelis do not serve in the Israeli army. At the same time, it is also true that the taxes paid by Palestinian Israelis comprise a significant portion of the state budget, which has never (thus far) been allocated on an equal per-capita basis between Jewish and Arab citizens.

Much more could be said, in general and in detail, against the policies of the state of Israel regarding Palestinian Israelis individually and collectively. The important point here is that we can choose either to continue arguing, accusing, and complaining or to propose new ideas that would change the situation in this land for the better.

Even if the idea of the undivided land is too complicated to promote, as many people from both sides believe, then perhaps we could accept the divided-land solution without making the evacuation of established Jewish settlements necessary. A solution as generous in spirit as this one would neutralize much of the Israeli opposition and offer us a great opportunity to model for the Israelis how they might more generously absorb the Israeli-Palestinian minorities within their state. Demonstrating by our example how coexistence between Palestinians and Jews is possible, we could start by declaring that the settlers could remain in the Palestinian state as equal citizens like all other citizens.

On an even more positive note, I recently heard a presentation in our community by an Israeli and a Palestinian about the idea of two states with open borders. This group is an initiative by Meron Rapoport, an Israeli journalist from Tel Aviv, and Awni Almishni, a Palestinian political activist from Beit Lahem who spent twelve years in Israeli prisons. Their motto is "One Homeland, Two States." I believe that their proposal is the most humane idea presented thus far for the resolution of the Israeli-Palestinian conflict.

I know that what I am suggesting here will be difficult for many Palestinians to accept and that it will be totally rejected by the Israeli establishment and the majority of Israeli settlers. But we Palestinians would not lose much by making such a declaration. If the Israelis were to accept it, we would gain an opportunity to prove our sincerity; if they were to reject it, then it would be their challenge to present a better, more humane solution.

Jerusalem

East Jerusalem is often analyzed separately, because it was claimed as part of the unified and eternal capital of the state of Israel. Since that step, however, it has remained easy to notice the discrimination practiced against its Palestinian population by successive Israeli administrations, whether in Jerusalem's city hall or nationally. The infrastructure of Arab neighborhoods is clearly underdeveloped, to put it mildly, when compared to the infrastructure supporting Jewish neighborhoods in and around Jerusalem.

In addition, the Palestinian inhabitants of the city of Jerusalem hold the status of "permanent residents" of the state of Israel, rather than citizenship, entitling them to vote in local elections but not in elections for representatives to the Knesset (parliament).

Since 1967, and even more so since more draconian policies were promulgated in 1995, this permanent-residency status has caused thousands of Palestinians to lose their right to continue living in Jerusalem or to return to it if they have left (typically to study or work abroad for more than a few years). From any objective standpoint, it is a very strange practice that Palestinians are not allowed to return to live in the place of their birth at the same time that any Jewish person from anywhere can automatically become a citizen of Israel while having no relation by birth to the land. In addition to the East-Jerusalem Palestinians, many similar cases can be cited that involve Arab-Israeli citizens whose spouses were denied the permits they needed to allow them to stay in Israel because they happened to be from the West Bank or the Gaza Strip.

I only wish the Palestinian leadership would consider withdrawing its opposition to allowing Palestinian residents of East Jerusalem to participate in electing Jerusalem's municipal (Israeli) government. This is, after all, something that Palestinian residents of East Jerusalem are permitted under Israeli law. As of this writing, the population of Jerusalem is comprised of half a million Jews and three hundred thousand Palestinians (according to the Central Bureau of Statistics of Israel). Might Palestinian participation in voting have an influence on who would become mayor of Jerusalem? Could not a Palestinian's presence in the city council influence and shape the policy of the city regarding major issues, such as the wrongful confiscation of Palestinian property, the unlawful demolition of Palestinian houses, the unbending refusal to issue building permits to Palestinian residents, and their routine exclusion from participation in city planning regarding their neighborhoods? What could be more important at the moment than considering ways to create and to guarantee better and more humane living conditions for Jerusalem's Palestinians? Consider the previously mentioned example of Upper Nazareth/Natzrat Illit (chapter 2).

Note that Arab East Jerusalem, due to its annexation by Israel right after the June 1967 war, is not subject to the military rule (the "Civil Administration") Israel created to control the rest of the West Bank and originally the Gaza Strip (the latter is now technically no longer occupied but effectively is still under Israel military control of its borders, airspace, seafront, and access to the outside world). Hence the Palestinians of the annexed part of East Jerusalem and its surroundings have generally had much more freedom of movement within Israel than have Palestinian residents of the West Bank and Gaza Strip. In addition, the extension of Israeli law, jurisdiction, and administration to include East Jerusalem explains why most Palestinian publications were based in East Jerusalem from 1967 (under Israeli occupation, freedom of the press and freedom to publish were not available in the rest of the occupied territories) until the advent of the Palestinian authority in 1993, when much of this activity shifted to Ramallah.

My impression is that Israelis—the public and the government—are relatively indifferent to the refusal of Palestinians thus far to vote in Jerusalem's municipal elections. Moreover, I believe Palestinian participation could create changes that would not only enhance the material well-being of East Jerusalem residents but also create more humane relationships between all the inhabitants of the city. If East Jerusalem Palestinians don't seize the initiative, no help will be forthcoming from elsewhere, because despite their very real distress and all their appeals for external aid, no solution or promise of help has come from the outside—not from the Arabs, not from the Muslims, not from America or Europe, and not from the United Nations. Meanwhile, Israeli plans for the city and its suburbs move ahead regardless. The participation of the Jerusalemite Palestinians in the city elections need not necessarily signify, as many Palestinians fear, our acceptance of Israel's annexation of the Arab part of the city. We could decide unilaterally that this would be a temporary stage until a comprehensive Israeli-Palestinian political agreement is achieved.

Until we see what God's map is for this region, nothing can justifiably be called sacred geography. What is truly sacred is not a piece of land but our willingness to allow the inner territory of all our lives to become sacred. This can happen only if we meet the moral challenge of extending our goodwill to others. This includes our willingness to recognize others' rights despite artificial political borders. My understanding of God's map is that it is not designed to cause pain to anyone.

Every reality, whether dismal or promising, is a product of a process. Dreaming about a better reality, however, does not require that we

The Anteater And The Jaguar

answer all questions optimally from the beginning. What is important is that we start with good intentions. The processes arising out of these intentions might then carry us onward to better outcomes, perhaps even vastly better than dreamed of. Wahat Assalam began as the dream of one man whose intentions were noble. Had we been required before embracing his idea to find answers for every problem that might arise or solutions for every eventuality we might encounter along the path, then nothing would have ever come of his vision. Even now we struggle and fumble our way through difficulties. We do not have an answer for every problem, and we never will. Yet our willingness to respect our differences and to care about one another has enabled us, despite all our limitations, to create a small miracle that may be the closest thing to what the Promised Land was meant to be.

An example on a larger scale is Europe, where, after perhaps the bloodiest conflicts in human history (World Wars I and II), leaders decided to put aside national grievances and differences and embrace a new future. It was mainly the good intentions of those involved that brought a new era there.

During my stay in Bradford, England, in 2000–2001, I used to listen to the local affiliate of the BBC when it transmitted a few minutes of live discussions from the British Parliament in addition to its program of classical music and soft pop. To my surprise, one lively parliamentary discussion centered on the passing of a law intended to require farmers raising pigs to provide piglets with toys, because piglets like to play with toys just as puppies do. Of course, animal-rights activists favored the proposal. Others, however, opposed the bill, because it would require significant additional costs for the farmers.

Listening to this discussion made me wonder about the extremes we manage to live with in this world. One parliament gives itself over to the luxury of discussing the rights of piglets, while others still get stuck in discussions over whether minorities should be forbidden the right to use their own language, the right to commemorate their national occasions, and the right to teach their own history. Some might think that granting piglets rights is almost insane, but it gives those of us struggling for basic human rights reason to hope. If the rights of pigs can actually become the concern of a society, then may there not be hope that the rights of human beings in our part of the world might one day be considered, too?

It still amazes me that some countries still insist on choosing governing systems that have proven to be inhumane, easily corrupted, and futile instead of choosing a system that has proven to work more effectively and humanely. All in all, there are many models of governance in this world that work and others that do not. Clearly, the systems that promote dignity and equality for all citizens, despite myriad differences among them, have proven much more effective in the long run than have systems that fail to guarantee those things. We can see the contrast in quality of life, judged by any criteria imaginable, enjoyed by those who choose to live by the most enlightened moral values and human achievements, compared with those who still insist on organizing principles based on irrelevant convictions and ideas from ages long past. Why do we continue to insist on choosing the hard and costly path that has been tried, to their sorrow, by so many others before us? What makes us think our story, employing the same methods, is going to reach a different conclusion? When will we stop trying to reinvent the wheel?

Thirty-One

The Choice is Ours

I have searched for the good things that have happened in our shared human history to show how world peace is possible. I want to dwell on these things, hoping they may become possible again. I have also decided *not* to spend my life digging up stories of past atrocities simply for the purpose of sustaining enmity and hatred among peoples on this planet. I choose to remember them only for the purpose of avoiding them, but I do not want to fashion them into a weapon that will injure others.

In the spectrum of choice bounded by these two options, we reflect on what is inside ourselves. If we live with a tumultuous and conflicted personality, then we will seek to satisfy our psychological needs by reveling in conflicts and enjoying despair. We will try continuously to feed them and sustain them. On the other hand, if we live in peace and contentment with ourselves and other people, then we will strengthen and feed this psychological state. We will do so by connecting to a bright hope instead of giving in to crippling despair, by exercising a positive faith instead of clinging to paralyzing doubt, and by relating to others in a spirit of love that seeks unity and forgiveness rather than offering ourselves as fuel for endless, exhausting conflict. We must choose between being on the side of destruction or the side of construction.

Rayek R. Rizek

How many media pundits, politicians, and so-called experts on international politics and relations appear every evening on television, using their positions of influence to convince people about the need to use force and to wage more wars against others? How many popular religious leaders use their positions of authority to spread hatred and enmity among people when they are supposed to be promoting tolerance and mutual respect? How much responsibility does the film industry bear for sometimes retelling history in a distorted manner and for reinforcing harmful stereotypes that feed anger and hatred among people and justify future wars? How many of these people of influence try to convince us that the violence of our enemies results from their inborn evil natures? Why do they avoid the modern sciences of psychology and sociology, which can give us a much better rational understanding for the reasons underlying human behavior? How many of these people of influence tend to explain current events without relating to the context provided by past events that could have motivated what happens today? Is it not the case that much of the tale of our human history, after all, is an accumulation of injustice, violence, and error prompting us to perpetrate yet more injustice, more violence, and similar mistakes? Who are those people we are hurting and victimizing if not our brothers and our sisters, since we were all created in God's image? I wonder why, thus far, we have still been unable to create the change we yearn for after so many lessons in our human history. For how long are we going to believe the mantra that we have no other choice but to hit them hard and, if that doesn't work, harder? How long will we go on ignoring and covering up the embarrassing past chapters of our story, instead of taking responsibility by recognizing them and also apologizing when necessary? Could this cycle of mutual violence, tending toward mutual destruction, be brought to an end in any other way?

I used to think about local peace, but lately I have realized I should talk about world peace as well, for I have realized that the arguments and pretexts are similar on all sides of every other conflict. A central issue is always one of ego and the need for self-justification. The same

The Anteater And The Jaguar

"we are right, and you are wrong" mentality exists everywhere. Indeed, the more we justify thinking we are right, the more we blame others for being wrong.

Always we hear the same allegations that one group is more civilized than another and therefore deserves to live more than the other does. We encounter the same assertions that the other group cannot reason and that all they understand is force and punishment, which justifies our using it against them. We hear always the same accusations that their violence is unjustified terror, while ours is legitimate self-defense—even when the victims are innocent civilians—and the same claims that we are different, as if we do not all belong to the human race. We need to stop all these classifications, because not long ago, we were all cave people.

No person or group is totally innocent, and none is totally guilty. All communities and nations are arbitrarily created out of the human imagination. Just as this is true for others, it is also true for us. We are broadly divided in this land between Jews and Palestinians, but when we draw closer, we realize these broad divisions do not really define who we are. Jews are divided from other Jews ethnically, politically, culturally, and religiously, just as Palestinians are divided from other Palestinians in the same ways. There is no better time to realize the acuteness of these divisions than during governmental, municipal, and communal elections. The intensity of these divisions is not limited to the different parties but also appears within them, as each has to choose its representatives, council, and committees. Even when elections take place within my own Arab Christian Orthodox community in Nazareth to elect the community's council every four years, it is possible to hear the different competing parties denigrating and condemning one another. This community is also divided over issues regarding its Patriarchate and the Patriarch who sits in Jerusalem. These issues are an outcome of the domination of the Greek branch of the church over the Patriarchate and its affairs, over the Patriarch's continuous dealings with lands that are the property of the local community, and over the exclusion of local Arab priests from occupying high positions in the church establishment. I can remember my mother's obvious pride when she spoke of her grandfather, Priest Saleh Farah, who criticized and rebelled against the Greek monopoly over our church and its affairs back in the 1920s. At some point, her grandfather opened his own church in a rented house, causing a split within the local church community in Nazareth. After a few years, he agreed to return to serve in the main church after he was promised his grievances would be addressed. But he passed away a short time later, and from that day to this, nothing has been done to introduce any changes that would treat the local community as equal partners in the church.

Separate communities, moreover, are made up of separate families. Some families look down on other families, even within their own community. They do this because they believe they are nobler than others. Even within the same family, one branch may feel superior to another.

Though we know these facts about human behavior, most of us still prefer to see and to judge one another according to artificial national and communal divisions. Each of us, however, should make the choice between what is factual and what is fictional. I have chosen to belong to the human community, for I have realized that not every member of my religious or national community can be my friend, my partner, or my neighbor. The same is true of my religious group. My affiliation with it should not make strangers or enemies out of every member of another religion or nationality. It is not necessary for every member of one religion or national community to be a stranger or an enemy of every member of the other.

How could I be blinded by my loyalty to a specific community when some of my best friends are Muslims, Jews, and citizens of other countries? How could I be so blinded by my allegiance to my own nationality when I realize how many different ideological and cultural affinities and preferences this nationality represents? Subgroups exist in nations as well, and some individuals belonging to them hate, dehumanize, and even murder one another. I know many foreigners, including many Jews, who have served the Palestinian cause more faithfully and sincerely than many Palestinians and Arabs have, for some of the latter have exploited

The Anteater And The Jaguar

the cause and used it to pursue their own personal aggrandizement and to prosper materially. Indeed, how could I give blind allegiance to any group when sometimes I find my so-called enemies acting more mercifully than my own people?

How much longer will we go on living with primitive tribal divisions? How much longer will we go on dehumanizing one another just so we can massage our egos? How much longer will we go on dehumanizing others so we can justify our hatred, our anger, and our violence toward them? How much longer will we insist on passing on to our children and future generations our own complexes, prejudices, and fears? Why should our children have to continue a war started generations ago by people who lived long before we were even born?

What are we really fighting about? Most of our present arguments and justifications for continuing our hatred of others are based on what has happened in the past. But how much do we really know about the past? Can we ever fully know the truth of everything that happened then? If so, where does our information come from? Is it reliable or biased toward one point of view? We all have had the experience immediately after witnessing a recent event of hearing divergent opinions, explanations, and interpretations of what happened and why. How then can we be so sure about events that happened decades, centuries, or millennia ago and talk about them as if we were there? How can we justify acts of revenge today against the descendants of people who supposedly committed acts of violence against our people when they are innocent of their ancestors' crimes? How many times have we had one friend who does not share our opinion about a third friend? How often do people with a vested interest in getting their point of view across selectively choose what information supports that interest while obscuring information that does not? Is it not a fact that throughout history, politicians and religious leaders have used lies, distortions, and demagoguery to justify wars and continue oppressing other people?

Ironically, many people claim to be descendants of a pure race. They forget that many thousands of wars have been fought during our common human history, where the first actions engaged in by invading and conquering armies usually were to kill the men and rape the women. It is also ironic that some people claim to be descendants of noble families when all our ancestors lived for thousands of years under the law of the jungle, where the strong exploited and abused the weak.

In any situation or challenge we face, I believe we always have a choice of dealing with it honestly or dishonestly. Why should we believe that expelling the Palestinians from their homes in 1947–48 was the only solution to the problem back then? The same question could be asked about any other war, for that matter, irrespective of whether it took place recently or long ago.

Why should we totally trust our decision makers? Do they disclose to us all their true plans and motives when they make the decision to start a war? How come there always seem to be dark secrets about the launching of a war, secrets that may come to light only long after the war ends? Is it not usually the case that secrets are kept in classified archives and revealed only after thirty or fifty years, if they are ever revealed at all? How many times have we changed our minds about certain historical events once those secrets came to light? How much longer will we continue to believe those who sit on the top of the pyramid? How many times will we allow them to fool us? Haven't we learned that political corruption and money often go hand in hand?

People who profit monetarily from wars do not have a vested interest in peace. The weapons industry has become a main source of income for many countries. Though these countries may claim neutrality, their complicity in supplying weapons to those actually engaged in the practice of war makes them no less guilty. Could countries for which weapons manufacturing is big business afford to close down this lucrative industry? Are we going to be fooled over and over again about the necessity of wars that are in fact unnecessary? Are we going to go on selling new and improved, yet-more-lethal weapons and weapons that inflict maximal damage on the basis that we will be unable to avert future wars and will need those things to defend ourselves? Are not those who sell

The Anteater And The Jaguar

weapons glad when wars break out and persist for prolonged lengths of time, because this gives them ample time and opportunity to test their new and improved weapons? These are issues we should consider whenever war breaks out.

I believe that all human history should be read with a degree of skepticism, especially when we are dealing with interpretations of history. If our interpretations of history are biased in support of our own agenda to the degree that we disqualify an entire people from receiving a fair hearing in the court of human opinion, then there will be little hope on which to build a common future for all humanity. So how much longer will we allow the revisers of fact and manipulators of opinion to cite "evidence" that convinces us to hate and kill one another when, as science proves and religion teaches, we are all brothers and sisters in one large human family? If we can live by receiving blood transfusions and organ transplants from other people, then why is it so hard for us to recognize our common humanity in life's higher pursuits? In our case specifically, hundreds of Palestinians and Jews have been granted a second chance at life after they received a needed organ from a Jewish or Palestinian donor. For inspiration in that regard, I recommend you see a documentary, *The Heart of Jenin—the Story of Ahmad Khatib*, about a Palestinian boy shot by Israeli soldiers. When he died, his father decided as a gesture of peace to donate his son's organs to Israeli children waiting for transplants.

I always try to view our common humanity through the tears and pain of fellow human beings from all over the planet who have lost loved ones in wars, accidents, and natural catastrophes. I see our common humanity through the tears and emotions of athletes who represent their countries in the Olympic Games, whether these are tears and emotions of joy at winning or disappointment at losing. I see our common humanity in airports, where people express the same emotions when their relatives arrive or depart. No matter who they are or what language they speak, the emotions are identical. I observe our common humanity in hospitals, where people express the same emotions, no matter who they are, when their loved ones are recovering, are dying, or are bringing a new baby into the world. I also see our common humanity in our hospitals when I watch Jewish and Arab physicians and nurses attending to and caring for Arab and Jewish patients as equal human beings. I have been there myself and have seen this with my own eyes not long ago, when I had to spend a few weeks in an Israeli hospital. The physicians and nurses are Israeli Jews and Palestinians, Christian and Muslim, men and women, religious and secular. The patient can't know ahead of time who will attend him from the medical staff. Will his doctor be an Arab or a Jew? And his nurses? I felt I was discovering another Oasis of Peace, when I had always thought the community where Dyana and I live was the only one. At the hospital, I saw a group of people who, as healthcare professionals, are involved in the most humane mission I've ever witnessed in practice by any combined Jewish-Palestinian group. This experience suggested to me that, if this level of cooperation is possible in the hospital, perhaps it might also be achievable in the whole country.

Most people tend to blame politicians as the reason there is no peace between us. But our politicians reflect us, their constituencies, and their electorate. Why is it that throughout our common history so many leaders have been mentally unstable psychopaths and warmongers? We allow people to lead us who spend their lives either killing or multiplying the pain and misery of thousands and even millions of people. Such leaders cannot tolerate any objection or criticism of their authority or their convictions. Many are unusually arrogant and have inflated egos. Some are even persuaded that they are divine or, at the least, are the spokespeople of God on Earth.

Can we really say we had nothing to do with the accession to power of such leaders? We cannot say they just fell on us from the sky. The truth is that they are the manifestations of our collective psychological state. How much have we really changed as human beings over the thousands of years that our species has lived on Earth? Do we not still today commonly elevate the same sort of mentally unstable and morally bankrupt leaders, hypocrites, and demagogues as we have always done? How long

The Anteater And The Jaguar

will it take for us to realize that, in order to fix our external reality, we must fix our internal problems first? If we do, then we will have a better chance to avoid producing leaders who traffic primarily in corruption, blood, and the aggrandizement of their own egos.

Throughout my life, people have asked me which political party or group or ideology I support or belong to. And when I replied with a laconic "none, so far," they generally seemed to think there must be something wrong with me or that I was just immature. The truth is that I tried but have never succeeded in totally identifying myself with any specific political group or ideology. I don't know why, but I could hazard a guess that it has to do with my parents' injunction to stay away from politics, or perhaps the way I find it hard to adopt any one framework exclusively, while my natural curiosity prompts me to continue investigating the merits of others. Today I believe I have done the right thing by remaining nonpartisan. My nonassociation with any political group has allowed me to remain in a place that is more open and generous toward differences, the merits of which are usually subjective. My determined individuality has helped me to choose humanity as my reference and not any particular political ideology; this choice seems right to me, especially when this or that ideology begins to justify violence committed against other human beings in its name. As I write this, violence is raging in the Middle East, and wherever I look, I see many people aligned in support of this or that movement or faction or party—despite the fact that all of them are involved in violence. I keep asking why: Why can't we choose an option that rejects violence as the sole means to resolve our disagreements? How shall we create a different and more humane reality if we limit our spectrum of choices to the immoral versus the evil? Regrettably, there are a great many people whose political affiliations apparently enable them to justify violence, even when its victims are innocent civilians.

For some years during the eighties, we kept a herd of sheep in the Oasis of Peace, the sale of which helped us pay for some of our needs. I was glad when we decided to get out of that business. The idea was not proving itself from a financial standpoint, but in addition, we were concerned about the inherent moral contradiction. Some of us had begun to ask how we could be so deeply committed to the idea of promoting peaceful coexistence between people while raising sheep destined for the slaughterhouse.

While we still had the sheep, I sometimes used to join the shepherds, most of them young foreign volunteers, when they took the herd out to pasture. Sitting on some rock and surveying the scene, I used to wonder about the whole dynamic. The sheep would graze, kept in line by border collies who kept them moving along, patrolled their perimeter, and drove back strays when they wandered away from the herd. All the shepherd had to do was to whistle or call, and the dogs would faithfully obey orders and do the job required. At the end of the day, the dogs were rewarded with a good meal, and the shepherd's work was appreciated by the village administration. I came to see this scene as a metaphor for our behavior and our relations as humans. There are always those who give the orders and those who obey them when both are in the service of a higher authority. Stay with the herd and you are considered normal. Dare to leave the herd and you will encounter intimidation, rejection, and punishment. Don't we all pay that sort of price any time we try to break away from the herd?

I believe it is up to each of us to insist on his and her individual right to think freely and not to cede this right to the authority of someone else. I believe it is up to each of us to choose between accepting a role as a member of a herd serving some fraction of humanity or to be a messenger for a better human connection among us all, serving a vision of our shared humanity that transcends enmity and abhors violence. Isn't it true that although the prophets of old were ridiculed, even put to death, their message lived on? What is politics if not the art of separating us into herds and inciting us against one another for the benefit of just a few?

Thity-Two

Our Destiny

"Hopefully, this whole country will someday be like your village!" This wish is one I often hear expressed by lots of different visitors to our community—especially the Jews and Palestinians who visit. However, most of these people still think, and earnestly believe, that others should do the changing first if such a reality is ever to be reached. Few are willing to start by changing their own firmly entrenched opinions and attitudes first.

I have learned that if we truly want our circumstances to change, then we cannot afford to wait for others to do it; we must start with ourselves. I am convinced that this is just what we have done and are continuing to do—those of us who came to live in Wahat Assalam and have remained here. I wouldn't say we all came to the Oasis of Peace fully aware of what we were going to need to do to create peace between us. As I have repeatedly noted, most of us came here believing that our story was right and that it was the duty of others to change before the situation in our country could improve. This is why we ended up facing so many disappointments and so much anxiety and pain when others seemed unwilling to accept our stories in the way we thought they should. Those of us who stayed on here, however, had to think hard and search bravely for the peace we desired; we had to work much harder at this than most people are willing to do. Most people have never faced the diverse human, social, political, educational, and administrative challenges we ended up facing here as partners in our one shared community.

In our community, we are all constitutionally equal. No one sees a need to carry weapons to use against others. Indeed, we here have chosen, in the well-known phrase from Isaiah 2:4, to "beat our swords into plowshares and our spears into pruning hooks." We all enjoy the same rights, and we all accept the same obligations. Somehow, over time, we have all realized we are in the same boat. We knew we had to cooperate if we were to succeed in persevering on our common journey. What fostered this cooperation? A primary factor, I think, has been our understanding that our responsibility toward our community and the idea it represents is much bigger and much more important than our personal needs, desires, and comforts.

At some point during my life here, despite all the frustration and pain I went through, I became convinced that none of us could let this idea fail, no matter what might happen. *I* could not let it fail, because if it were to fail, then our story for many years to come would be about one small community of Palestinians and Jews that failed. We would then have had to agree that the state of affairs in this land is beyond fixing—and perhaps beyond redemption.

After visiting our community and talking to its people, a person will come away having heard different stories, different experiences, and different conclusions; despite these differences, most of us in our community have reached one main conclusion—we share a common humanity. We can argue that the process we have undergone together in the Oasis of Peace has been one in which the priorities of our identities have changed. At the beginning of our encounter with one another, it was our national identity that mattered most. Eventually, though, we started to see more and more of others' human sides, despite our many differences. With time, the other became a person, and whether that person was Jewish or Palestinian or other no longer mattered. Dealing

The Anteater And The Jaguar

with one another from this perspective has made it easier for most of us to consider one another's different needs and commitments.

Therefore, if we in this land ever want to liberate ourselves from the deadly embrace of the anteater and the jaguar, we must deal with our conflicts on the basis of our primary identity as human beings relating to fellow human beings, for in this identity we are all surely equal. On the other hand, to attempt to resolve our conflict as Jews and as Palestinians will forever be impossible, because the preconditions inherent in our ethnic, religious, political, and national identities will always throw major obstacles in the way or create rifts of inequality that cannot be bridged. To insist on dealing with one another on the basis of these secondary identities is a reflection of our reluctance to resolve the conflict by viewing our opponents as our equals. Secondary identities only support the myth that we deserve more than others do.

Furthermore, it is perfectly fine if these secondary identities are important to people, because these give meaning and purpose to life. But to use them to assert our own rights at the expense of the rights of others is unacceptable. If there must be a precondition for recognition, then it must be mutual; each party must accept the other's preconditions.

In our community, our close encounters were the cause of our awakening to one another's humanity. I have learned that such close encounters advance our ability to overcome personal and collective fears and complications. Humanization is the main key needed to help change the situation from one of conflict to one of a common and shared existence. Having honest and sincere intentions also makes complicated issues easier to deal with. Instilling these kinds of intentions in our young people can be achieved through education, without necessarily having most people live in mixed communities or sending their children to mixed schools like ours.

Education must do more than provide children with the opportunity to acquire knowledge and cultivate their minds; educating our children for a shared egalitarian future must encompass content and practices that enhance children's awareness of our common humanity.

Such education can happen only when self-limiting national, communal, and religious frameworks are made comprehensible in the light of our common interests as human beings. We cannot permit these frameworks to be used destructively—to sustain and feed our egos, sharpen the divisions between us, or make us believe those with whom we disagree are subhuman.

Isn't it true that neither the achievements nor the failures of the human race have been limited to a single civilization, nation, religion, or group? Whether we are Middle Easterners, Asians, Europeans, Africans, or Americans, our societies and civilizations have all had their day in the sun during different periods of human history. Hence, whether we talk today about nations, religions, groups, or individuals, all of us have deeds to be proud of and things to regret or feel shame about.

We are not better than other people by virtue of being a member of this nation or that religion; of this community or that family; or by being richer, more educated, or more "modern." If we believe that this sort of affiliation or label elevates us above others, the import is purely psychological. It is not a result of being genetically different, as though "they" are less evolved than "we" are. We shall never reach contentment if we continually compare ourselves to others, because we will envy those we see as above us and disrespect those we see as below us. These negative thoughts, with their negative emotions, are simply another cause for suffering and conflict.

I have talked about my personal experiences of mental anguish and how I found relief and hope. Nonetheless, I am aware that the pain I have endured is not as tragic when I view it in the context of what many others have experienced. There are many traumatized people all over the world who have gone through heartbreaking psychological pain as a result of physical illness; terrible accidents; or the loss of a dear family member or even the whole family to violence, accidents, or natural disasters. When I am in the presence of such people, I am overwhelmed and speechless. All I can do is to be supportive by listening to them without minimizing their agony or requiring them to work through it as though it is something that could be easily accomplished. In the end, what remains important is how we deal with our pain on the personal level, in the long run. Do we choose to live with our pain in a manner that will hurt us even more? Can we live in pain without projecting it onto others, or do we recognize at some point that it is neither right nor fair to do that?

A well-known Arabic proverb says, "Your calamity can become more bearable when you recognize the calamity of others."

I first learned some sixteen years ago of a group of people who had lost precious family members as a result of the mutual violence stemming from the political conflict in our land. In spite of what they had to endure, these unique people decided to seek the way of peace rather than to retaliate. This group started as a Jewish-Israeli group who supported Prime Minister Yitzhak Rabin in his peace initiative with the Palestinians. The work of this group later provided a forum in which Israeli Jewish and West Bank Palestinian families could share with one another the similar tragedies they had endured, and gradually, they began educational initiatives for peace—in the hope that no more families would have to endure the same pain. I very much admire and appreciate the courage and humanity of these people, whose group today is known as Palestinian Israeli Bereaved Families for Peace.[16] Boaz and Daniella Kitain, parents of Tom, whose story is told elsewhere in this book, are active with this group. They and their comrades have chosen to share their suffering as a means of reconciliation, rather than to use it as a justification for seeking revenge. There can be no better way than this to halt the cycle of mutual violence, for revenge is rarely justified (and some would say it is never justified). Too often, revenge is not directed against a specific person who committed an act of killing in the first place but is instead directed toward innocent people who provide a convenient scapegoat against whom others blindly vent their fury.

On the subject of revenge and healing, I recommend reading about the work of Imam Muhammad Ashafa and Pastor James Wuye.

---

16 Founded in 1995 by Yitzhak Frankenthal and Roni Hirshenzon

Rayek R. Rizek

These Nigerian spiritual leaders worked toward reconciliation between Muslims and Christians in their homeland after the mutual massacres that took place between them during the 1990s.

Particular wars between people may eventually come to an end, but to guarantee they do not recur, reconciliation is essential. Suppose for the sake of argument that the political leadership of the two peoples in our land someday agree to implement a solution based on partitioning the country into two states. Once this is accomplished, what story will each side tell its people? What will future generations be taught about it? Will the two sides say they reached their agreement and ended the conflict as a result of their recognizing each other's historical and religious rights in this land? Or will each side say they had to accept an unfair solution by giving up a piece of their ancestral real estate to people who did not deserve it? This latter possibility reveals that the embers of resentment and anger still smolder and that the right fuel could easily reignite the conflict yet again.

Regrettably, the issue of reconciliation has not been addressed very much thus far as part of the various initiatives seeking to end our conflict over this land. We are still stuck in an unproductive who-is-right-and-who-is-wrong mentality, with all the associated attempts on both sides at historical justification for the two opposing positions. For this reason, a viable peace document between our two peoples must include reconciliation, because we will continue to live in close proximity to each other.

This reconciliation effort must include a more objective reinterpretation of history. By that I mean that both sides must face up to what history truly reveals about the good each group has achieved and the bad each group has been responsible for perpetrating. Using history to distort and dehumanize others must cease. Both sides will need to extend apologies for past actions and attitudes that were hurtful and destructive and for all their attempts to justify these actions and attitudes. We must emphasize human rights and moral values that unite us rather than divide us. Only when these changes are reflected in history textbooks as well as media headlines can we hope for a lasting peace

The Anteater And The Jaguar

that will guarantee security, progress, and prosperity for future generations as well.

Finally, Jews and Palestinians who are directly involved in the present conflict would do well to internalize an important fact: Regardless of how many countries or people champion our side in the conflict, we are the ones who will continue paying if the conflict remains unresolved. Only we, together, can find the path to a better life beyond dehumanization, distortion, violence, and denial of responsibility. No one else can find it for us.

I believe it is part of our destiny to end up sharing the same land at this time in our human history, and I believe it is up to each person to decide how to help shape this destiny. I believe it is not by chance that we ended up together, not only as members of two nationalities but also as followers of three linked monotheistic religions, the sons and daughters of Avraham/Abraham/Ibrahim and of Sarah and Hagar. It is true that the conflict has a very strong political aspect, but I believe it has an equally powerful religious side to it. We can move ahead if we can but realize that we are living in the twenty-first century now. In simple terms, our choice is between letting the mostly ambiguous past continue to control our thinking and our attitudes or opting to view that past as a valuable lesson in what is possible and ethical and what is not. We must, all of us, realize we will always reap what we sow.

Our shared destiny will evolve in one of two ways: either we will remain together in this darkness of pain, or we will choose to reconcile and build a new shared reality that might help awaken all the people on this planet to our common humanity.

This is what we have been doing, as best we can, at the Oasis of Peace, Neve Shalom/Wahat Assalam.

If the heart is upright, deeds will be good.[17]

---

17 From the Shinto scriptures

Made in the USA
San Bernardino, CA
22 July 2018